D1259682

DEFENSE XXI

Shaping a Way Ahead for
the United States and Its Allies

ROBBIN F. LAIRD

Editor

Defense XXI:

Shaping a Way Ahead for the United States and Its Allies

©2022 Robbin F. Laird

Photo Credit: Training military technology.
Rawpixel.com rights purchased from Bigstock.com

print ISBN: 978-1-66783-134-3
ebook ISBN: 978-1-66783-135-0

Cover Design @ OPS
Contact @operationnels.com

CONTENTS

This book is dedicated to my mother Miriam Luger Laird,
in celebration of her 102nd birthday.

She has lived through many decades of global turbulence and conflict
and her generation knows that constant vigilance is the only defense of
free men and women.

FORWARD BY MICHAEL W. WYNNE, 21ST SECRETARY OF THE U.S. AIR FORCE

There has been a myriad of discussion, discourse, and symposia about the impact of technology on military oriented strategic agility, be it for units, theater operations, or allied operations across theaters. Seldom do we come across a compendium that doesn't of itself, in some detail, provide further insight; but rather one that solicits insight from the leadership and operators of the types of technologies and tools allowing strategic agility. Approaching the subject from this direction allows range and maneuver space which mirrors the concept of strategic agility.

Discussion about deterrence and dominance are exciting, yet from the perspective of the national decision makers, so much is presumed, and under some conditions modified based upon insights from think tanks and behavior of their allies. But as Secretary Rumsfeld was often quoted as saying "you go to war with the weapons you have, not the weapons you want." What was left out of this notion was the one that operators performing the missions assigned have a tendency to extract more performance, and even use the weapons they have in unique and different ways to essentially extend the lifetime and usage potential from systems in hand. It is quite refreshing to hear from the performing team how they see their role in providing the support, and fact-based evidence to bolster the quality of national decisions. My hat is off to the author's herein that go where defense writers seldom go; that is into the fields of training, techniques, tactics and procedures and asks for an honest assessment as to the quality of the combined forces.

The authors and I have had many a cup of coffee concerning the betterment of joint operation by allowing and in fact encouraging distributed battlefield information as well as battlefield damage data. We talked of minimizing weapons requirement, by yielding weapons employment across the theater of operations. We even opined as to the separation of sensors and shooters, such that sensors could guide to a target a distant fired munition, or system, and it is here somewhat pleasing to note that the emergence of manned or unmanned sensors being asked to perform this very duty. We were necessarily neutral as to the impact of technology on allies' decision making.

However, one of the most promising areas of analysis found here is a concept that was expounded by the then Vice Chief of the Joint Chiefs, Michael Mullen, who spoke of a thousand ship navy, and in that pronouncement cited evidence of allied combined force structure across a wider naval enterprise. This concept has taken on additional meaning with the expansive export of the F-35 fifth generation weapons system. By itself it has essentially force multiplied across many potential flash points in the world. But herein, the reader will find some evidence through leadership insights and unit training, together with an underlying expansion of the integration aspect, treating the entirety of the battle space as an integrable space. Exactly as Admiral Mullen had hoped would occur. This took not just vision, but lots of talented and diplomatic serving military leaders inside U.S. forces as well as inside allied forces, and then the requisite training and even joint battle exercises of the disparate national forces to work compatibly.

Each of these actions and activities, though good by themselves, cannot thwart a bad political decision, or the belligerent action that might separate a former ally into a neutral party, or a detriment to what could have been a formidable alliance. This part of the general discussion has two elements, first the diplomatic character of the relationship must deteriorate, and second the peer competitor must act to establish a different relationship using what the United States describes as a whole of government approach to diplomacy. As some of these interviews might point to, there is a deepening suspicion as to the fealty of some nations as to treaties. This is forcing nations to determine separate strategies and perhaps more concentrated defenses. As some might say, the content of these articles and discussions may prove to be disturbing as they might differ from established narratives.

The fascination that comes through this compendium is the clear approach taken by both serving military leaders, and political leadership that is willing to foresee the distinct possibility of a miscalculation on one or both sides of conflict. Whether due to distraction by differing levels of crises; or due only to a separable need internal to their nation, the historical miscalculation takes many decades, if ever to right themselves. Once while in Hungary, I was in a discussion with a learned source, and he said, "in the run up to World War One, we made a bad choice, and then watched as Germany lost the war, and we lost our Empire."

Such can be the impact of bad national decisions. Thus, the management of escalation may be the natural follow on to mismanagement of deterrence and dominance. Clearly, in the age of nuclear weapons, the definition of limited war gets fuzzy.

The following articles, organized as they are by natural topics, will undoubtedly enhance the reader's understanding as to just how weapons and information technology and the distribution and relationship knowledge have affected and impacted the age-old concept that military action is simply an extension of diplomacy by other means.

PREFACE

This book is the second book in a tribology of defense books we are publishing this year. The first book published this year focused on the USMC and its transformation since 2007. In that book, I focused on the strategic shift from the land wars to the return of great power competition and peer competitor conflict. It beings with a brief primer on the key elements of change and then in the book, Marines discuss how they are reshaping the force to deal with the new historical era.

This book focuses on key drivers for change in defense which are reshaping force capabilities and the strategic context within which those capabilities are being shaped. It is about technology, concepts of operations and strategic purposes for defense. The final book for 2022 focuses on the evolution of the maritime forces and the effort to combine evolving concepts of operations with evolutions in the conduct of conflict and war and the broader strategic competition,

This book brings together several of the articles we published in 2021 on *Second Line of Defense* and *Defense.info,* which highlight key trends in the defense policies and challenges facing the United States and its allies. It is a follow-up to our book published in 2021, which highlighted trends in 2020 and was entitled: *2020: A Pivotal Year?* There are new pieces as well which were previously unpublished as well included in the book.

The 2020 book focused on the pandemic, notably as it played out in France and Britain. The book also dealt with the evolving global dynamics affecting defense and security for the liberal democracies and ended with a look at the enhanced tension between Australia and Europe regarding China.

That tension continued into 2021 and one of the themes which we highlight in this book is the evolving Australian approach to national security policy, which includes enhanced national resilience and augmenting the reach and range of its defense forces in the Pacific. The reach and range piece are at the heart of the Australian decision to shift from a conventional to a nuclear submarine acquisition program, which entailed shifting from the working relationship between Australia and France to a new tripartite working relationship with the UK and the United States in terms of shaping a transfer of the technical knowledge necessary to acquire nuclear attack submarines for Australia.

This was despite the uncertainly affecting U.S. defense policy best underscored by the Biden administration's blitzkrieg strategy of withdrawal from Afghanistan. While the narrative press quickly put this decision and its consequences into the rearview mirror, the world has not. And the long-term consequences for U.S. credibility and for the U.S. military are yet to be fully determine but already tested in the Ukraine crisis 2022.

One theme which we explored in 2021 associated with the enhanced challenge from the authoritarian powers is that of escalation management and reduced warning time in terms of the threats which authoritarian powers can deliver. Here we focused on the work of Australian strategists, who have focused specifically on the threats posed by China to Australia in these terms.

During 2021, we visited several U.S. Naval and Marine Corps bases, as well as France and Poland as well as "virtually" Denmark and the United Kingdom. During those visits, we interviewed many senior commanders about how they are focused on shaping a more effective military to deal with the evolving challenges from the authoritarian powers. In this book, we have included the interview with those senior commanders as well as insights from discussions "virtually" with Australians and Danes, as well as in-person visits in France and Poland.

There are new capabilities being pursued to add to the combat and crisis management capabilities for U.S. and allied forces, and we have included discussions of two such capabilities. The first is the coming of autonomous systems to the force. This assessment was built upon the Williams Foundation

Seminar in Australia in April 2021, which focused on this theme as well as the evolving capabilities for maritime autonomous systems seen most recently in the formation of the U.S. Navy's Task Force 59. In early September 2021, the U.S. Navy set up a new task force to deliver usable unmanned systems for enhanced maritime capabilities in the 5th Fleet Area of Operations.[1]

The second is the shift in how training is being crafted in order to enable the force to fight in interactive kill webs. The historical focus on Tactics, Techniques and Procedures (TTPs) needs to become Training, Tactics, Techniques and Procedures (TTTPs) to get to where we need to go with regard to advanced warfighting. In that shift, the training piece expands the role of the digital space and the role of digital warriors in evolving the warfighting capabilities of a multi-domain blue force facing an evolving red multi-domain force, changing both in terms of technology and in terms of concepts of operations.

In short, this compendium of articles published in 2021 and early 2022 provides an overview of several key trends and key themes regarding the evolution of U.S. and allied defense. Many of these articles have been written by the editor but other members of the team contributed significantly throughout the year as well. But some of those pieces, notably dealing with Europe are being published separately in another book to be published in 2023 entitled *French Defense Policy Under President Macron*.

Throughout the book, the date the article first appeared on our websites is highlighted. But we have worked through several themes throughout the year, rather than randomly publishing pieces as events drive commentary. A key reason we publish our book series is precisely to be able to highlight the thematic approaches we take to events and to be able to present those themes on a more permanent basis to a broader audience.

And I would like to close this preface by noting that one of our contributors, Brendan Sargeant, has died in a tragic accident in February 2022 as this book was being prepared for publication. His piece in chapter one focuses on the challenge and the need for strategic imagination to guide us

---

1   "Task Force 59: Creating Maritime Capabilities for the 5th Fleet Area of Operations," *Second Line of Defense* (October 24, 2021), https://sldinfo.com/2021/10/ task-force-59-creating-maritime-capabilities-for-the-5th-fleet-area-of-operations/.

in effectively transitioning challenging times. His piece is really an epitaph in many ways to his own capabilities and accomplishments in helping his native Australia navigate in his lifetime through historical changes. He is seriously missed and leaves behind a huge gap for those who do strategic analysis and an even greater one for his loving family. More of Brendan's pieces including interviews can be found in *2020: A Pivotal Year?*

CHAPTER ONE:

CRISIS CAPABILITIES AND ESCALATION MANAGEMENT

Our focus over the past few years has been on the shift from the Middle Eastern land wars to the strategic competition with peer competitors. The preparation for the high-end fight is a key part of this refocus, but not the sole focus; rather the key challenge is to have the capabilities and skill to shape effective crisis management and to be able to deliver escalation control.

The peers we are talking about are nuclear powers. Any high-end fight will be shaped by the presence of nuclear weapons in such an engagement. Clearly, there is need for the United States to protect its interests short of nuclear engagement, but the United States is not the only player in such calculations.

This means that building out conventional war-fighting capabilities entails thinking through from the outset how packages of conventional forces can be clustered for crisis management events in ways that provide for effective escalation control. This requires civilians to prepare for escalation management, rather than when facing an event which can spin out of control, either ignoring or capitulating to the peer competitor. It is about doing more than verbal admonishment or zoom meetings, or being reduced to invoking economic sanctions, or otherwise limited use tasks, which often have little real effect on deterring an authoritarian peer competitor.

The mindset of the peer competitor is a key part of preparing for crisis management as well.

This means understanding what might allow for successful crisis management when dealing with such different cultural manifestations of global authoritarians such as Russia or China. This has a clear effect on the forces which might be tasked with performing crisis management tasks. How to avoid the seams that the Russians exploit in normal times, and that they will accentuate through various means of coercion in a crisis?

In our discussions with both Commander Second Fleet (C2F), and with Allied Joint Force Command Norfolk, it is clear Vice Admiral Lewis and his team focused from the outset of the 2018 standup of the new C2F on how to shape a fleet which is optimized for crisis management and on how to operate in such a way that the Russians can exploit the operational seams in the North Atlantic.

The emphasis of the Nordics on a significant strengthening of their collaborative capabilities and the North Atlantic Treaty Organization (NATO) reset in the region have provided a key context within which the U.S. and allied fleets are working new ways to distribute the force to the point of effect but to do so in a way that the force is integrable across the region. What this means is the key role of the "relevant nations" in North Atlantic defense needs to be to understand events in their region from the standpoint of crisis management. And to be able to correlate that understanding with clear and decisive military and civilian leadership actions to convey to the Russian leadership what deterrence means in a specific case.

Deterrence is not a universal state; it is delivered in times of key events shaping pre-crisis or crisis challenges. As Dr. Paul Bracken, the noted strategist who recently retired from Yale University, put it in a 2018 piece: "The key point for today is that there are many levels of intensity above counterinsurgency and counterterrorism, yet well short of total war. In terms of escalation intensity, this is about one-third up the escalation ladder. Here, there are issues of war termination, disengagement, maneuvering for advantage, signaling—and yes, further escalation—in a war that is quite limited compared to World War II, but far above the intensity of combat in Iraq and Afghanistan….

"A particular area of focus should be exemplary attacks. Examples include select attack of U.S. ships, Chinese or Russian bases, and command and control. These are above crisis management as it is usually conceived in the West. But they are well below total war. Each side had better think through the dynamics of scenarios in this space.

"Deep strike for exemplary attacks, precise targeting, option packages for limited war, and command and control in a degraded environment need to be thought through beforehand. The Russians have done this, with their escalate to deescalate strategy. I recently played a war game where Russian exemplary attacks were a turning point, and they were used quite effectively to terminate a conflict on favorable terms. In East Asia, exemplary attacks are also important as the ability to track U.S. ships increases.

"Great power rivalry has returned. A wider range of possibilities has opened up. But binary thinking—that strategy is either low intensity or all-out war—has not."[2]

Warning Time, Events, and Crisis Management

In an important paper by Paul Dibb and Richard Brabin-Smith, both Professors currently at the Strategic and defence studies centre of the Australian national University, the authors address the question of the impact of reduced warning time upon Australian defense and security.[3] This comes from both the nature of the Chinese challenge, and the changing nature of threats, such as cyber-attacks. How best to defend Australia in an environment with reduced warning time?

Although obviously about Australia, the discussion in the report raises a broader set of questions on how to know when an event is setting in motion

---

2   Paul Bracken, "One-Third Up the Escalation Ladder," *Second Line of Defense* (April 25, 2018), https://sldinfo.com/2018/04/one-third-up-the-escalation-ladder/.

3   Paul Dibb and Richard Brabin-Smith, *Deterrence Through Denial: A Strategy for an Era of Reduced Warning Time* (ASPI, May 2021).

a chain of events which provide a direct threat to a liberal democratic nation and how to respond. It also raises the question of shaping capabilities which can be inserted into a crisis early enough to provide confidence in an ability to have effective escalation management tools available as well.

The question of an ability to move force rapidly to a crisis becomes increasingly significant as escalation control returns as a key element of constraining, managing, and protecting one's interests in a crisis. This is why I have preferred to focus on full spectrum crisis management as the challenge facing the liberal democracies in meeting the challenges of 21st century authoritarian powers, rather than simply preparing for the high-end fight. And there is another reason: it is very likely that a high-end fight between the major powers will end up entailing nuclear use. The reality is that we are engaged in ongoing limited war with the authoritarian powers, if one considers gray zone conflict and hybrid operations as subsumed under a concept of 21st century limited war.

But for Australia, what the authors underscore is the importance of deterrence through denial with regard to the Chinese threat. And to deal with this threat, the government's emphasis on long-range strike is a key part of what the authors see as a way ahead.

As the authors of the report argue: "Having a deterrent force based on the concept of denial—as distinct from deterrence through the much more demanding concept of deterrence through punishment—should be more affordable. Deterrence through punishment involves attacking the adversary's territory, whereas deterrence through denial is limited to attacking the adversary's forces and associated infrastructure directly threatening us. In any case, the idea of Australia being able to inflict unacceptable punishment on a big power such as China would be ridiculous. The bottom-line for defense policy is that as confidence in deterrence by denial goes up, our dependence on early response to warnings should go down."

Paul Dibb Outside the Hedley Bull Centre, Australian National University, November 2013. Credit: SDSC Photograph Collection.

A key part of expanding the buffer to manage crises entails Australia enhancing self-sufficiency and self-reliance through expanded stockpiling of fuel and key war stocks. And over time, some new systems will be added through domestic production as well, notably as the autonomous weapons revolution evolves and accelerates.

As the authors warn:

> "Australia now needs to implement serious changes to how warning time is considered in defense planning. The need to plan for reduced warning time has implications for the Australian intelligence community, defense strategic policy, force structure priorities, readiness, and sustainability. Important changes will also be needed with respect to personnel, stockpiles of missiles and munitions, and fuel supplies.

> "We can no longer assume that Australia will have time gradually to adjust military capability and preparedness in response to emerging threats. In other words, there must be a new approach

in defense to managing warning, capability, and preparedness, and detailed planning for rapid expansion and sustainment."

The United States remains the indispensable ally for many reasons, but the U.S. will be preoccupied in crises impacting its own interests as well. This means that an expanded focus on building out Australian buffer capabilities will be significant to shaping an effective response to reduced warning times.

New digital technologies have altered the question of what warning time is all about. Notably, with regard to the cyber threats, when is there an attack, and what does it mean? As the authors note:

"A campaign of cyberattack and intensified cyber-exploitation against Australia could be launched with little notice, given the right level of motivation, and would have the advantage of having at least a level of plausible deniability while imposing limits to what might be envisaged as a proportional response. Such response options available to Australia would include retaliation, such as a government-sanctioned cyberattack—a capability that the Australian Government has acknowledged it has. (This capability has already been used against terrorists, but whether it has been used more widely isn't publicly known.)

"The warning time for the need to conduct such operations is potentially very short, meaning that there needs to be a high level of preparedness, including the ability quickly to expand the cyber workforce (with a concomitant need for expedited security clearances), and cyberattack campaigns that are thought out well in advance. There's a strong argument that such planning should include within its scope the possibility of causing high levels of damage to the adversary's infrastructure."

They end their report with five policy recommendations. The first is to establish a National Intelligence Officer for Warning. The second is to establish a Directorate of Net Assessments. And the authors highlight the focus of such a Directorate as follows:

"While it's unlikely that China would directly attack our continent, we must prepare for credible contingencies involving Chinese military coercion in our immediate strategic space. That coercion could involve the threatened use of military force, including from future Chinese military bases located to our north and east. Ignoring such probabilities risks strategic surprise involving our key national security interests. If the Directorate of Net Assessments is to have relevance, it will need to simulate high-level political and policy decision-making in real time. Without such time-urgent inputs, it won't be possible to play other than theoretical war games."

The third is establishing a priority for long-range missile strike. Here they reinforce the importance of the commitment the current government has made to this task, but I would add that Australia can work much more effectively with its allies, including the United States in shaping a new generation of strike weapons, rather than simply replicating what the United States is already doing.

The fourth is realistically assessing their U.S. ally. For the authors, this means:

"We need to accept in our strategic thinking that America is now a more inward-looking country that will foreseeably give more attention to its domestic social and political challenges. It also needs to be remembered that the U.S. has from time-to-time undergone severe bouts of isolationism. We don't think that's likely to happen under the Biden administration, but it could recur under a differently motivated presidency.

"We need prudent analysis about how the U.S. will react to its own warning indicators of potential military attack and what it would expect of Australia. In our own broader region, we can't afford not to be fully informed about U.S. contingencies in Taiwan or the Korean Peninsula, so we need to assess U.S. military capabilities as well as Washington's intentions."

I would add my own comments to this judgment. For me, one of the challenges for either the United States or our allies is to understand what a good ally actually is. It is one which has a realistic understanding of what it can and cannot do and an ability to assess realistically the global environment. I would argue that that is in shorter supply in both the United States and in many of our allied Departments or Ministries of Defense.

I would note as well that the concerns about paying more attention at home than abroad are true of the United States and all or most of our partners. The challenge then is how can the liberal democracies realistically work together to deal with global authoritarian states who see global influence and adventurism as a coin of the realm for enhancing their power?

And as for the political comment about the Biden administration, given the dominance of identity politics in the administration, one might see considerable inward preoccupation. President Trump, for all his tweeting and rhetoric, enhanced the capabilities of the U.S. in many ways, although his inability to support multilateralism conceptually was always a limiting factor in his global policy.

And the final factor is increased preparedness and force expansion. As the authors put this challenge: "For the first time since World War II, Defense needs to also take seriously the conditions under which force expansion and mobilization would happen. It wouldn't be acceptable to defer such consideration until Australia were within warning time of a serious military attack against us or our key interests. Planning for timely and effective mobilization doesn't at this stage require a detailed plan but rather the development of principles that would be applied to the development of the force structure and defense policy for industry. The place to start would be to identify those steps that should be taken now to ensure that force expansion and mobilization would achieve their goals."

I would add that in their approach to deterrence through denial, a major effort over the next decade could well be working a new defense approach for integrated defense from Western to Northern Australia to the first island chain (the Solomon Islands). And in so doing, air and maritime integration, the introduction of new force multipliers through autonomous systems, the ground forces learning how to do expeditionary basing, and working that basing with air-sea integration, will be a key part of deterrence through denial.

When that chessboard is established and worked, the question of what the strike force can achieve in terms of longer range becomes an even more formidable consideration than simply having longer-range missiles. And in this context, shaping the best ways to work with the partners and allies in the region, and working new integrated distributed concepts of operations with the United States and Japan will be critical as well.

Events, Policy Making and Strategic Imagination

Professor Brendan Sargeant, the noted Australian strategist, gave an inaugural lecture in a new series of lectures at the Australian National University on the evolving challenges facing Australia in 2021. He argued that underlying strategic policy is a set of assumptions about the world, which make up the driving force of interpretative reality. As the world changes, simply continuing a particular path forward, which is a projection into the future of past assumptions about the world, can lead to policy disasters.

As he put in his lecture:

> "One feature of any crisis is that it highlights a need for change. When this is understood, the question becomes, how should this change occur? What are its costs and gains? How should we understand success? What is failure? Why does success or failure occur?

> "One way of thinking about strategy is to consider it as preparation for a future crisis. Yet, our capacity to envisage and prepare for a future crisis can be constrained by the limits of our strategic imagination, even as the crisis becomes visible and demands a response.

> "My central proposition is that a strategic challenge of any magnitude is first a challenge to imagination. The quality of the imagination that responds to that challenge determines

the shape of the strategy that follows. An understanding of the relationship between strategy and imagination can deepen our understanding of what strategy is and how we might assess the utility of strategy in specific circumstances."

In effect, events happen in the world. Public and policy makers interpret those events on the basis of their preexisting assumptions, and in the case of a nation's policy making, preexisting policy proclivities are likely to be followed unless discontinuity is recognized and understood.

It is especially important to grasp the nature of change and to debate it for there is no certainty that the assumptions held by any particular group are correct.

What Sargeant is calling for is greater capability to understand the proclivities of a policy system and how those proclivities and assumptions drive a policy decision no matter what the actual event may suggest is happening. In effect, this requires a restoration, in the case of the United States, of an ability to debate policy without descending into the catacombs of social media assertion of one's particular group's operational theology.

In the case of Washington, I have always found it fascinating how when a new administration comes to town within a couple of years, new definitions of reality dominate no matter what has really happened in the big world. How then to be able to look at a global event and determine what it means? My own proclivity is to think in terms of case studies, to take alternative assumptions to what that event might actually mean and how best to shape a response or not? In the world of following the soccer ball approach to news and policy making, often what is really important is not even the focus of attention.

Sargeant underscores that a country's identity is closely tied up with what its strategic assumptions and how those assumptions craft a narrative.

"A country is an imagined community—it possesses an identity created by the people who live within it, the stories these people embody and tell, both as individuals and communities. A country is a larger and more complex entity than any individual human being, but as an imagined community, a country does not exist without the people who have created it out of their actions, stories, desires, and their sense of who they are and where they belong.

"A country will possess a strategic imagination which will have evolved over time in response to the influence of geography, history, culture, and the many other tangible and intangible forces that go to create a community and its vision of itself. A country's strategic imagination is a living thing, dynamic and evolving in contact with the world, and full of contradictions. In those rare moments in a country's history where a genuine choice must be made and action taken, a country's strategic imagination becomes most visible."

If we take this characterization to the American case, the rise of identity politics clearly fragments the underlying culture which drives the assumptions under which that country then can imagine its place in the world. Or put bluntly, even though the United States is the key ally of Australia, how will the United States interpret events going forward in the presence of a fragmenting identity politics cross-cutting interpretation of events going on in the big world?

This is of course important for Australia as Australia faces a major shift in its strategic focus to find its leadership role in the Indo-Pacific world. As Sargeant puts it:

"Perhaps the deep purpose of strategic policy is to help create Australia by charting a future and giving meaning to the past. Strategic policy and its expression in action through strategy builds national identity; national identity validates strategy. Yet our language can lack authenticity. We use terms such as 'creative middle power' to describe ourselves—or we 'punch above our weight.'

"These are clichés, a tired rhetoric designed to mobilize political support and unlock resources, provide talking points for politicians and officials. Our policy and strategic documents repeatedly reference the "rules-based global order" and of the U.S. Alliance as the foundation of our security. We avoid the arduous task of self-creation and instead deploy these clichés as a shield against our anxieties. Yet the Indo-Pacific asks us: how long will this rhetoric, increasingly nostalgic in tone, make sense?"

The question of where Australia fits into the evolving Indo-Pacific world, and how to shape a realistic and effective leadership role is a key one for the liberal democracies. With the 21st century authoritarian states clearly focused on making the world a thriving place for their culture, their economies, and their way of life, they have worked inside the systems of the liberal democracies through various means as well as directly assaulted them globally.

And as the global authoritarian powers shape global reach, how does this change the situation for Australia? Sargeant addressed this in part in his discussion of strategic space.

"Australian strategic policy and strategy have always grappled with the profound influence of geography as both a constraint and an opportunity. Australia's geography provides challenges in communications, logistics, and force disposition.

"From a strategic perspective, it provides both the luxury and the challenge of distance. In a strategic environment of reducing strategic space, the challenge for Australian strategy is to determine which force disposition and design is going to provide the most flexibility and embody the best recognition of the reality of our strategic environment.

"In this context, how we conceptualize our strategic geography in the context of a changing strategic order is a challenge to strategic imagination at many levels and in many ways. We live in a maritime environment, but on a continent-sized island. Australia has a history of sending expeditionary forces to other parts of the world as part of a larger alliance or coalition engagement on the basis that Australian security is often best served by participation and maintenance of larger global strategic systems from which Australia benefits. Yet Australia is also an island continent, which brings with it a concomitant obligation to provide for its defense, but also creates a sense of security because any invading adversary would face almost insurmountable obstacles.

"But is this changing? We have always thought about geography as providing us with space. But in a world where space as a strategic resource is diminishing, do we need to reconceptualize our strategic geography to take us beyond, for example, the demarcation of continent versus archipelago, or do we need to see that geographical space as a single continuous environment? In this context, recent developments in Australian strategic environment have emphasized the need to focus on our near region as an arena for strategic contestation.

"This has given a renewed prominence to the question of our strategic geography, our capacity for self-reliance and the terms of our participation in larger regional and global strategic systems. How we understand and conceptualize our geography is an imaginative challenge before it becomes a challenge for policy and strategy."

What is the meaning of current events which occur? How to place those in a dynamic context of change? The policy community is largely lemming-like, so where does this imagination come from? How can we roll back the social media cramping of the space in which to DEBATE and exchange perceptions and assumptions with regard to what we see?

Although Sergeant's lecture is about Australia, it is clearly more than that. As he concludes:

"The work of policy, an art of desire, is to say what the world might be. The work of strategy is to create the path towards that world, responding to all the known and unknown impediments that are likely to emerge. Policy lives mostly in the world of imagination; strategy lives mostly in the world of experience. The art of the policy maker and the strategist is to bring imagination into the world of experience and through this to create strategy that can change the world. In times of great change, the challenge is to imagination, for continuity in strategy is likely to lead to failure."[4]

Crisis Management and Strategic Imagination: Meeting the Challenge

I will close this chapter with the interview which I did with Professor Sargeant in the summer of 2021, to focus further on the importance of strategic imagination when addressing great power conflicts and crisis management.

This is how Sargeant put it at the beginning of our discussion.

"I actually think policy is a secondary discussion. The first discussion is, what's driving the way you think about policy? And to me, there are two big drivers. One is the future. We don't know what the future is, so we can only speculate about it. We can try and create various futures, but we cannot know what the future that will emerge will be. We must step in and think about what the various futures might be, and what are the pathways from those futures back to now, and what are the pathways forward.

"We need to think very specifically. If you want to create a particular future or you think a particular future might emerge, what are you going to do about it between now and then. That's where the strategy piece comes in because strategy is a pathway.

"The other big driver is how you understand yourself and your situation. What is driving the way you think about the world? Are you sufficiently self-aware, or sufficiently self-critical of the

---

4   The quotes by Brendan Sargeant are taken from his lecture. Brendan Sargeant, "Challenges to the Australian Strategic Imagination," Australian National University (May 2021), http://sdsc.bellschool.anu.edu.au/sites/default/files/publications/attachments/2021-05/centre-of-gravity-58-challenges-to-australias-strategic-imagination.pdf.

assumptions that, in a sense, lead you to a particular perspective, out of which emerge policy solutions?

Brendan Sargeant speaking at the Williams Foundation Conference on "Hi-Intensity Operations and Sustaining Self-Reliance," April 2019.
Photo Credit: *Second Line of Defense.*

"One of the things I think is problematic about large, embedded, very stable institutions is that they start working for themselves and they see the world as a reflection of themselves, rather than seeing the world and thinking about, well, what sort of relationships should they have with the world? If, for example, you make, say, a force disposition decision for internal institutional reasons, without thinking about its impact on the world, that is a failure of understanding, a failure of thinking about the future. It also means that your decision-making is driven by your own needs rather than the needs of having to deal with strategic reality.

"Let me give an example which is derived also from your work on the Nordics and European defense. When you talk about the Nordics, you don't talk about them trying to defeat Russia. You talk about them 'managing' the challenge of Russia. We are in a world of continuous process management, of continuing adaptation to constantly changing circumstances. One feature of crises is that they call you to challenge yourself and your assumptions about the world. You need to continue to do this because the world is always changing. You are continuously managing your relationship with a changing reality.

"And because you don't know what tomorrow will be, you have to have sufficient adaptiveness to be able to respond and change. That is a very different world to the one where you just sit and forget, or because you have built a big force, you can assume that it will take care of everything. Or you live in a world that no longer exists. That is what I talk about when I talk about nostalgia.

"For me, when I look at a lot of our planning, it is very linear. It builds a set of assumptions. Those assumptions are built on what we've done in the past, and they project a linear projection into the future. As we know, the future is not what we think it will be. We need a much richer, broader understanding of possibilities, built on a richer understanding of ourselves and our situation.

"We need to try to create future worlds by what we do, even though the world is not going to be what we seek to create. The question then is, how do we have sufficient adaptiveness and capacity to live in a range of future worlds, and to be constantly testing our assumptions of the nature of the world that we are in?

"Crises challenge our sense of identity; If they are big enough, they will challenge a country's sense of what it is, and how it will operate into the world. You can succeed or fail on the basis of the extent to which you're able to understand the challenge to identity as part of the challenge that a major crisis will create.

"Strategy, then, is preparation for the future crisis. We live in a world where we are not sure what the future crisis is. We are also living in a time of crisis. In this context, strategy becomes something about the relationship between where you are, who and what you are, and the range of possible futures that might emerge."

We then turned to the specific Australian case. Australia is facing significant change as America's role in the world has changed, as China is seeking its definition of the global order, and as technology reduces the traditional comfort of Australian geographical isolation.

"We have outsourced a lot of strategic policy to our senior partner, and we are paying for that at the moment. We need to develop a diplomatic and strategic culture, which is far more aware of the contingency and volatility of the world, and far more willing to, in a sense, take risks. What I think we are seeing in Australia at the moment, with this COVID lockdown, with the closing of the borders, and the focus on domestic policies, is that our energy has turned inwards because there is a real fear and reluctance to step out.

"The real danger is that the world will force us to change before we realize that we have to change ourselves. There is a clear commitment to reshaping our military and rethinking policy in relation to our regional strategic environment, but the rethink is too slow, and it is not conceptually adventurous enough. As Paul Dibb has argued, we don't have the luxury of warning time anymore. We don't really have the luxury of space, which means that we cannot continue to operate at the pace or the rate of change that we have been used to.

"We need to be ruthless in our self-analysis, about our strengths and weaknesses, and who we are. We need to have a clear sense of the range of possible futures and the various responses that we may need to make. That is why I say a crisis is a challenge to imagination, a challenge to identity before it becomes a policy or a strategy challenge."

We then discussed a major challenge, which is understanding the nature of your friends and adversaries. The words 'allies' and 'partners' are frequently used in describing relationships for the United States or Australia, but what does that actual mean in a specific event and case? The core competitors Russia and China and other authoritarian powers, like Iran, do not think like the leaders or publics of the democracies. Understanding what a particular competitor or adversary is doing (and why) in a particular event which becomes a crisis and a step in the escalation ladder is obviously crucial for escalation management.

"Your adversary is not a reflection of yourself. I think the hardest thing in policy and strategy is to be prepared to try and see reality as it is, not as you want it to be. Then it is a relationship between that and the pathways you build into the range of futures that might emerge. And to have adaptive capacities, to support a range of options and solutions.

"Robbin, you have emphasized the importance of case study thinking as a way to do strategy. This makes a great deal of sense. With the case study method, every situation is different. If you are thinking about the future, you need to think about multiple futures, not a single future. One of the advantages of case studies is that that it actually gives you a methodology to test the future. When you are testing the future, you are not just testing the future, you are testing yourself in the present, because you have to think of two places in time at once. We don't see enough of that in strategic thinking. Bureaucracies are designed to create consistent outcomes over time. Bureaucracies assume that time is an infinite resource. That is certainly not the case in today's strategic challenges and realities facing Australia."

CHAPTER TWO:

COMMANDER'S PERSPECTIVES

VADM Lewis: Commander of Second Fleet and of Allied Joint Force Command Norfolk

By Robbin Laird and Ed Timperlake
May 26, 2021

With the strategic shift from the land wars, and meeting the evolving Russian challenges, Admiral Richardson, then the Chief of Naval Operations (CNO), directed the reestablishment of the U.S. 2nd Fleet in 2018. He put VADM Lewis in charge of the command, but it was a new departure not simply a reestablishment of the 2nd Fleet.

We had the chance to meet with the three commands under his leadership, 2nd Fleet (C2F) and NATO's Joint Force Command Norfolk (JFCNF) and the Combined Joint Operations from the Sea Centre of Excellence (CJOS COE), which has been folded into C2F. That Centre has played an important role in working the kind of allied integration which Lewis has sought and is working to employ.

Left-to-right Commander, U.S. Fleet Forces Adm. Grady, Chief of Naval Operations Adm. John Richardson, Commander, U.S. 2nd Fleet Vice Adm. Andrew Lewis and Fleet Master Chief U.S. 2nd Fleet Smalts salute the Ensign during the 2nd Fleet Establishment Ceremony. August 24, 2018. Photo by Petty Officer 1st Class Gary Prill.

VADM Lewis provided insights throughout the span of our conversations and meeting with his commands, and we sat down in his office on May 10, 2021, at the end of those engagements to discuss how he saw the way ahead. We started by discussing the original standup of the command in 2018. The CNO had a clear desire to reestablish a command that could address North Atlantic defense, and notably the growing importance of coalition operations in the high north. C2F is not a large command, certainly when compared with other numbered fleets. And VADM Lewis worked the first three months with less than 10 staff members, during which time he worked the foundation of how the fleet should be established and how best to work its concepts of operations.

Question: How did you do the initial launch process?

VADM Lewis: We had a charter to reestablish the fleet. Using the newly published national defense strategy and national security strategy as the prevailing guide, we spent a good amount of time defining the problem.

My team put together an offsite with the Naval Post-Graduate School to think about the way ahead, to take time to define the problem we were established to solve and determine how best to organize ourselves to solve those challenges. We used the Einstein approach: We spent 55 minutes of the hour defining the problem and five minutes in solving it. Similarly, we spent the first two-and-a-half months of our three-month prelaunch period working to develop our mission statement along with the functions and tasks associated with those missions.

From the beginning, our focus was on developing an all-domain and all-function command. To date, we clearly have focused on the high-end warfighting, but in a way that we can encompass all aspects of warfare from seabed to space as well.

Question: We are very impressed with the template you and your team have put together in shaping a way ahead. It is clearly an integrated distributed approach encompassing the allies as well. As you mentioned, resources are tight, and clearly effectively organizing the U.S. with allied resources in the region provides significantly greater capability than simply focusing on the U.S Navy alone. How would you characterize the shift which you and your team are shaping?

VADM Lewis: Our Allies and partners across the Atlantic and into the Nordic region are also rethinking collective defense. These are both NATO and non-NATO nations that are clearly engaged in enhancing their national and collaborative capabilities.

With regard to new strategies and policies, they are not simply checklists. The effort involves reworking the art of warfare, innovating, overcoming things that do not work, and leveraging tools and processes that do work in reshaping force capability. We are clearly focused with our Allies on reshaping what we can do now with the forces we have now, in order to ensure a solid foundation for adding new capabilities in the future.

I think that the challenge with overarching guidance from above is when it is too prescriptive. It is a question of working at the operational force level on new ways of doing things effectively. For example, there is an emphasis on shifting to distributed maritime operations. At C2F we are focused on concrete ways to operate from distributed maritime operations centers as a way to exercise agility at the fleet level.

Although it is conceptual, our focus is on how to develop the Maritime Operations Center (MOC) as an effective weapon system. We're talking about a distributed operation center across the battle space that is able to command and control forces from various locations. This allows for ease of communication or the ability to command more effectively and provide command functions in order to receive timely feedback from the tactical forces.

I think to do this you have to have some imagination and flexibility in order to put the pieces together. We have exercised this concept through several distributed operations centers to various locations—the USS Mount Whitney for BALTOPS 2019, Iceland, Tampa, Camp Lejeune, New York (with the Comfort), and again on the Mount Whitney this month for Steadfast Defender 2021.

Question: The template which you and your team have put in place, shaping an integrated distributed force, is well-positioned to encompass a number of the new technologies, such as maritime autonomous systems. How do you see the relationship between reworking concepts of operations and technologies?

VADM Lewis: I've become somewhat jaded with technology because technology is just a means to an end. To put it another way, it's just a tool. You have to ask what are we trying to get out of it? What's the objective? And then, how are we going to use that technology? The key point is that our processes need to be agile enough to absorb new technology without missing a beat. That's where I think we need to focus our efforts.

An operational headquarters or a high-end tactical headquarters is a weapons system. Normally, when war fighters discuss weapon systems, they refer to their platforms. But the operational or tactical headquarters should be looked at as being a key weapons system, the glue that pulls a multitude of different weapons systems together in a coherent manner—both kinetic and non-kinetic. They can mass fires, mass effects, and maneuver in a coordinated fashion at the fleet level. That's what operational and tactical headquarters do.

But we need to get better at being able to craft, shape, and leverage operational or tactical headquarters as a weapon system. We have to get a lot better at doing so, and new technologies can be helpful here, which is one of my objectives for working with the Mid-Atlantic Tech Bridge.

Question: There are other command challenges, such as the division between Second and Sixth fleets in the Atlantic or how C2F will work going forward with II MEF, for example. How do you see the way ahead?

VADM Lewis: We are working hard on this challenge. My main effort as the Commander of two NATO commands and a U.S. Fleet command is to ensure there are no seams in the Atlantic, seams that our adversaries can exploit. By communicating and working closely with our counterparts on the other side of the Atlantic, we can ensure we are working to close any perceived gaps. As an example, we recently conducted staff talks with Second Fleet, Sixth Fleet and II MEF. We are making progress thanks to the relationships we have spent time developing.

In terms of C^2, we can always be better about how we talk about and exercise command and control. My focus has been on the principles of mission command in which you emphasize trust with your commanders to lead distributed forces. You have to first understand the environment, and then you have to give clear intent. Once you have given this guidance, you let the distributed forces operate in a way that allows them to self-organize in order to meet the mission. This doesn't involve a whole lot of detailed control from various headquarters, rather it only provides enabling guidance that allows them to take initiative at the right level and to manage risk at the right level. My role with regard to my subordinate commands is to mentor the commanders below me. My goal is to give them the right guidance and then let them command.

I have two discussions each week with the operational strike group commanders that work for me—the first is focused on man, train and equip issues, and the second is focused on mission command and operational issues. It's an opportunity for me to hear about various issues and spend time listening. At other times, we'll bring in a guest speaker and discuss operational dilemmas others have faced to use as case studies for the group. It is truly time well spent with the strike group commanders who make up our waterfront leadership.

Question: How do you view the way ahead with integration with the USMC?

VADM Lewis: We have a fantastic relationship with our USMC counterparts, and because of that relationship, we have made great progress with integration. We have a few Marine staff officers working at 2nd Fleet, but I think we would also benefit from an exchange of sorts at the Flag level. I think we could make additional progress if we integrate a Marine as the deputy commander of C2F, and vice versa, a Navy commander as the deputy commander at II Marine Expeditionary Force (MEF). I have such an approach with my NATO JFCNF command, and it works well as we shape very concrete ways ahead to build more effective fleet operations with our NATO counterparts.

Rear Adm. Steve Waddell: Second Fleet

By Robbin Laird and Ed Timperlake
March 19, 2021

During our visit to C2F in March 2021, we had an opportunity to discuss the standup of the command in 2018 and its evolution since then. One clearly important fact cannot be missed when visiting VADM Lewis, the CO of C2F. In his frugal office space, one finds his office flanked on one side by a Canadian Rear Admiral and on the other by a British Rear Admiral. The first is his C2F deputy, and the second is his NATO deputy.

It is hard to miss the point: this is a command focused on integration of maritime capability across the North Atlantic. The importance of having a Canadian Rear Admiral within the American command cannot be overstated. While it is not unheard of to have members of partner militaries embedded within large U.S. commands, U.S. 2nd Fleet has taken this further by integrating them into the actual command and decision-making structure of the fleet at a very senior level.

International cooperation and coalition building is key to having a force that is capable of operating together, in peacetime as well as war. Integration does not begin at the senior level. Waddell has worked with and embedded with the U.S. Navy throughout his career. "Much like the U.S., we in Canada have an entire generation of sailors and naval officers, myself included, that have routinely deployed around the world, often integrated as part of a NATO task group or a U.S. carrier strike group," said Waddell. "Those opportunities have allowed my colleagues and me to become accustomed to working with partners and the U.S. Navy. Trust is built over time."

As the U.S. Navy begins to shift its attention from decades of operations in the Middle East back to blue water and high-north engagement, ensuring strong partnerships between the U.S. and allied Arctic nations becomes of paramount importance. Waddell and the other allied officers on U.S. 2nd Fleet's staff bridge gaps in understanding, strengthen relationships, and are central to U.S. 2nd Fleet's mission accomplishment.

Not surprisingly, Rear Adm. Steve Waddell has a very impressive background, which includes serving in the Pacific Area of Operations, most recently at Canadian Forces Base Esquimalt from July 2014 through June 2017. In other words, he brings a perspective on the challenges facing maritime forces in both the Pacific and the Atlantic to his work as the Vice Commander.

In our discussion with him, he underscored how important the standup of this command was from his point of view to defend the interests of the United States and its partners in the Atlantic area of operations. He underscored that C2F is best understood as a startup command, rather than having stood up an existing command template as seen elsewhere in the U.S. Navy, and as such sees this effort as a driver for change for 21st century naval operations.

Vice Adm. Andrew Lewis, commander, U.S. 2nd Fleet, left, stands alongside U.S. 2nd Fleet Vice Commander, Rear Adm. Steve Waddell. (U.S. Navy photo by Mass Communication Specialist 2nd Class Joshua M. Tolbert, August 12, 2019.)

According to Waddell:

"We will not be as large a command as other numbered fleets. We are designed to max out at about 250 people and currently are around 200. We have to be different and innovative in how we get after the missions. We need to make sure we're using tools and alternative resources, because we don't have that depth and capacity of people, so you have to find a different way."

As a startup command that is now Fully Operationally Capable or FOC, they are not emulating other numbered commands in many ways.

"We are not primarily focused on the business of force generation, but we focus on how to use assigned forces to shape a desired outcome. We don't want to get in the space of those responsible for force generation: we just want to be able to advocate for timely, effective outputs that optimize the use of the fleet."

He noted that the assumption that the 2nd Fleet was going to be the 2nd Fleet of old was misplaced.

> "The old 2nd Fleet was interested in sea lines of communication. But the new 2nd Fleet is focused on strategic lines of communication. This is an all-domain perspective, and not just the convoy missions of past battles of the Atlantic."

He referred to C2F as the maneuver arm in providing for defense, deterrence, and warfighting but as part of a whole of government approach to defending the United States, Canada, and NATO allies against threats. He underscored that "we are flexible and unconcerned with regard to whom we will work for. Operationally, we work for NAVNORTH (Fleet Forces Command) for the Homeland Defense Mission, but we can seamlessly transfer and work for NAVEUR/ EUCOM to defend forward, or to work in the GIUK Gap for an Allied Joint Force Command."

Rear Admiral Waddell drove home the point throughout our discussion that they were building an agile command structure, one that can work through mission command and with expeditionary operations centers. As he explained it, "For us, a Maritime Operations Center is not a room with equipment. It is a capability, based on technology, process, and people. We distribute it all the time, whether it's been afloat or ashore. Previously, we were in Iceland. Right now, they're down in Tampa for an exercise. I'll be joining them in a couple of days."

How did we end up with a Vice Commander who is Canadian? As Rear Admiral Waddell tells it, VADM Lewis was asked to stand up 2nd Fleet and given much latitude to do so. He went to a senior Canadian official to ask for a Royal Canadian Navy officer to serve as his deputy.

Waddell felt that bringing a Canadian officer into the force made a lot of sense for a number of reasons. First, because of the partnership nature of operations in the area of interest. Second, because the Canadians have experience in operating in the high north, which could be brought to the renewed efforts on the part of the United States' side to do so.

Finally, as Waddell himself works the C2F experience, he can weave what he learns into the Canadian approach to operations:

"It's not lost on me that we as a Canadian service honed our teeth in the battle of the Atlantic in the Second World War in the North Atlantic and then in the Anti-Submarine (ASW) fight through the Cold War. Those competencies, although we were collectively distracted a little bit from iterations to U.S. Central Command (CENTCOM) and in the Persian Gulf for some time, are crucial going forward. I think we've reinforced those capabilities and are investing in new capabilities at home in Canada, such as with the Type 26 surface combatant program, a very robust platform."

He highlighted that the distances involved in the High North are generally not realized.

"People forget that it's a longer distance to go from, not even Norfolk but Halifax up into the Arctic than it is to cross the Atlantic."

The logistics infrastructure in the High North is very limited compared to Europe, which means that for C2F, working through the kind of operational infrastructure needed to operate in the area is part of the equation as well.

"There is renewed focus on getting the East Coast Fleet involved in more northern activities. Canada does a series of annual Arctic exercises called NANOOK. C2F is involved in this exercise. Typically, every other year there is a major warfare exercise off of Halifax called CUTLASS FURY, where we will send ships and aircraft to participate as well. We are working to be able to reinforce operations in more northern latitudes."

Rear Admiral Waddell emphasized that the focus was upon the Atlantic challenge, and not narrowly focusing on a specific Combatant Command's (COCOM's) area of interest.

"You need all of that to have an informed and meaningful conversation that really comes down to priority, level of effort, and force apportionment. Our reality is that combatant commanders are assigned resources, but the fight needs to be contiguous across COCOM boundaries. It's not a NORTHCOM problem. It's not a EUCOM problem. It's an Atlantic problem."

He discussed various tools and approaches being used to understand how to scope the challenges and priorities, including hosting a Battle of the Atlantic tabletop exercise. The goal of efforts like these is to scope out the various interactions across an extended battlespace to understand how combat operations in one area of interest influence those in other areas of interest.

All of this leads to a very significant conclusion about the U.S. Navy and allies integrating across an extended battlespace and operating distributed forces.

"For the web of capabilities, you need to be ready to fight tonight, you need to be able to seamlessly integrate together across the fleet, inclusive of U.S. and allied forces. You fight as a fleet."

That means fundamental change from a cultural assumption that the U.S. Navy has run with for many years. "You need to understand and accept that a fighting force needs to be reconfigurable such that others can seamlessly bolt on, participate in, or integrate into that force. That might mean changes from the assumptions of how the Navy has operated in the past in order to operate successfully with allies."

Vice Admiral John Mustin: Chief of Navy Reserves

By Robbin Laird and Ed Timperlake
April 26, 2021

The U.S. Navy is reworking its approaches to shape new capabilities for the high-end fight. Obviously, a refocus from a two-decade primary role in supporting land wars to a return to blue water expeditionary operations is a significant one. And clearly one which affects the Navy's reserve forces as well. Recently, we talked with Vice Admiral John Mustin, Chief of Navy

Reserves, N095, to find out how he was working the way ahead to make sure the reserves integrate into full spectrum crisis management, which if deterrence fails, will lead to a high-end U.S. and Allied Air/Sea combat campaign.

The key point which he made in the guidance he released last Fall on the way ahead for the Navy reserves is visionary:

> "...the changing geopolitical environment forces us to modernize our thinking, our force structure, our training and our operations to address the realities of a future conflict. Simply said, we cannot assume tomorrow's war will look like yesterday's. Hence my Theory of the Fight includes accelerating our transformation to ensure we get, and remain, 'future-ready.'"

Vice Admiral Mustin went on to state:

> "The reserve force today is optimized perfectly to support the global war on terror. Many of our processes, our unit structures, billets, training procedures, even the way that we mobilize sailors do a fantastic job meeting the specific requirements of a counterinsurgency, counterterrorism, non-maritime, land-based conflict, particularly in CENTCOM and the horn of Africa.

> "My comment in my commander's guidance was that is not likely to be effective to address the next conflict, and if I am reading the tea leaves properly in this era of great power competition, we're going to need very different skills.

> "The Navy has recognized this, and the Navy is transforming. And I did not feel that the reserve force was working quickly enough to reflect that transformation in our reserve-specific force structure, processes, and procedures.

> "We are working very closely with the fleet commanders. We are focusing on answering their needs. 'What is it that you need and value?" And equally important; "What does the reserve team do for you today that you don't value?

"My job has been to take fleet feedback and then shape the future structure of the reserve force, to address those specific needs. For the numbered fleets there are several capabilities that leap to the fore, specifically emphasis on their maritime operations centers, both capacity and capability. Related but not explicitly tied to the maritime ops center is expeditionary logistics that are explicitly tied to our distributed maritime concept of operations. And one echelon down is a focus on expeditionary advanced base operations.

"Everything I just described is ripe for reserve force contribution. We've begun the process now to determine where we have elements of the reserve force that are relatively low value as it relates to CNO and fleet priorities. How can I harvest some of the current existing units and billets to meet priority needs, and how can I take our sailors out of low value jobs and create new high value jobs, given the strategic shift to the high-end fight?

"That's an initiative underway right now, and I'm happy to report there are a number of things that I'm able to do in this fiscal year. There are also certainly things that are on the roadmap for fiscal year '22 and some for '23 and '24 and beyond. But I want to move out now because I just don't know that we're going to have a lot of time to make those changes when the shooting starts."

In World War II, a well-respected historian Max Hastings in a seminal work, *Inferno*, determined that after a difficult start, the U.S. Navy was at the end of the war the most effective fighting force of all combatant forces of all nations. Admiral Mustin took pride in that historical example but correctly observed that today the U.S. Sea Services may not have the luxury of time. They must be trained and equipped to win the fight and get it right, right now.

Great Lakes, ILL (March 13, 2021) Vice Admiral John Mustin, Chief of Navy Reserve, speaks with Naval Region Midwest Reserve Component Command Sailors at 2021 CO-SEL conference. U.S. Navy photo by Cdr. Todd Spitler.

Question: We are focused on the strategic shift and how that demands significant change in warfighting and escalation dominance. A different set of skill sets are clearly required. Clearly, we have seen at Second Fleet that a key priority is C² for a distributed integrated fleet. This requires different skill sets as well. There is a whole new generation of digital warriors in our society as well. How are you focusing on reshaping the reserves to harvest the opportunities in civil society and to focus on the critical skill sets for the "new" Navy, so to speak?

Vice Admiral Mustin: That's a perfect scene-setter. I completely agree that what made us successful over the last 20 years, post 9/11 is not what's going to make us successful into the next few decades.

Working with Vice Admiral Lewis has been important as well. As Second Fleet Commander, he clearly understands that we need to shape a new approach. When I was in high school in the 80s, my father was Second Fleet Commander, so I can legitimately say that "The new Second Fleet is not your father's Second Fleet."

What VADM Lewis wants and what we are offering started with a clean sheet of paper as it relates to the design of the reserve force for C2F.

I've looked at every other numbered fleet to determine which model works best for us. And then, perhaps not surprisingly, I recognized the reserve design supporting each fleet was different. What that tells me is that there is a need for us to establish a template where we can get at 80% of the core competencies, the missions, functions, and tasks associated with the C^2 in the maritime element. And then there's certainly some peripheral amount, call it 20% hypothetically, tailored to the region, the Area of Responsibility (AOR), the theater. Shaping a template for C^2 is a key element around which we can shape fleet design going forward, as well as shaping the skills required to support that design.

If you go on the second fleet watch floor right now, there will be a handful of reserve officers and sailors that are standing watch. And early in my tenure I mentioned to Vice Admiral Lewis, that rather than build a team that shows up a weekend a month, two weeks a year during exercise support requirements, why don't we build a team that's fully integrated so that they work with their chiefs of staff, their division directors, their 'N codes,' as we call them, their department heads by function. And let's have them plugged in every day, not just on weekends.

And I don't mean 365 days, but if an average sailor can do roughly 38 days a year—that's just the sum of a weekend a month, and two weeks a year. There's nothing that says it has to be a weekend a month and two weeks a year, I could do 30 days consecutively and then not see them again for six months, or we could do groups of five days or 10 days. We can be as flexible as we want.

If we invest time upfront to training them to their watch station, then we get production time out of them by having them show up and actually stand the watch. And that's good for second fleet as well as for the reserve sailors, because they earn a credential that is permeable and enduring. They can then take a billet at their next job at another fleet. That means that the skills that we've invested in them are permeable and they can plug in immediately to another fleet.

Admiral Lewis was very receptive to the idea, and frankly, after hearing it, said, "Okay, this isn't a course of action. This is your tasking, make it happen." He has been very receptive to saying, let's build full integration. I don't want there to be a distinction. And I told him if we do this right, no one will ever know the difference between a reserve and an active sailor. You're just a sailor. And you're a sailor that's contributing to the requirements of second fleet, whether that's at an expeditionary environment or operating at the headquarters building.

Question: The reserves bring significant experience to the active-duty force. This has been a key to navy success in the past. How do you see this going forward?

Vice Admiral Mustin: The focus on fleet ops is critically important to me. I just had a conversation with CNO today about the strategic imperative of restoring seagoing ratings to the reserve force. Right now, we do a fine job in staff headquarters, but when it comes to getting folks on the waterfront, it's more of a challenge. For every sailor that says I've got the time and the inclination, we can get them afloat, so that's a goal of mine.

A key problem we face is not having a lot of time to mobilize in the face of significant conflict. With regard to our reserve component, there are two kinds of readiness. There is mobilization readiness, and there's warfighting readiness. Mobilization readiness is the cost of being a reserve sailor. You need to maintain your readiness to mobilize when asked. And that means you've done your dental checks and your medical checks, and you've done your physical fitness assessments and your general military training. That's kind of the standard stuff that Title 10 pays for in the number of days, the weekend a month and the two weeks a year, and that's up to you.

You don't get a Navy Achievement Medal for being mobilization ready. In fact, if our sailors can't maintain mobilization readiness, I will ask them to leave the service because it's a privilege to serve, not a jobs program.

The more challenging side is the warfighting readiness piece. And that's where I'm investing a lot of time and effort to understand the training pipelines, the timelines, the costs, the billets, the units, etc, because my assumption is we need to be ready on day one of a conflict. I'm also working very diligently to improve the processes to mass mobilize our people.

And I've committed to the CNO that in January of 2022, we will be able to mobilize 49,000 sailors in 30 days, which is about 15 times the throughput capacity we had when I took office here.

We need to be ready to go because we're not going to have five years to ramp up, to get good at our jobs like we did in World War Two. We have to be good at our jobs now. I want to use every penny of training dollars and every iota of time when we have our precious sailors in uniform and get them training to be good at their billets, because I just don't feel like we've got the luxury frankly, of waiting.

And that said, I will tell you, I'm thrilled that we just celebrated our hundred- and six-year anniversary as a reserve force. And though we have contributed in every significant conflict in our nation's history, post-World War I, we've never been caught by surprise in mobilizing the reserve force.

What does that mean? Well, I told you, we have to be ready because it's likely to be short notice. This means having the reserves as a key contributor to the active-duty force, particularly as it builds out for conflict, and that means having the kind of experienced reserve sailors that you referred to as key players in the process.

Question: How important is tapping into the right kind of civilian skill sets in the reserves to meet current and future warfighting challenges?

Vice Admiral Mustin: You hit the nail on the head. I can write a book on the countless stories of folks who have a unique set of civilian skills, who are ready to serve the nation in uniform. There is a wide variety of critical skills that the reserve force brings to bear: think big data and analytics, data visualization, predictive analytics, 3D manufacturing, space, cyber, unmanned, and autonomous systems. We've got folks who work in all of those program areas as civilians, and also in units that support the operations or the concepts of employment. We've got Silicon Valley folks, we've got venture capitalists, private equity players, who understand what's happening in the technology sector and areas where we can take advantage and apply their skills and insights to what we do in uniform. The challenge I wrestle with frankly, is how do you scale that?

Rear Admiral Betton, Royal Navy: JFC Norfolk

By Robbin Laird and Ed Timperlake
March 24, 2021

When you visit 2nd Fleet and JFC Norfolk, you are acutely aware of the key role they play in working together to build out 21st century North Atlantic defense. Vice Admiral Lewis is the head of both commands, and the two commands work closely together in shaping the kind of integrated distributed force crucial to 21st century warfighting and deterrence.

JFC Norfolk was created at the 2018 Brussels Summit as a new joint operational level command for the Atlantic. It reached an important milestone in September 2020, when it declared Initial Operational Capability. JFC Norfolk is the only operational NATO command in North America and is closely integrated with the newly reactivated U.S. Second Fleet. We had a chance to visit with Deputy Commander, JFCNF Rear Admiral Betton during our March 2021 visit to Norfolk.

It is notable that Betton comes to this command as part of the Royal Navy's significant reworking due to the impact of the new carrier and its onboard F-35s. The Queen Elizabeth class is the only carrier built around the F-35 and for the Brits, it also drives integration between the RAF and the Royal Navy.

The sense we had from the C2F staff of the excitement of working a startup command and innovating from the ground up was underscored as well by Rear Admiral Betton with regard to his command.

> "Coming here 18 months ago has been a really exciting professional opportunity, and genuinely a pleasure to have another run at setting up a team pretty much from scratch. The Second Fleet team was well on the way by the time I got here, but the NATO team was just about at conception, but not much beyond that."

The geography and three-dimensional operational space of the NATO zone of responsibility is very wide indeed. As Betton put it:

> "SACEUR's area of responsibility goes all the way from the Yucatan peninsula in the Gulf of Mexico to the North Pole. I've

always loved the phrase "from Finnmark to Florida" or Florida to Finnmark[5]. But it is also important to realize all domain challenges and threats that we face. It's everything from seabed infrastructure, through the sub sea water column, the surface, the airspace above it, and up into the satellite constellation above that."

As the former commander of the Queen Elizabeth Strike Group, Rear Admiral Betton is very familiar with the coming of the F-35 as an allied capability to Atlantic defense. The USMC has been a key partner of the UK as the Brits have stood up their F-35B capability afloat, have integrated with the British carrier in the North Atlantic, and have generated new ways to integrate USMC-Naval forces with the new aircraft.

Betton also noted that first the Italians and now the Norwegians have brought their F-35s to conduct air patrols from Iceland. Indeed, one could note that the F-35 capability operational today in the North Atlantic is indeed largely allied—or to put it another way, the most advanced combat airpower in the region is provided by the allies.

Royal Navy Rear Adm. A. Betton, Deputy Commander, JFCNF, (left) and U.S. Vice Adm. A. Lewis, Commander, JFCNF at JFCNF's Initial Operational Capability ceremony at Naval Support Activity (NSA) Hampton Roads, Virginia. September 2020. Photo Petty Off. 1st Cl. Th. Green.

---

5   Finnmark is the northernmost part of Norway. It reaches around Sweden and meets Finland. It is part of Norwegian Lapland.

We also discussed the importance of innovation in the maritime domain awareness NATO community as well. The Brits preserved their ASW skill sets after having cancelled Nimrod and in anticipation of adding the P-8, which is being deployed from RAF Lossiemouth in Scotland, where there are P-8 facilities for allies as well.[6] The Norwegians are operating P-8s as well. With P-8s and the U.S. Navy operating Triton, which operates in an orbital cycle complementary to the sortie generation approach of the P-8s, there is a continuous belt of ASW, and anti-surface fleet information being provided for the U.S. and allied forces in the North Atlantic.

These new capabilities have their most important impact in supporting rapid decision-making cycles. The C2F focus on reworking C^2 to provide for effective mission command and distributed operations is a key effort for JFC Norfolk as well. And the two staffs work interactively on shaping a way ahead in the crucial C^2 domain.

Betton underscored the importance of reworking of how allies work together in the North Atlantic:

"The U.S. is by far the dominant figure of NATO, but it's not the only piece. And it's not always just the heavy metal that is relevant. It's the connectivity, it's the infrastructure and the architecture that enables the 30 nations of NATO to get so much more than the sum of the parts out of their combined effort. But it's particularly the relevant nations in the operational area and their ability to work together which is an important consideration."

The Rear Admiral underscored the importance of the only operational NATO command on U.S. soil.

"The idea of integrating it with the second fleet headquarters under a dual hatted command was a fantastic move because it emphasizes bluntly to Europe that the U.S. is fully committed to NATO. It's not NATO and the U.S., the U.S. is part of NATO.

---

6   Robbin Laird and Murielle Delaporte, "Canada, the UK and the Seedcorn Program: Keeping UK ASW Skill Sets Alive," *Second Line of Defense* (October 18, 2017), https://sldinfo.com/2017/10/canada-the-uk-and-the-seedcorn-program-keeping-uk-asw-skill-sets-alive/.

And having an operational headquarters here in Continental United States (CONUS) really emphasizes that point in both directions."

He noted that there are 16 nations at the command currently with three more arriving in the next few months, namely, Portugal, the Netherlands, and Bulgaria. It is crucial to shape a better understanding of how central air-maritime forces are to NATO defense.

And reworking how to do the most effective defense is also a work in progress. As Rear Admiral Betton put it:

> "One of the key efforts we are pursuing in this integrated command is not just stitching together NATO and U.S. assets, but it's also stitching together teams within teams. It could be the U.S. cooperating with Norway, Sweden, and Finland, with Admiral Lewis commanding a multinational command.

> "And a crisis might grow and evolve into something that the North Atlantic Council agrees to respond to and therefore activate the JFC to command in a NATO sense. But because the Commander has that flexibility to go from a unilateral U.S. only under second fleet, through a growing coalition, there's the opportunity to coordinate activity with a whole diverse range of entities before it becomes a formal NATO response."

Agility and scalability are a key part of the way ahead for 21st century full spectrum crisis management. And the JFC working in an integrated manner with C2F certainly is working such capabilities. This is a case of startup fleets working core capabilities, which are clearly needed across the combat force. This is why what is happening in Norfolk is certainly of strategic impact and significance.

MajGen Cederholm: Second Marine Air Wing
July 29, 2021

The Marines are undergoing a change with a sense of urgency associated with the strategic shift from the Middle East land wars to being effective in strategic competition. The Marine Corps exists to provide a globally deployable Naval Expeditionary Force in readiness, this means preparing for initial engagements in contested areas of operation and working within the Joint Force and our alliances to support the high-end fight, if called upon to do so.

This is a strategic shift, but in many ways, it is a strategic shock moving away from the combat conditions and training associated with the Middle East to a wider variety of mission engagements in the Pacific and North Atlantic areas of operation. One noticeable constant is 2nd MAW never stopped training to fight in any clime and place, to include spending more time training in the Nordic region with the Nordic allies.

But the blunt fact is that this generation of Marines has been engaged in the Middle East in counterterror and related operations, not focused largely on operations in the littoral against strategic competitors. And to be clear, this requires crisis management skill sets specific to a wide diversity of situations which are likely to occur dealing with competitors in any region.

There have been new phrases coined suggesting how the Russians or Chinese operate in the new strategic environment such as hybrid war and operations in the gray zone. Clearly, the reset of the USMC involves being able to dominate in those situations as well as enabling the Joint Force and our allies to ramp up escalation capabilities as required.

During my July 2020 visit to 2nd MAW, I discussed this shift and its challenges with Marines, and with the CG of 2nd MAW, MajGen Cederholm. When I met with him last December, he highlighted the importance of increasing readiness for the force, and we started the July meeting by focusing on the Wing's success in readiness over the past few years.

According to Cederholm, "We are in the process of approaching readiness levels that have not been seen in decades. On some days, our readiness rate has approached 73% of all our assets being flown. Marines at all levels have contributed to this success, one which is critical to enable us to meet our mission of being able to fight today."

He then indicated that this was one of four key priorities being pursued by the Wing going forward.

> "Our first priority is to continue increasing our readiness rates by adding more combat depth through our formations. The second is to drive more lethality into our training and readiness (T&R) manuals. The third one is a combination of force preservation and force development, ensuring that we are training Marines, protecting Marines, and understanding risk, both organizational and institutional risk. The fourth is alignment to the future, or alignment to the 2030 force design effort."

2nd MAW is clearly focused on the training piece as a key part of the way ahead. Major General Cederholm highlighted the need to train to fight today but to find ways in reshaping training and the T&R manuals to better position the Wing for the future fight. What he argued is that even though the Marine Corps continues to clearly have capabilities to engage with peer competitors, the T&R manuals over the years of engagement in the Middle East appropriately focused largely on the operations in support of CENTCOM.

Maj. Gen. Michael Cederholm speaks with Col. Michael McCarthy visiting Marine Air Control Group 28. July 23, 2020. U.S. Marine Corps photo by Staff Sgt Andrew Ochoa.

This clearly needs to change going forward. The Wing leadership is focused on finding ways to do this more effectively going into the future.

> "What types of missions do we need to do for the evolving peer fight? How can we write T&R manuals that train to those missions, and not just what we have done over the past twenty years?"

He argued that there is a clear need to shape an understanding of predictive readiness to be able to do the evolving missions which are required for the peer fight, something the Commandant of the Marine Corps and Chief of Staff of the Air Force have written about.

> "If we take our target as 2030, and we plan back from that, we can better inform our force design and development efforts.

> "2D MAW currently has planners in the EUCOM AOR who are looking to smooth out any inhibitors or barriers that would hinder our ability to operate in and around the European continent, but they're also eyeballing the future to fall in alignment with our priorities, which is alignment to force design in the future.

> "How do we plug into the 2030 operating concept, what tools do they need, and what missions do they need to train to? How do they integrate more effectively with the Joint Force and our alliances? How do they integrate into the kill web? We are working on that roadmap right now, and it will require a significant shift in how we educate and train our formations.

> "We are retooling for the future fight. At the same time, we're prepared to answer the phone, time now, takeoff, and beat any and all potential adversaries out there."

Although F-35s are in 2nd MAW, they are there as part of the training effort. 2nd MAW will be receiving its F-35s over the next five years and will see the CH-53K as the latest USMC aircraft come to 2nd MAW prior to the rest of the USMC. Given that the VMX-1 detachment working the operational testing is actually at New River, this makes a great deal of sense.

But given the approach which MajGen Cederholm outlined, he clearly thinks the Marines need to look at their new platforms in a specific way. That way was highlighted in a quote he cited from an individual he described as an "incredible defense leader" who asked him several years ago:

> "Why do we stuff the F-35 into our current operating concepts? Why don't we take our current operating concepts and revise them based on the capabilities which the F-35 brings?"

But the Wing is receiving a new aircraft soon into the operational force, namely, the CH-53K and the CG have recently flown on the aircraft. He underscored:

> "I was amazed at the automation that's built into the aircraft. To be honest with you, I can't stop thinking about what the different possibilities are of how we can make this platform support our operating concept on the battlefield of today—and not just today, but on the battlefield of the future."

And that is the real advantage of the reset which MajGen Cederholm is highlighting and working with his team at 2nd MAW: focusing on evolving missions, leveraging new capabilities to expand their capabilities to execute those missions, and to build out the Marines so they continue to be able to be a highly effective and lethal contributor to the defense wherever and whenever our Nation may need.

LtGen Rudder: Commander, U.S. Marine Corps Forces, Pacific
September 8, 2021

My last visit to Hawaii and meetings with the Marine Corps Forces Pacific (MARFORPAC) commander and his staff was in 2014. In August 2021, I visited again and spent several days in the Islands, during which I visited both MARFORPAC and Pacific Air Forces Pacific (PACAF). Since my last visit, what the Marines refer to as the "pacing threat" has gained enhanced momentum. The People's Republic of China, both in policies and capabilities, has ramped up the threat and challenge envelope for the United States and its allies. The Russians are a Pacific power as well, and the direct threat posed by North Korea is an evolving one as well.

At the onset of my visit to the Marine Corps in Honolulu, I had a chance to talk with LtGen Steven Rudder, commander, U.S. Marine Corps Forces, Pacific. I have known "Stick" ever since he served as Deputy to the then-Deputy Commandant of Aviation, LtGen George Trautman.

We started the conversation by focusing on how he sees the challenge facing the Marines in the Pacific.

This is how LtGen Rudder put it:

> "Our first challenge is about having the right force postured with the right capabilities. Our starting point is today's posture, which for the most part is centered in Northeast Asia. Because of the vast distances in the Pacific, our additive challenge is being able to maneuver capabilities into places where you may not have a dedicated sustainment structure. Regardless, you have to be able to rapidly get there, set up, and operate using organic lift and logistics."

The current Commandant of the USMC has highlighted the importance of the Marines being able to leverage their position as part of an "inside force" that is able to "stand in" and operate inside the adversary's weapons engagement zone. LtGen Rudder underscored that part of the USMC current posture means, that on a daily basis, the Marine Corps must operate inside an adversary's threat ring.

> "I think the key advantage for us is the daily posture of Marines in Japan and within ongoing partner operations in Southeast Asia. We are persistently in the first island chain ready to maneuver to seize or defend key maritime terrain. Continued integration with the joint force in Japan and in the Republic of Korea is critical within the context of any contingency. The question then becomes: what capabilities does the Marine and the Joint Force need to maneuver into the right tactical position to get the desired effects?"

Since I last visited MARFORPAC in 2014, the Marines have reworked the force projection trajectories, and are in the process of making these trajectories realities to shape a more effective engagement force in the region. Notably, since 2014, the initial Marine Rotational Force in Australia (MRF-D) has deepened its cooperation with the Australian Defence Force (ADF).

And Australia has itself enhanced its joint force capabilities, including the introduction of the F-35 and an amphibious surface fleet and air/ground capability. The focus on operations in the direct defense of Australia and wider Indo-Pacific region creates significant and evolving opportunities for US/Australia interoperability.

Also, the Marines are building up their presence in Guam at Camp Blaz. This is the first new Marine Corps base since 1952. This is how LtGen Rudder highlighted several opportunities for force projection. "We are focused on shaping an effective posture that combines forward bases with rotational partnerships with key Allies. I have already highlighted how important our posture is in Japan. Employing Infantry and MV-22s from Okinawa and F-35s from Iwakuni (in southwest Honshu) we readily integrate with Japan's Amphibious Rapid Deployment Brigade."

"MRF-D plays a role as well. Six months out of the year, we rotate 2,000 Marines into Australia with ground forces, MV-22s, fires, and logistics capability. Now that the Australians are operating the F-35 and routinely exercising amphibious operations, we can work jointly on expanding high-end bi-lateral and multi-lateral operations. As a combined force, we have already increased the complexity of operations as recently demonstrated during Talisman Saber 21.

"And as we build up and deploy greater numbers of forces to Camp Blaz, Guam, we will use this location as an additional posture location for 5,000 Marines and Sailors. All of these posture developments allow us to have various operational touch points from which one could aggregate force capabilities. With a combination of air and sea lift, we are designing a force with the ability to rapidly move into positions of advantage."

We then discussed the evolution of fires which the Marines can bring to the Pacific fight. With the end of the Intermediate-Range Nuclear Forces (INF) treaty, the United States can now build longer range conventional capabilities. The Marines are looking to participate in this effort and employ them from expeditionary forward bases well inside the adversary's weapons engagement area. The objective is to contribute to Sea Lines of Communication (SLOC) defense or be additive to offensive naval fires.

According to LtGen Rudder:

> "If we look forward in the not-too-distant future, we'll have the ability to have land-based, long-range fires, aviation fires, and persistent high endurance Intelligence, Surveillance and Reconnaissance (ISR) with the MQ-9. We'll be able to move those capabilities with KC-130s, MV-22s, or amphibious lift allowing us to project long-range fires forward anywhere in Asia, much like we do with the HIMARS (High-Mobility Artillery Rocket System) today.

> "HIMARS fits in the back of a KC-130 allowing rapid mobilization and insertion. We will exercise the same operational tactic with anti-ship capability. We want to project sea denial capabilities to cut off a strait of our choosing or maneuver into positions to create our own maritime chokepoint. As we saw with hunting mobile missiles in the past, having long-range fires on maneuvering platforms makes them really hard to hit. As we distribute our long-range fires on mobile platforms, we now become a hard platform to find.

> "Our desire is to create our own anti-access and area denial capability. For the last several years, we were thinking about the adversary's missiles, and how they could be used to deny us access to forward locations. Now we want to be the sea denial force that is pointed in the other direction. Land-based fires are perfectly suited to support naval maneuver.

"We want rapidly to move by air or sea, deliver sea denial capabilities onto land, maneuver to position of advantage, deliver fires, maneuver for another shot, or egress by air or sea. We are training current forces on concepts for sea denial missions supported by maneuver of long-range fires. This is a key element of the naval integration."

With a growing capability of joint sensor networks, the potential for more effective joint targeting is a reality. As the joint force focuses on dynamic targeting, services are closely coordinating fires networks and authorities. The advantage of land-based expeditionary fires is that it provides persistence cover within an established air and surface targeting solution.

This is how LtGen Rudder characterized how he saw the way ahead.

"We are completely integrated with naval maneuver and working hand and hand with the joint force. I MEF and III MEF have been operating seamlessly as three-star naval task forces astride Seventh and Third Fleets. During crises, I become the deputy JFMCC (Joint Force Maritime Component Commander) to the Pacific Fleet Commander. The MARFORPAC staff integrates with the PacFleet staff. Even during day-to-day operations, we have Marines at PacFleet planning and integrating across multiple domains. Should we ramp up towards crisis or conflict, we will reinforce our JFMCC contribution to ensure we remain fully prepared for all-domain naval force execution.

"This means that our anti-ship missiles will integrate into naval maneuver. We also aggressively pursue PACAF integration for bomber, fighter, and 5th Generation support. Daily, our F-35s are integrated into the PACAF AOC (Air Operations Center). We are focused on better integration to ensure we have a common operating picture for an integrated firing solution."

The USMC F-35s play a key role in all of this. Although there is a clear focus on enhanced integration with the U.S. Navy, the integration with the USAF is crucial for both the U.S. Navy and the USMC. LtGen Rudder highlighted the role which USMC F-35s play in Pacific defense and force integration.

"We count on pulling fifth-gen capability forward in times of crisis. We are committed to having forward deployed F-35s conducting integrated training on a regular basis with our PACAF counterparts. We will also conduct integrated training with our Korean, Japanese, Singaporean, and Australian partners. We are also training with aircraft carriers when they operate in the region—notably, the USS Carl Vinson, the first U.S. Navy F-35C variant carrier aircraft.

"And the F-35B has caught the operational attention of the rest of the world. The United Kingdom's HMS Queen Elizabeth is the largest fifth-generation fighter deployment ever conducted on an aircraft carrier. We are proud to be a part of that UK deployment, with a Marine F-35B squadron, VMFA-211, embarked and operating with our British partners. They are currently doing combined operations in the Western Pacific.

"We are excited to see the Italians operating F-35s off the ITS Cavour, and we hope by the fall of this year that we'll be landing an F-35B on the Japan ship Izumo, as the Japanese look ahead to the purchase of F-35Bs. The South Koreans are considering going down a similar path, with Singapore also adding F-35s to their inventory.

"Aside from shipboard operations, the F-35B can do distributed operations like no other combat aircraft. We can go into a variety of airfields, which may not be accessible by other fighter aircraft, reload and refuel, and take back off again, making the both aircraft and the airfields more survivable."

LtGen Steven R. Rudder salutes Marines with III Marine expeditionary Force before giving his remarks during the III Marine Expeditionary Force change of command ceremony on Marine Corps Air Station Futenma, Okinawa, Japan, Nov. 9, 2021. U.S. Marine Corps photo by Cpl Benjamin M. Whitehurst.

The Marines are the only combat force that tactically combine fifth generation with tiltrotor capabilities. This combined capability is crucial for operations in an area characterized by the tyranny of distance.

The MV-22 Ospreys can also carry a wide variety of payloads that can encompass the C^2 and ISR revolutions underway. And if you are focused on flexible basing, the combination of the two aircraft (Osprey and F-35B) provide possibilities which no other force in the world currently possesses.

But shortfalls in the numbers of aircraft forward create challenges in unleashing their full potential for enabling the Marines as a crisis management force and enhancing the Marine Corps contribution to the joint force. The nature of distributed operations in the Pacific demands long-range aircraft like the MV-22 to sustain the force. The amphibious operating capability of the USMC becomes more significant as flexible basing and the enhanced capabilities which a family of amphibious ships could bring to the force.

This is how LtGen Rudder put it:

"We can reconfigure our amphibious ships to take on many different assault functions. I think when people talk about amphibious assault, they have singular visions of near-beach operations. Instead, we need to think of our amphibious capability from the standpoint of our ability to maneuver from range. Rather than focusing on the 3,000 or 5,000-meter closure from ship to shore, I think about the 600, 700, 1,000-mile closure, with amphibs able to distribute and put people in place or to conduct resupply once you're there.

"Amphibious lift, with its ability to bring its own connectors for logistics support, is increasingly significant for the operational force. In addition, we have to make sure that we're able to close the force when lethal and non-lethal shaping has done its course.

"At some point, you're going to need to seize and defend land. We have two ways to tactically accomplish this mission, either by air or by surface assault. There's no other way to get forces ashore unless you secure a port that has the space to offload and a road network to move ashore. Open port options are highly unlikely during crisis, thus amphibious lift is increasingly becoming more valuable for maneuvering forces in the maritime domain."

The Marines are launching a new capability in the next couple of years, the Marine Littoral Regiment (MLR). According to the MARFORPAC commander:

"We are working towards initial operating capability (IOC) of the MLR in 2023. We want to demonstrate the maneuverability of the MLR as well as the capabilities it can bring to naval operations. Near term, we will work to exercise new capabilities in the region, such as loading the NEMESIS (Navy/Marine Corps Expeditionary Ship Interdiction System) system on the KC-130s or LCAC for integrated operations with F-35s, MQ-9s, and other maritime targeting capabilities."

In short, the USMC is in transition in the Pacific, and working towards greater interoperability with the joint force, notably, the U.S. Navy and the USAF.

LtGen Heckl: I MEF Commander

July 9, 2021

During my lifetime, the USMC has been the initial crisis management for the nation. It continues to be so, but after a long interlude of becoming land-centric due to the demands of the nation's leaders. With the return of direct defense in Europe and with the changing strategic situation in the Pacific, the USMC is in transformation to recalibrate how to play its crisis management role with the presence of peer competitors.

The Marines as we underscored in our book on Pacific defense published in 2013 already have several key elements necessary to play a more agile and flexible role in the Pacific.[7] The Osprey coupled with the F-35 offers significant tools in providing an entry insertion point which is a significant one. The Marines are building on this advantage and looking to find new ways to shape their force forward in the Pacific and to do so with enhanced joint and allied cooperation.

I had a chance to discuss the way forward with the CG of I MEF, LtGen Karsten Heckl. I last talked with him when he was the CG of 2nd Marine Air Wing. Before that, I talked with him in Norway when he was COS STRIKEFORNATO, and before that when he was the Deputy to the Deputy Commandant of Aviation.

We started by discussing how he saw the challenge. He underscored that a key part of understanding the nature of the threat environment is to understand the nature of the Chinese regime. Although this can be labeled great power competition, in the Pacific the great power is run by leaders of the Chinese Communist Party. They are communists, they are authoritarians, and they wish to play by their rules.

---

7   Robbin Laird, Edward Timperlake and Richard Weitz, *Rebuilding American Military Power in the Pacific: A 21st Century Strategy* (2013).

It is not simply a military challenge but a political-military and cultural one as well. Certainly, a key part of working the Marine Corps' role in the Pacific is political military as well as a narrowly warfighting role. We often hear about hybrid war and the gray zone; with a Marine Corps well-respected in the Pacific and working relationships with partners and allies in the region, the Marine Corps can play a more effective role as a crisis management force.

LtGen Heckl underscored that a major challenge facing I MEF was enhancing its ability to operate forward or west of the international dateline.

"I have a 7,000 nautical mile physics problem, but we're doing a lot of things already that have us operating West of International Dateline."

U.S. Marine leaders from I Marine Expeditionary Force Information Group (MIG) speak to LtGen Karsten S. Heckl, the commanding general of I Marine Expeditionary Force, during a visit at the I MIG headquarters building at Marine Corps Base Camp Pendleton, California, Aug. 19, 2020. U.S. Marine Corps photo by Cpl Tia Carr.

He noted that the strategic shift provided in the defense guidance to focus on the great power competition is a key driver for change, but the transformation necessary to do so needs to be accelerated. This includes the question of augmenting Indo-Pac exercises as well.

Clearly, the Marines like the rest of the joint force is working through how best to deter the Chinese and to engage in operations over an extended area or over an extended battlespace. This is clearly a work in progress. He noted that I MEF has a great working relationship and is enhancing integration with Third Fleet, but both are located on the West Coast of the United States. How best to operate forward?

This entails the question of how to do effective blue water expeditionary operations. This entails the question of how to work the Pacific geography with allies and partners to get the maximum political-military and combat effect. It is also a question of taking advantage of new ways to operate as well. For example, as seen in the Black Widow Exercise in the North Atlantic, the Marines can certainly contribute to ASW operations. How might the Marines more effectively assist the Navy in sea denial and sea control in the Pacific?

A key limitation for the Marines in the Pacific for sure is size and state of the amphibious fleet. Operating at sea and from the sea with Marine Corps air assets provides very agile and powerful force insertion assets to deliver crisis management effects. But the decline in the numbers of amphibious ships is a critical problem, and how best to rebuild the fleet is a work in progress.

When I was last in Hawaii, the MARFORPAC team was focused on ways to expand the amphibious force in the Pacific with allies, or to enhance what they referred to as "amphibiosity". That was 5 years ago, and now allies are indeed expanding their amphibious forces, in South Korea, Japan, and Australia. And allies are adding F-35Bs and Ospreys to their force. How can the USMC best leverage this upsurge in capabilities? It makes little sense to further devolve the U.S. amphibious fleet as allies themselves see greater utility in this force for crisis management and warfighting.

As LtGen Heckl put it: "My biggest concern right now is amphibious shipping and connectors." And in this sense, the expeditionary force leverages what the Navy and Marines have now, but creative thinking about how to build out an amphibious fleet is clearly needed. There is also a need to build actual integratable assets as well.

He concluded: "The challenge seen from I MEF is that for us to be effective, we need to be credible. To be credible, we need to be forward with credible forces. We are focused on positioning the MEF to be in a position to be an effective deterrent force."

Brigadier General Michael Winkler: Pacific Air Force

September 21, 2021

During my recent visit to Hawaii, I had a chance to talk with Brigadier General Michael Winkler, Director of Strategic Plans, Requirements and Programs at the Pacific Air Force. We discussed the way ahead for PACAF in the evolving strategic situation.

The U.S. services and our allies are focused on shaping innovative ways to deliver effective warfighting and deterrent capabilities. For the USAF, a key focus is upon building out fifth generation airpower, leveraging that capability across the joint force, crafting, shaping, and delivering a more distributed force labeled as Agile Combat Employment, and preparing the ground for the coming of the new bomber as a key weapon system for the Pacific.

BG Winkler underscored that PACAF is focused on the importance of operating as a joint force and doing so by learning from its ongoing operational engagements. As he put it:

"Our vision for the Pacific is to operationalize the Pacific AOR. In so doing, we need to take a proactive approach. Too often we operate in the Pacific theater at the speed of staff. What we need to do in the Pacific theater is to act at the speed of operations."

With the current force, a key path to unleash enhanced capabilities is being able to leverage airpower and enhance the capabilities of the air-maritime force, up to and including the role of the USCG. The presence force throughout the Pacific, whether American, partner or coalition provides the baseline for engagement with competitors and adversaries. Leveraging presence to connect to a wider integrated force is an important way ahead to deal with the challenges in the Pacific.

BG Winkler put it this way:

"A United States Coast Guard National Security Cutter might be facing a challenge. And because we haven't fully integrated their sensor suite in with the rest of the Department of Defense (DoD) capabilities, they aren't going to be as informed as they need to be because we haven't made those connections or haven't been able to leverage the full range of U.S. combat power.

"We are working towards enhanced integratability in the force. A game changing capability is based on ensuring that every sensor out there is connected to a network, and that network shares information with everybody that we allow access to it. And we would want to make sure that all of our allies and partners have access to that network.

"Certainly, all the U.S. forces forward deployed would have access to that network, as well. We've got a lot of work to get from where we are today actually to being able to build that capability, but that's one of the things that we need to redouble efforts on. Access to the right information is going to be the key to the next conflict. I also think that both parties in the next conflict will probably be trying to prevent the other country from being able to have an information advantage."

Throughout the discussion, he highlighted the importance of what I have referred to as full spectrum crisis management capability. The USAF needs to be able to contribute across the conflict spectrum, precisely because deterrence works only if demonstrated power is engaged from the lower to higher ends of conflict.

BG Winker argued:

"The more we build out our phase zero peacetime capabilities, the more we organize, train, and equip our force right now to be able to have that information advantage. We need to continue to practice those tactics, techniques, and procedures in phase zero, as we're doing normal training operations, or even normal real-world operations in phase zero.

"Every single Humanitarian Assistance and Disaster Relief (HADR) event is an opportunity to shape a mixed force that can then share that same type of data. I think that using those training reps as an opportunity to better build our joint inter-agency situational awareness is a step in the right direction.

"We have tools to do that right now. We don't have to wait for a 5-year, or 10-year advanced battle management solution. We've got Link 16 networks, radios, and a lot of different ways in which we can communicate information. To the degree that we can do that more machine-to-machine data processing, I think that'll be a more efficient way of doing it, because we're going to start to develop large amounts of data. So much data… that the human trying to assimilate all that data now becomes the choke point in the process. So, the more we get the machines and the artificial intelligence finding the anomalies in the normal activity for us, the easier it will be for us to be able to process that data and start to capitalize on information advantage.

"But we certainly don't need to wait for future capabilities; we can enhance joint capabilities across the spectrum of warfare now by working more integration with the key elements of air, sea and land power."

PACAF is working the agile employment concept as a key part of shaping the ability of the Air Force to operate across the expanse of the Pacific and to do so in a more survivable mode. When I met the current PACAF Commander in Australia, he was the commander of 11th Air Force. And during a 2018 Williams Seminar, he discussed the need for what would now be called Agile Combat Employment. I wrote about his assessment in my book on the evolution of Australian defense strategy published earlier this year.[8]

At the Williams Foundation Seminar in Canberra in March 2018, the 11th Commander, Lt. General Kenneth Wilsbach, highlighted the nature of the challenge requiring the shift to mobile basing as follows:

"From a USAF standpoint, we are organized for efficiency, and in the high intensity conflict that we might find ourselves in, in

8   Robbin Laird, *Joint by Design: The Evolution of Australian Defence Strategy*, (2021)

the Pacific, that efficiency might be our Achilles heel, because it requires us to put massive amounts of equipment on a few bases. Those bases, as we know, are within the weapons engagement zone of potential adversaries.

"So, the United States Air Force, along with the Australian Air Force, has been working on a concept called, Agile Combat Employment, which seeks to disperse the force, and make it difficult for the enemy to know where you are at, when are you going to be there, and how long are you are going to be there.

"We're at the very preliminary stages of being able to do this but the organization is part of the problem for us, because we are very used to, over the last several decades, being in very large bases, very large organizations, and we stovepipe the various career fields, and one commander is not in charge of the force that you need to disperse. We're looking at this, and learning how we might reorganize, and be able to employ this concept in the Pacific, and other places."

Now PACAF Commander Wilsbach has made this a core effort. And this is how BG Winkler underscored the effort:

"PACAF has done a pretty decent job over the last three years of getting the Air Force to embrace this idea of agile combat operations and to export it to Europe as well. The whole idea, if you rewind the clock to the mid 80s, early 90s, was that every single base in the United States Air Force that was training for conflict would do an exercise where you'd run around in chemical gear. At that point in time, there was a large chemical biological threat, and the Air Force recognized that it needed to be able to survive and operate in that chemical threat. So, we trained to do it.

"I think the new version of that chemical biological threat is the anti-access area denial umbrella. The idea of agile combat employment is our capability to survive and operate and keep combat momentum underneath the adversary's anti-access area denial umbrella. Basically, we are focusing on our ability to survive and operate in a contested environment.

"PACAF has taken a realistic approach that is fiscally informed because it would be very difficult for us to try to build multiple bases with 10,000-foot runways, and dorms, and ammunition storage all over the Pacific. What we've done instead is concentrated on a hub and spoke mentality, where you build a base cluster. That cluster has got a hub that provides quite a bit of logistic support to these different spoke airfields. The spokes are more expeditionary than most folks in the Air Force are used to.

"The expeditionary airfield is a spoke or a place that we operate from. It's not 10,000 feet of runway; it's maybe 7,000 feet. We're probably not going to have big munitions storage areas, there's probably going to be weapons carts that have missiles on them inside of sandbag bunkers. And we're going to look a lot more like a Marine Expeditionary base than your traditional big Air Force base. It'll be fairly expeditionary."

We then discussed the challenge of reducing the number of USAF personnel necessary to sustain air operations, along the lines which the Marines have focused upon.

"The MOS challenge is a very real problem for us. And I think we're starting to figure out how we're going to get around that. We're calling it multi capable airman, where we do some degree of cross training. So, your average crew chief now can actually do other flight line tasks like load missiles, and vice versa, your fuels folks actually can do some minor maintenance tasks. It is very much more along the lines of the USMC model. The goal is to have airmen do more things, which then means we don't need to deploy as many of them to one location to still get the job done. And then, we'll work a logistics schema maneuver from the hubs to the spokes to do the things you'd mentioned previously—the fuel resupply, the munitions resupply, any other expendables."

We then focused on the shift of ISR from Intelligence, Surveillance, Reconnaissance to Information, Surveillance, Reconnaissance, and the shift to decision making at the tactical edge. As BG Winkler underscored:

"Our allies and partners are a huge part of everything that we're going to end up doing out here in the theater. We like to think that they are an asymmetric advantage, and the more that we can get the coalition plugged in the more effective we can be. It's not just U.S. sensors that are out there feeding the rest of the joint coalition force, but it is important to tap into the allied and partner sensors.

"I do think that we're at a precipice for information warfare, and the fact that some of the forward based sensors that we have, like the F-35, can generate way more intelligence data than our traditional ISR fleet, like the E3. Australia's flying the E7—fairly modernized, very robust ISR capabilities on those. I think there's been some discussion within the United States Air Force about whether we need to up the game and maybe make an E7 purchase, as well.

"But we are getting to that point where the forward base fighters are so much more technologically advanced than our ISR fleet, that it makes you question where the ISR node should be. I agree it doesn't necessarily need to be all the way back in Hawaii. It could be somewhere else in the theater.

"But the Air Force, as you're aware, has traditionally operated with AOC as the central node for command and control in the Pacific. We're trying to figure out as an Air Force what the future looks like. But I don't think that future is going to be five years from now. I think it might be 10 years from now.

"And in the short term, what you'll probably see is a something that allows us to operate from the AOC, protect our capabilities to operate from the air operation center, to be able to help synchronize fighters throughout the entire AOR, but then set up subordinate nodes that are probably forward of the AOC. If the AOC does get cut off or shut down, for some reason, you do still have subordinate C2 nodes in the theater that can keep the continuity of operations, and keep some battlefield momentum up, to continue to take the fight to the enemy.

"And I think we're all getting more serious about electronic warfare. I'll be interested to see how those capabilities mature over the next 10 years. I think we're at a situation right now, where electronic warfare in a lot of ways is still a supporting force to the kinetic stuff. The big question in the electronic warfare is knowing you've got a limited number of assets that can do it, where do you want to prioritize that? And that question drives you back right to who is doing the command and control? How are you integrating the most effective electronic warfare to support the highest priority kinetic warfare? That's a commander's decision, so the important part of that is the Joint Force Commander or the Joint Task Force Commander, or whoever is running the fight, needs to very clearly articulate to his subordinate commanders, who is the supported commander for synchronizing those joint fires. Because without knowing that ahead of time, we may possess all of the capability in the world as a joint force but we will never employ it as effectively as we could."

The official USAF photo of Brigadier General Michael P. Winkler. Credit: USAF

We then discussed training. And with the coming of the B-21 in the mid-term, preparing for the coming of the B-21, not as a platform, but a weapons system, notably integrated in the air-maritime fight is a key consideration. The role of an expanded ability to work in the synthetic environment is important, but BG Winkler felt that progress has not been rapid enough in this domain, and live training is critical and so to do so in ways that better emulate the red side threat is even more critical.

Here he noted that building new capabilities in Alaska, on the U.S. side, and in Australia, on the Australian side, were significant in shaping a way ahead. And although we did not discuss this, in my view, being able to operate the new bomber from these two trajectories as an air-maritime asset, or one that can work with the tactical air forces, or the fleet is a key leverage for the mid-term for the United States and the allied forces.

BG Winkler closed by linking the training discussion with where we had started the conversation, namely, working from operations to con-ops evolution.

"Admiral Aquilino, INDOPACOM commander, believes that the entire Pacific Ocean right now should be our training space.

Every single time that China sails a Surface Action Group, out here into the Philippine Sea, we ought to be working as a joint force to integrate and bring in additional assets that maybe we haven't used in the past. For example, maybe that's an opportunity for us to partner with the Coast Guard to figure out how we can get them added into a Link 16 network to share situational awareness.

"But we need to take advantage of the opportunities our adversaries provide us by getting out and about in the Pacific. And that's how you get that training level down to the operators that are going to be pulling triggers and assimilating information in a combat environment as you let them train. Do it every single day in their weapons platform. I think any situation in this theater is an opportunity for us to practice."

MajGen James F. Glynn: The CG of MARSOC

November 18, 2021

The Marine Forces Special Operations Command (MARSOC) provides an interesting case study for the USMC transformation path. It was stood up in 2006 and was clearly part of the response to the land wars and one of its goals was to enable the Marines to work more effectively within the key role which Special Operations Forces were playing in how the land war was being fought.[9]

With the Middle Eastern land wars no longer the U.S. defense priority (although counterterrorism operations sadly not), should MARSOC be abolished? Some have argued this. But as the Marine Corps is reworking how to operate force distribution and integration, why aren't the small unit operational capabilities of the Raider teams a key element of the next phase of transformation?

---

9   Sgt. Jesula Jeanlouis, "Marine Forces Special Operations Command Celebrates 15th Anniversary," (February 22, 2021), https://www.dvidshub.net/news/389559/marine-forces-special-operations-command-celebrates-15th-anniversary.

The idea behind the Inside Force is to find ways that smaller clusters of Marines can deploy within a Weapons Engagement Zone, and connect with an Outside Force, either to empower that Outside Force or to deliver decisive effect in a special area of operations.

Also, a key element of the peer fight is to understand how to deal with a core challenge posed by our peer competitors, namely, being able to counter their focus on operating at a level of lethality below outright war but using military and other means to coerce outcomes in their favor. Or put in other words, we are facing ongoing limited wars with peer adversaries with a learning curve on escalation management and control, rather than simply dealing with hybrid war or gray zones.

MARSOC forces could contribute significantly to working at this level of warfare, and with focus on ways to connect more effectively indigenous or partner groups with the Outside Force, whether Marines, or the joint or coalition forces, the work which MARSOC has done with joint and coalition forces in the past would seem as well to be a key asset to leverage going forward.[10]

MARSOC while preparing for a peer fight could also provide a significant real world force element for innovation at the small group level, which can be leveraged and introduced into the wider Marine Corps force. They also could assist in rethinking how to use the assets the Marines already possess to enhance combat capability now rather than waiting for whatever innovations arrive and are credible the decade out.

Given the importance of small group operations distributed but integratable with a larger force, the Marine Raiders should be a key part of this next phase of transformation. In effect, the Marines need to take full advantage of MARSOC opportunities and to leverage their potential contributions to shape change going forward.

---

10 An interesting look at some of these dynamics is an article by Paul Baily, "Enabling Strategic Success; How MARSOC can help overcome 'simple minded' militarism," *Small Wars Journal* (January 11, 2021), https://smallwarsjournal.com/jrnl/art/enabling-strategic-success-how-marsoc-can-help-overcome-simple-minded-militarism.

MajGen James F. Glynn during his promotion ceremony aboard Marine Corps Air Station Beaufort on May 5, 2020. U.S. Marine Corps photo by LCpl Aidan Parker.

I had a chance to discuss in November 2021 the challenges and opportunities for shaping the way ahead for MARSOC within the overall transformation of the USMC and its role in the Joint Force with MajGen James F. Glynn, the CG of MARSOC. We started by discussing the nature of the change being focused upon at MARSOC. As MajGen Glynn put it:

> "From the outset of the standing up of MARSOC, we focused on a concept often referred to as I-3: Interoperability, Integration, and Interdependence. And I believe, based on competitors and what their study of our Joint Force capabilities are, the time is now to focus very purposefully on interdependence as a core element going forward.

> "How are we going to be ready for the future? A stand-in-force approach means that we need to be very deliberate about the development of our capabilities going forward, with a thought towards the interdependencies of what special operations forces are expected to do in support of, and as part of, such a force.

> "By virtue of Title 10, services tend toward the responsibility to engage in crisis response as a core function, and certainly the Marine Corps is crucial to such a mission. The Navy performs

some actions in competition, such as freedom of navigation, and all the services focus on reassuring partners and allies. But SOF in general, and MARSOC in particular, focuses on activities that begin before crisis. We are part of the overall engagement in precrisis actions and do so by operating and developing relationships with partners and allies to enable them to do their own crisis prevention and response and enable them to tamp down violent extremist organizations that can turn into insurgencies. What we do on behalf of the naval services is provide access and placement to friends, partners and allies in shaping relevant capability in that precrisis to crisis phase."

We then discussed the advantages which flow from smaller group operations to drive innovation in the larger force. I argued that one of the advantages of having small groups like MARSOC is you can be more cutting edge because you're smaller, and you have less large force consensus building to try something new. And in my view, the Marines have capabilities from the aviation side, right now, Ospreys, F-35s, Vipers/Yankees, and CH-53Ks, which can be tapped in new ways to shape innovation going forward while other innovations are shaped in the decade ahead, which in my view will be shaped by actual modular task forces in operations and combat.

MajGen Glynn provided his perspective on this aspect of driving change as follows:

> "Our size is our strength. We have the agility to make a decision, take one step and pivot 90 degrees to enable that decision. We've demonstrated that in a number of areas. That's obviously considerably more cumbersome to larger formations.

> "What that enables Special Operations Command (SOCOM), and the Marine Corps is an outsized return on investment for a relatively miniscule investment in time, money and equipment. We can leverage the SOCOM acquisitions mindset of buy, try, decide; in other words, get one, try it. If it's not good, then don't use it. If it just needs to be modified, make some modifications, and try it again. And if it's worthy of investment, then on behalf

of the service we can turn it into a program of record and a larger scale investment.

"We are focused on strategic shaping and reconnaissance with a specific emphasis in the electromagnetic spectrum and information environment. Our ability to bring multi-domain awareness and effects to the precrisis and crisis phases to, for example, the MARFORPAC commander in his role with the Joint Force Maritime Component Commander, is a key focus for us.

"Returning to my point regarding interdependencies, I look at MARSOC operations as part of a Venn diagram, or the image of the Olympic rings. If the capabilities of the service and the SOF component are thought of as rings, how purposeful can we be about where, how, and why they overlap? What are those capabilities that intersect and represent purposeful interdependencies? The Marine Corps prides itself on mission analysis and task organizing for the mission. We have that opportunity on a larger scale right now, and MARSOC, as the Service SOF component, is optimized to be the vanguard of experimenting with interdependencies required for stand-in forces."

The focus on MARSOC as an Inside Force or Stand in Force, as the Marines call it, does highlight the interdependency nature of their operations. What do they bring to an area of operation? What do they link to enhance their own impact, and to enhance the other elements of the force which operates in or comes to an area of interest? Working innovations in interdependencies to shape effective precrisis and crisis responses is a core driver of change for the evolving MARSOC force.

This is how MajGen Glynn put it:

"Our name, Marine Raiders, highlights an innovative tradition dating back to 1942. Our company commanders in this organization are Majors and each unit has the capability to engage in multi-domain operations. Throughout these initial 15 years, MARSOC units have significant experience in expeditionary operations, sets and reps as expeditionary advanced operators and that experience is crucial in shaping the way ahead as we work with new approaches and new technologies. At the same time, we have joint and coalition experience, and working with partners and allies is a key part of our operational DNA.

"For the naval forces, our approach to basing and logistics is a key driver of change as well. We are agnostic to where we operate from, but it is influenced by aspects of support like logistics. As long as we get what we need to operate, we are not concerned with how it arrives. If it is by a CH-53, or an unmanned USV, it's that the logistics capability contributes to enabling where we are. We operate from ships, ashore, can be air dropped, however, we will stay where necessary for the time needed, and a noteworthy aspect of it is about logistical enablement for what can be done in the area of interest.

"From this perspective, we are clearly interested in adopting new technologies. We can operationally test, evaluate, and take equipment and techniques to a remote location where we're training or deployed and learn from it. With that experience, we've said, "Hey, we're going to need to fix that thing, but the other thing works. From there, we've been able to influence the pace of investment and adoption. I think this approach can become very impactful to the way ahead for the coming Marine Littoral Regiments.

"Our ability to leverage what we already have, but to do so in new ways, is crucial to innovation with today's force, as we develop tomorrow's force. Our ability to operate with the Viper, with the 53K, with the F-35 now, we definitely have an opportunity and are working towards realizing enhanced combat effects from such interdependencies."

We then concluded by discussing the changing nature of warfare, and how MARSOC can enable the force to enhance its ability to prevail within that changing warfare calculus. In my view, the 21st century authoritarian powers who are peer competitors operate in the warfare spectrum from the use of lethal force designed to achieve tactical or strategic objectives below the threshold of triggering a wider conventional conflict up to the level of nuclear force informed conventional operations.

MARSOC from this perspective is a clear player in frankly both ends of the spectrum, but certainly is a meat and potatoes player in deploying to counter the lethal force supporting the political objectives of what people like to call "hybrid warfare" or operating in the "gray zone". And with its focus on shaping the kind of relevant interdependencies with other force elements, which can play from either partner or coalition or joint forces, MARSOC can learn how to be an effective tip of the spear, but even more importantly, help shape what indeed the most relevant spear would be in such situations. From this perspective, MARSOC is not a force focused on irregular warfare, but about ongoing limited warfare 21st century peer competitor style.

MajGen Glynn noted that from such a perspective one could consider MARSOC as focused on optimizing for the 21st century version of ongoing limited warfare 21st century peer competitor style.

> "We're leveraging capabilities in order to bring cross-domain awareness of peer adversary actions and activities that are going on right now."

He argued that bringing their combat experience to the evolving warfare context is a key advantage for the MARSOC force.

> "The reality of our deployments around the world is that our force is getting very relevant warfighting sets and reps. They know what it's like to be in a denied environment, at least for a period of time, and they know what it's like to be in a contested environment for extended periods of time. They're adapting and adopting both the technology, the techniques, and the manner in which they do business on an evolving basis to operate in such environments.

"We take lessons from our deployed forces now and apply them into the process that we have to certify, validate, and verify every formation that we send in support of Special Operations Command. We run a validation process flexible enough to adapt to emergent requirements to make sure we stay relevant and remain current, because that's our assessment of how quickly things are changing, particularly below the threshold of declared armed conflict."

LtGen Beaudreault: Looking Back and Forward

July 15, 2021

I first met LtGen Beaudreault during my visit to II MEF in April 2021. I returned on June 29, 2021, prior to the General's retirement in July. I asked him to look back on the evolution of the USMC during his time of service, and to provide some thoughts about the challenges going forward. As his career spanned the end of the Cold War and the global competition with a peer competitor, through the long period of the priority on the Middle Eastern land wars, and now with the return of global competition but this time now with peer competitors, his thoughts are especially helpful as we refocus on the new strategic context.

LtGen Beaudreault:

"As I reflect on my time with the USMC, the most capable USMC during my time of service was the force we had in the 1988–1991 period. I should be clear at the outset that I am not suggesting the Marines of today are not as capable as those in that period. I am referring to the size and capabilities we had available to us at the end of the Cold War. We were very lethal, agile, and combat flexible. In terms of naval integration, we had MEB elements which Saddam Hussein had to consider a serious threat of amphibious invasion. We could do either deception or forcible entry. We had a much more robust amphibious capability than today.

"We had a significant Force Reconnaissance capacity organic to the USMC. They embarked as part of the force and relationships are important in this business. There was nothing like having them eat in the wardroom or on the mess decks and interact with those that they supported. They were trained in *in extremis* hostage rescue, ship take-downs, gas-oil platform seizures, and in combination with the embarked SEALS were a tremendously capable force. Some of those skills have migrated to special operations forces, which are not always co-located or physically present for integrated crisis planning.

"That was a very, very capable Marine Corps. For example, Force Reconnaissance had an ability to conduct insertion operations out of submarines, that might come in handy in the future. We need to recover some of that capability."

LtGen Brian Beaudreault, left, the commanding general of II Marine Expeditionary Force at a forward combat service support area established by Combat Logistics Battalion 252 at Marine Corps Air Ground Combat Center Twentynine Palms, California, Oct. 25, 2019. U.S. Marine Corps photo by Cpl Scott Jenkins.

With the coming of 9/11 and the focus on counterinsurgency and counterterrorism, the mission focus changed significantly. The Marines, out of necessity, supplemented what the U.S. Army and the nation required in order to be successful in those wars.

But as the Marines now refocus on the challenge of dealing with peer competitors, the question is, how best to do so?

As LtGen Beaudreault highlighted:

> "The Commandant is dealing with the challenge of making hard choices about the way ahead. But the nation needs to realize that we need a larger USMC to do our job more effectively. We need a bigger Marine Corps. We need a bigger amphibious fleet. We need a bigger Navy.

> "We are a maritime nation, but with the force we have, we have limited shock absorption capability. Where's the shock absorption capacity? If we have to replace the number of combat losses we might experience in a peer-to-peer conflict, how are we going to do so? How do you sustain the fight? That gets into the industrial base and all other areas. We don't have enough shock absorption capacity in the department right now, in my view.

> "We have just enough to meet requirements and get to a one to three deployment to dwell ratio under the current steady state environment. We've got enough to generate combat replacements. But creating whole cloth units is going to be challenging. And I'm very concerned about if we take losses, the ability to rapidly replace those losses. And the affordability and time factors that go with our modernization and fielding in having to replace our damaged equipment.

> "What I worry about is insufficient capacity. And after your initial salvos, what does the buy look like? I do like the conceptual pieces of where the Commandant's going under his Force Design 2030 initiatives. I think you can complicate the adversary's targeting with some discreet units that are out there. But not everybody can be like MARSOC with small teams that are going to have this effect. I do share some of the concerns on how you sustain distributed forces.

"I think the strength of the Corps, as compared to the Army, is our relationship with the Navy and the organic mobility we get out of our sea lift. We are facing a declining amphibious fleet with potential decommissioning of the LSDs—that's a concern. What impact will this have on the nation and the nation's ability to have the Marine Corps-Navy team deploy to the crisis with sufficient shock absorption capability in the event we take some losses due to adversary action?"

The air power transformation the Marines have gone through over the past twenty years, with the coming of the Osprey, then the F-35B, and now the CH-53K transforms what an integrated Marine Corps-Navy team can bring to crisis management, but II MEF does not yet have F-35s in its force and currently is relying on allied F-35s to play their role.

According to LtGen Beaudreault:

"By 2024, we start replacing our fighters at 2nd MAW with F-35s and should be full up by 2030. USMC F-35s have been prioritized for the Pacific, but this creates some challenges for us. The Harriers and the F-35s are not the same at all, and our deployments in the Atlantic region without F-35s creates a gap. But we are getting the CH-53Ks into our force as the initial operating force, which will clearly augment our ability to provide greater capability to operate in the air-sea-ground domain as well."

In short, LtGen Beaudreault has lived through the last peer fight and led the II MEF in its initial process of adapting to the new strategic context. As he underscored:

"We're all watching China, but you know what? There's another actor out there who merits watching."

LtGen Beaudreault retired from the USMC on July 9, 2021.

CHAPTER THREE:

WORKING WITH ALLIES

Joint Force Command Norfolk

By Robbin Laird and Ed Timperlake
April 7, 2021

A key driver of change for North Atlantic defense has been the dynamic growth in Nordic defense cooperation. In the book co-authored by Laird with Murielle Delaporte, a significant part of the analysis on the reworking of European direct defense focuses on the impact of this Nordic dynamic on reworking how collaboration of the "coalition of the willing" or the "relevant nations" working together with key NATO partners is reshaping European defense.

As we put it in that book:

> "Europe and its defense are not one narrative but several. The Russians face an increasingly unified Nordic Northern Flank with enhanced UK focus on the region, backed by reach into North America. The central part of Europe is a mosaic of former Warsaw Pact states with varying degrees of concern about the Russian challenge, backed by a German French alliance with the nuclear-armed France in this key area. And the southern zone of Europe in which Greece, Turkey, Spain, and Italy have about as much solidarity today as they have had historically, which means that aggregation management is crucial to deal with any alliance-wide challenges."

And the Nordic Northern flank and the redesign of direct defense is high-lighted in that book as follows:

"A key part of shaping a new approach to direct defense in Europe is winning the fourth battle of the Atlantic (which rests on dealing with) a key aspect of the Russian challenge, which is crucial for the Nordics, namely, the need to hold the Russian Kola bastion at risk.

"For the United States and Canada, it is about reinforcing Europe and holding the Russians at bay, notably with Putin threatening a nuclear strike via his projected new hypersonic missile to be launched via a submarine. But for the Nordics, it is about homeland defense, and not letting the Russians have a free ride to use the Kola Peninsula and its extended perimeter defense without a significant capability by the West to attrite and destroy the Russian bastion. When you come out from the land into the air and sea corridors, is where the West for sure needs to be able to operate its own anti-access and area denial capability. Two can play at this game."[11]

We had a chance during our visit to Norfolk to talk with the Vice Admiral's political advisor located in JFC Norfolk, Snorri Matthiasson. He is a senior Icelandic diplomat, who had just returned from the European visit of Vice Admiral Lewis. We conducted the interview by phone because of COVID-19 restrictions, but his insights on the "startup" command were very significant.

Matthiasson noted that he first met Vice Admiral Lewis on a visit with the Icelandic Chief of Defense to Norfolk, shortly after C2F had been stood up. This was going to be Lewis's first NATO command, and he sought out a political advisor to assist in his efforts. He was the first foreigner to join the NATO command, just prior to the arrival of Rear Admiral Betton.

He underscored how the standup very much felt like a startup, which allowed them to think through how best to work the efforts for U.S.-European collaboration. He underscored that "Nordic states were engaged in defense

---

11   Robbin Laird and Murielle Delaporte, *The Return of Direct Defense in Europe: Meeting the 21st Century Authoritarian Challenges* (2021), chapter six.

and security activities in the region, and as they worked coordination efforts, there was a clear need to better coordinate with U.S. and other allied efforts, such as the United Kingdom, France, and German forces operating in the region as well. As Matthiasson put it:

> "Vice Admiral Lewis looks at the area from the East Coast of North America to Finnmark as a continuous battlespace, but there was an opportunity to do a much better job coordinating national efforts in the area to shape enhanced coalition capabilities.

For example, the Danes have been working for decades in Greenland and working maritime situational awareness. How to better leverage what they are doing, and how best to bring the capabilities of new maritime domain awareness systems into their operations?

As working crisis situations entails the whole of government responses, doing a better job of bringing together military operational concepts of operations with tactical or strategic diplomatic options is an important challenge to be met in North Atlantic defense. And that is clearly one thrust of the startup command's rethinking process for the evolving approaches to North Atlantic defense.

It is clear that the commands are not engaged in recreating the Cold War infrastructure but are engaged in shaping a very different approach. Notably, the F-35 enterprise is part of that new approach as an information and C^2 asset. With regard to Iceland, first the Italians and currently the Norwegians are operating F-35s from Iceland as part of the NATO air policing missions. The Brits will operate F-35s from their base in Mahram or at sea off their new Queen Elizabeth carriers. And this is prior to the U.S. Navy operating their F-35s in the region, but, of course, the U.S. Navy has an ability to work with those allied fifth generation aircraft. And this is true whether they come from Danish, or Norwegian, or British air bases in the future.

F-35B Lightning II Joint Strike Fighters assigned to Marine Fighter Attack Squadron (VMFA) 211 "The Wake Island Avengers" and the United Kingdom's Lightning 617 Squadron shortly after embarking onboard HMS Queen Elizabeth on September 22, 2020, off the coast of the United Kingdom. Royal Navy Photograph by LPhot Belinda Alker.

The impact on interoperability of U.S. with European forces is clearly enhanced by operating a common combat aircraft. This is how Matthiasson put it:

> "The Norwegians we met in Iceland emphasized that the F35 is an incredible capability, but it also allows them to jointly train with U.S. forces, which creates a new opportunity for joint and coalition warfighting approach as well."

As we wrapped up our discussion, NATO innovation was a key focus of attention. Obviously, the direct NATO missions and operations are tasked by Supreme Headquarters Allied Powers Europe (SHAPE) and Supreme Allied Commander Europe (SACEUR), after a North Atlantic Council (NAC) decision. But under that broader remit, JFC Norfolk provides a flexible umbrella organization to allow for cross-learning and cross-sharing of national efforts, which can be combined to provide for enhanced coalition capabilities.

As Matthiasson put it:

> "The nations have been very keen on working with us from the very beginning with the vision that we had of being an umbrella or nexus for the North Atlantic, because there is so

much national activity that is ongoing with some very advanced equipment. How best to shape collaboration and coordination in such a situation? Much of the activity in the region is under national rather than NATO mandates. But for the Russians, any NATO member's national activity is interpreted as being a NATO activity, so why not do a better job coordinating national efforts to get the right kind of coalition effect?"

Reshaping Nordic Defense Capability

February 8, 2021

During my recent visit to France, I had a chance to visit Denmark "virtually," and discuss the evolving Nordic approach to direct defense of the region with Hans Tino Hansen, the founder, and CEO of Risk Intelligence. His firm is working an assessment of what the Russians can project into the region and how the Poles, Balts and Nordics can collaborate more effectively to provide a defense belt which can absorb a Russian shock, slow it down, and prepare with NATO allies to reinforce the region, and ultimately, if necessary, to take back any lost territory. It also looks into the role of Ukraine and Belarus in an armed conflict and how it impacts on Russian options.

Various war games conducted by think tanks during the last five years have resulted in reported quick defeats for the exposed Baltic countries and NATO forces in the region due to the time lag of NATO reinforcements arriving to the region. With a more coordinated and comprehensive approach to collective defense in the region, it would be possible to do more with Nordics shaping more effective integration to thereby contribute more together.

As Hansen puts it:

> "We value and support a dialogue with the Russians. But the history and political culture of Russia, not just from the Cold War, is that the Russians respect strength and only from such a position, a meaningful dialogue is possible."

He then sketched out how the Nordic integration process could more effectively shape a dialogue from strength strategy even if two countries are members of NATO and two are not. He started from the fact that Russia is not the Soviet Union and does not have the advantages which flowed from Warsaw Pact geography or the forces of the Cold War.

Hans Tino Hansen, the CEO of Risk Intelligence, attending a conference sponsored by his firm in Copenhagen in 2018 entitled "Threat Perception 2018: The Northern European Perspective." Credit: *Second Line of Defense*.

"We have been looking at the conventional air-ground forces which could move into north-eastern European territory primarily from the Russian Western Military District. We have at the same time looked at how the national efforts of Poland, Estonia, Latvia, Lithuania, and the Nordics, if integrated more effectively, can provide for a more capable defense against different levels of direct action by the Russians.

"Our study is not yet ready, but the initial findings suggest that if you do such a correlation, there is almost a balance between the two even without NATO reinforcements in the basic and early scenarios of a conflict and not counting in the operational-strategic level assets on the Russian side. Furthermore, the Russians have at present a significant advantage of readiness, training and large exercises in higher levels of formations, electronic warfare as well as C^2.

"To get a good outcome, it is crucial to have the kind of integration tools such as C^2, which allow for a cohesive defense approach, but what such a process underscores is that integrated defense in the region holds great promise for shaping a stronger hand for the countries to initially defend themselves and to have a dialogue with Russia from a position of strength."

He underscored that the Ukrainian piece of this effort was crucial because stronger Ukrainian defense would require the Russians to have forces in place to deal with that challenge that could not be used elsewhere. At the same time the Belarus military and geography adds to the balance of Russia. Finland can mobilize a significant force to hold Russian forces at risk within the broader Nordic context and enhanced Swedish and Finnish collaboration creates new conventional capabilities which can affect Russian actions in the Baltic as well.

We discussed Kaliningrad, which is most often considered a source of strength for Russia and a danger to NATO and allied operations in the Baltic, but it is at the same time a source of vulnerability as well as strength for Russia. For example, the Russian enclave could if faced with a significant regional missile strike capability combined with a range of other conventional air, naval and land capabilities, face a formidable threat to its enclave. Hans pointed out that the Nordics and Poland must acquire such a capability, but that Denmark, for one is on the way to do so with the current study on strike missile capability as part of the current defense material acquisition plan.

We discussed a key missing piece as well which is the role of long-range artillery. By adding significant long-range artillery capabilities, Russian forces can be targeted in the enclave, as well as in terms of forces they would move into the Baltics, and in other areas where they would wish to project ground forces.

Hansen underscored that the United States is a key part of Northern European defense, but what he is suggesting is that the approach needs to change.

"By reducing what we need the United States to do in our defense in the initial period of armed conflict, the capabilities which the Americans can build for stand-off strike and defense capabilities as well as strategic capabilities become more important and part of the integration package."

He argued that "we need the right capability mix in the wider region. We need to be able to do both defensive and offensive (in a defensive context) operations for a period of time without having to depend initially on the UK or the United States."

And he returned to the evolving collaboration between Finland and Sweden and its impact.

"If Swedish/Finnish defense cooperation really takes off, it actually means that the soft bottom of the Kola Peninsula is clearly exposed. With strong integration of the Finnish and Swedish forces, that they are in a much better position to defend their airbases, which can be available to other Nordic defense forces and NATO forces as well in an armed conflict. It means that the Russians cannot take these areas, especially if the Finns and Swedes start to work together in a more coherent fashion. We're looking at ways to enhance cooperation between Sweden and Finland and between the NATO countries and these two key nations."

And if such cooperation accelerates, this allows the Nordic states to focus more attention on their reach from the "green" Arctic to the "white" Arctic and to shape enhanced capabilities for extended Nordic defense into the "white" Arctic as well. For especially Denmark, which is stretching its limited military resources from the Baltic Sea across the North Sea, North Atlantic and via Greenland to the North Pole, cooperation with the United States and the other Nordic countries as well as other NATO countries will be key to counter the increasing threat level of this vast area posed by Russia.

The Perspective of Major General Anders Rex

February 5, 2021

There is a growing emphasis on what is referred to as "multi-domain" C^2 as a key means to be able to operate in the extended battlespace. A new effort to do so is being spearheaded in the United States, which is referred to as Joint All-Domain Command and Control (JADC2). This is certainly an important effort and a key target to enable fully a future integrated distributed force.

But such a future force concept does not well describe what can be done now to enhance the capabilities of the United States and allied forces to deliver an enhanced capability to leverage data and C^2 in operations for today's forces. Indeed, a number of new capabilities already introduced into the force are driving changes which can be leveraged now, such as the arrival of the F-35 global fleet.

In the view of the commander of the Royal Danish Air Force, Major General Anders Rex, there are already significant opportunities now to build out enhanced integration. In an interview done with him while I was in Europe in January 2021, we discussed by teleconference his perspective and his approach. Major General Rex said:

> "For me, joint all domain C2 is clearly the future. But at the same time, we have to work on enhanced capabilities with the current force. We need to focus on both in parallel. Denmark does not have the muscle to shape the future of all domain command and control, but we also need to drive the change—we need to get the job done now.
>
> "What I have been focused on over the past couple of years is to make our force better now. Today, we actually already have the capability to shape more effective networks of ISR and C^2 without significant investments. For example, we are leveraging the Joint Range Extension Application Protocol (JREAP) that requires modest investments, and it is a way for us, our allies and coalition partners to build a modest combat cloud linking our data."

He argued that Denmark is building a national shared database structure to bring together Danish and allied assets more effectively. It can be forgotten by non-Danes that the Kingdom of Denmark reaches much farther than Europe and extends into the Arctic to include Greenland and the Faroe Islands.

When I visited Karup Airbase in 2018, I spent time with the team which mans the Danish Joint Data Link Operations Centre. And during that visit, Major Knud Aagis Larsen, the director of the Centre, underscored the Centre's role:

> "We design, establish, and maintain the infrastructure necessary for exchanging Tactical Data between C^2 units and fighting platforms. We are the hub between various C^2 systems, different tactical data link systems as well as across different domains."

As I highlighted at the time:

> "The expeditionary operations as well as Danish reach into the Arctic and into Greenland provide a challenge of operating over distance, that a non-Dane might simply not include, within the challenges of linking and communication of the force or between the force and military and civilian authorities.

> "But this means that the Danes have had to work non-line of sight capabilities for Link-16, which involves among other things, ways to move Link 16 data over various other networks as well. And with the IP revolution, the Centre has found ways to send Link 16 data over various IP systems as well."

The editor visiting the Danish Joint Data Link Operations Centre in 2018.
Credit: *Second Line of Defense.*

When discussing the way ahead with Major General Rex, he underscored that what had been laid down at the Centre was a key part of shaping the national way ahead but in close coordination with NATO as well.

> "We are building our national shared database in close coordination with the NATO coalition shared database structure. Taping into this data base allows us to leverage for instance pictures which we have just uploaded from one of our sensors, allowing the warfighter to tap into that information, and we can do that now."

He argued that learning how to best leverage information is part of the process of guiding near term innovation. He provided this example:

> "We fly our helicopters off our frigates and the captain of the frigate is using the helicopter in a certain operational way to achieve a specific operational goal. But data generated from the helicopters' onboard systems can be employed to inform other security or warfighting elements in the operational area. Who can use information generated from those helicopters sensors and how do we best get it to them? This problem can be worked

by shaping the operational networks to determine which data is usable by whom within an operational area."

He also highlighted the importance of focused integration in a particular specific operational area as a key consideration as well.

> "We should not focus simply on building a gold-plated multi-domain C² system designed to operate over very large geographical areas; we also need to have a system that is able to focus on local geographical areas, and for a certain amount of time."

He underscored the importance of expanding the capability and willingness of allies to share data. He talked about how the members of the Danish Joint Data Link Operations Centre work closely with other data experts in NATO and how that shared experience drives innovation in terms of shared intelligence underscoring what building an integrated force can drive.

Then Col. Anders Rex, Danish Air Force, addressing a 2015 conference in Copenhagen focused on the future of airpower. Credit: *Second Line of Defense.*

The future is now.

> "With regard to JREAP, we can tie the information we already have together using this technology. Let us just do that. And do it now. The networks that we already have, we have to be better at using them, and we have to distribute and share the information that we're already gathering. We need to change the culture of our militaries so that we are in a giving mode rather than a receiving mode. There needs to be a push of information rather than pull. And without that specific cultural change, new technologies will not matter as much as they could in shaping the way ahead for an integratable force."

Major General Rex underscored that this was especially important because of the need to work effectively in the range of crises affecting Denmark, Europe, and the NATO alliance.

> "We need to deliver spectrum elasticity. The Russians do not think in terms of peace, crisis, and then war; they have competition and war as their basic approach. The competition piece has a really wide range in which the use of all of a nation's tools of power can be escalated or deescalated in time, intensity or geography collectively or individually—so essentially the degree of conflict can continuously be expanded or compressed. This means that we too need to be able to move with elasticity along the spectrum of conflict. And our C^2 and ISR systems need to enable and facilitate spectrum elasticity."

Enhancing Australian Deterrence

By Robbin Laird and Ed Timperlake
July 14, 2021

In the first section of this book, we highlighted the Australian Strategic Policy Institute (ASPI) report by Paul Dibb and Richard Brabin-Smith that focuses on how to plan for Australia's defense in an environment with reduced warning time. The report raises a broad set of questions about how to know when an event might set in motion a chain of events that pose a direct threat to liberal democratic nations and how to respond early and effectively.

It also raises the question of how to shape the Australian Defence Force's capabilities so that they can be inserted into a crisis early enough to provide confidence that effective tools to manage escalation are available as well. In essence, the report focuses on ways for Australia to enhance the government's and the public's ability to understand the events that affect them and provide a warning in time for Australia to prepare for and manage any crises that arise...

A growing focus in the Australian defense community is on options for providing the ADF with a long-range strike capability more quickly. For example, Marcus Hellyer, a senior defense analyst with ASPI, recently raised the possibility of Australia acquiring B-21 Raiders from the United States, but that's a mid-term option at best.

Again, what can Australia do now to respond effectively to dangerous saber-rattling? Clearly, this is an area in which cooperation with the U.S. can provide both allies with enhanced deterrent options now and shape a more effective way ahead. For Australia, it's about how to build long-range strike into the ADF over the mid-to-long-term. For the U.S., it's about getting a better understanding of how bombers and the U.S. Navy fleet can work more effectively together.

In other words, there's an option that provides a building block for the way ahead to a long-range-strike-enabled ADF and for the U.S. to learn how to more effectively operate its joint naval and air capabilities in the Pacific both within its own services and with allies.

In the past, the U.S. has brought B-1 bombers to participate in exercises with the ADF in northern Australia. Now, a rotational force of B-2s could bring a stealth bomber capability to Australia's defense. It would not only be an important input in responding to China but would also underscore to the Chinese that their military build-up in the Pacific and specifically directed against Australia is not in their own interests.

For now, it would be a modest response, but the integration of U.S. Air Force bombers into the ADF has to be taken seriously in the face of continued direct threats against Australia. By training the Royal Australian Air Force and the Royal Australian Navy to work with the B-2s, B-1s and B-52s, those two key Australian power-projection forces can train with an operational long-range strike asset. That would demonstrate that long-range strike isn't primarily focused on reaching downtown Beijing, but rather on providing rapidly deployable enhancements to air–naval taskforces throughout the Indo-Pacific region.

Such a strategy would also enable Australia to determine if the B-21 is the right fit or whether there are other ways to bring long-range strike to the operating force. And it would help guide decisions on building the kind of sovereign missile industry Australia desires which is not simply about buying off-the-shelf U.S. or European equipment. For it's also clear that allies like the U.S. need a different approach to the one they have followed to date to get a less expensive and more effective mix of strike assets.

And as the U.S. shapes a more effective support strategy for allies' approaches in the region, the U.S. Navy and the U.S. Air Force will need to work on more effective integration of the bomber force with the operating fleet. And an evolving kill-web approach that integrates bomber and fleet operations can empower significantly greater collaboration between air and sea services and provide a more survivable, lethal, and distributed force. And this is not about preparing to fight World War III; it's about effective crisis and escalation management.

Part of the way ahead would be to build reinforced bases from which U.S. bombers could operate in the near to mid-term as Australia builds out its own desired capabilities. These bases could be used for rotations to exercise with the ADF or to reinforce Australian defense in a crisis.

These proposals are about taking the U.S.–Australia alliance forward in an effective way to deal with the defense of Australia today, and not simply speculating about the long-term options. It's also about demonstrating to Beijing that bullying isn't going to lead to the compliance of the liberal democratic states to a future Chinese global order. China's leaders need to pause and consider what Australia as an anchor and arsenal for democracy in the region might mean to their future as well.

We published multiple versions of this article, but this version was first published by ASPI on July 12, 2021.[12]

The Defence 24 Conference on Polish defense
October 1, 2021

During the last week of September 2021, there was a two-day conference held by Defence 24 on Polish defense. And that conference highlighted presentations from senior Polish officials and military officers as well as defense industrial presentations.

After 2014, Poland along with other states serious about defense, such as the Nordic states, shifted their focus from out-of-area forces, to reworking how to defend their own national territory against the authoritarian states and their challenges. And for the Poles, as a key state on the Eastern flank of Europe facing the unincorporated states in Europe, both Belarus and Ukraine, and the Putin-driven Russian state revival, how to do so is a work in progress.

The conference provided several insights with regard to the agenda for the Poles in shaping a way ahead. It should be noted that Poland is certainly focused on the challenges of enhanced national security, akin to the concerns discussed during earlier visits to Finland and in the Nordic region, and increasingly in Australia as well. There is a core concern with dealing with what have been called hybrid threats, namely, working wedges within a society and within that society's broader alliances by creating asymmetrical threats. For Poland currently, the Belarusian use of migrants to breach the Polish border on their way into Europe more generally is such a case. This challenge was extensively discussed at the conference, and the Polish response has been to mobilize the territorial forces to provide a new brigade to support border security.

---

12   Robbin Laird and Edward Timperlake, "Crafting a Way Ahead for Effective Australian Deterrence Against Chinese Threats," *ASPI* (July 12, 2021), https://www.aspistrategist.org.au/crafting-a-way-ahead-for-effective-australian-deterrence-against-chinese-threats/.

The Polish Minister of National Defence, Mariusz Błaszczak, addresses the Defence 24 conference. Credit: *Second Line of Defense*.

This has led to broader European concerns about how to secure European borders, with Poland receiving both criticism and support from a wider European community. And the wider community aspect is a key one. The Poles clearly see a Russian direct threat to them and to Europe. And they are closer to de Gaulle's vision of Europe, one of nations cooperating on common interests rather than on the views of the Commission, which sees the way ahead as creating a single set of rules for the entire European community. Here Poland is on a collision course with the European Commission.

At the same time, there is growing concern among nations who believe that Russia and China pose direct threats to Europe and see the need for enhanced cooperation among like-minded states. Certainly, there is scope for enhanced cooperation with the Nordic states that have deepened their own cooperation as well.

There were references as well about the United States and the dramatic Biden Blitzkrieg withdrawal strategy in Afghanistan and the Australian-UK-US (AUKUS) announcements. And the elephant in the room clearly is what the Biden administration is going to concretely do going forward regarding defense, both globally and in Europe.

The Polish government has raised its defense budget and is considering additional capabilities for its operational approach to direct defense. The challenge will be to build a more integrated joint force going forward and one which can work effectively with allies. How will the territorial force be shaped going forward? How will it intersect with more mobile capabilities, such as with its F-35 force?

In a period in which the allies of Poland are reworking their own defense templates, it is fair to say that there is no model for Poland to apply to its own direct defense which is congruent with what allies are doing themselves. The Nordics for example, are reworking how to shape a more integrated territorial defense but one in which air and missile power can expand the perimeter for their defense. The F-35 consortia is a key part of reworking how Europeans will deliver multi-domain capabilities to drive greater force integration, and Poland buying the F-35 will be able to participate in this ongoing development.

The United States is facing a significant change from its preoccupation on the land wars in the Middle East to shaping a new 21st century force, kill web-enabled, and crafted to provide for force distribution and integration. But this is a work in progress, one which I have focused on for several years with my colleagues. How does Poland then intersect with ongoing American and European allied warfighting developments, which are driving significant changes in the templates which will deliver relevant force capabilities against adversary forces, which themselves are undergoing fundamental change?

A notable challenge for Poland is how to both defend its national territory and to operate in its perimeter with mobile forces. The opportunity to integrate more effectively with its Nordic partners and operate in the defense of the Nordic states is not a task for Abrams tanks. How best to shape a realistic mobile force which can both operate in the perimeters and aid in the territorial defense? This applies as well to working with the states in the Black Sea region and when necessary, in the Polish perspective being able to participate in the defense of Ukraine.

In short, Poland is on the front lines of European defense. How they work their own defense is a key part of the broader allied approach.

The Changing Strategic and Security Situation for Poland
October 3, 2021

On Day One of the Defence 24 conference held in Warsaw, Poland, on September 28 and 29, 2021, Polish defense leaders highlighted the dynamics of change in the Polish defense and security situation. The initial presentation was by the Polish Minister of Defense, Mariusz Błaszczak, which was then followed by a presentation by Paweł Soloch, the Head of the National Security Bureau, and that was followed by a panel, which included Soloch, General Jarosław Mika, Commander-in-Chief of the Armed Forces, and General Wiesław Kukuła, Commander of the Territorial Defense Forces.

Together they outlined their general perspective regarding Poland and its defense. The border situation regarding Belarus and Russian cooperation with Belarus means that the migrant situation being used by the Belarusian government was a form of hybrid war. And in their view, Poland's response to close the border and to defend Poland was in the general interest of the European Union and should be seen as such.

The President of Poland had announced a continuation of the state of emergency regarding the border, and the Polish Territorial Defense Forces had organized a battalion to assist in border defense. And the Polish government has been reaching out for expanded diplomatic and security support in the region as well.

Paweł Soloch, the Head of National Security Bureau, on a panel during the conference. Credit: *Second Line of Defense.*

Soloch noted that the changes associated with Belarus and Russia were fundamentally changing not just Poland's but the entire European defense and security situation. Błaszczak also discussed the recently completed Russian Zapad exercise. He underscored that this exercise was not just a narrowly focused military operations exercise, but one which involved the Russian state and its political arm as well. It was a political-military integrated exercise.

The four officials variously discussed the Polish response. The first is to increase defense spending with Polish President Andrzej Duda eyeing a 2 ½ per cent of GNP goal. The second is to reinforce security mechanisms within Poland and to enhance the capability of the Territorial Forces to contribute to such efforts, including the use and further acquisition of Unmanned Aerial Vehicles (UAV) as part of the means for getting better intelligence to defend the homeland. General Kukula, the head of the Territorial Defense Forces (Wojska Obrony Terytorialnej or WOT), noted that his forces use UAVs every day and they are becoming an important part of their response to asymmetric threats.

The final consideration is their effort to continue to acquire new technologies from partners but to ramp up domestic industrial capabilities to integrate new technologies and to contribute to a more effective Polish defense and a more resilient Poland. Gen. Jarosław Mika, General Commander of the Armed Forces, underscored how important it was from his point of view to ramp up cooperation between the Polish Armed Forces and domestic industry to have a more resilient Poland in dealing with evolving security and defense threats. Notably, he sees a need in the missile area to ramp up Polish production capabilities.

The important efforts in missile defense were highlighted as well as working integration across this domain. Poland is the only foreign partner of the United States to acquire the integrated air and missile defense battle command system (IBCS) and is doing so at the same time launching its large-scale domestic missile defense program called Narew. This program and effort highlight a key direction forward for Polish defense, namely working ways to have a more integrated force. This is not easy when one is acquiring several new force elements, which have not been integrated in their home countries all that well.

The Defense Minister highlighted changes in the procurement system designed to facilitate more rapid and effective defense procurement in shaping out Poland's defense capabilities in the years ahead. Clearly, the Polish government is concerned with the deteriorating security environment, which explains in part the surprise decision to acquire Abrams tanks announced recently.

There are significant changes going on regarding Poland's partners, notably the United States and Germany, which clearly affect Polish perceptions as well regarding the best approaches to securing Polish defense and security. As Paweł Soloch put it: "We must be prepared for change. We must react flexibly."

Finland's Fighter Decisions

December 13, 2021

Recently, Finland announced their decision regarding a new fighter. They down-selected the F-35 and joined the F-35 global enterprise. At the same time, Belarus and Russia are using migrants as battering rams against Europe, Russia is moving force against Ukraine, and this summer Sea Breeze 21 turned into more of hybrid-warfare event than an exercise.

These events may seem disjointed, but they are not. When I did a study for Andy Marshall, the legendary head of Net Assessment, in the early 1990s after the Fall of the Wall and subsequent liberation of states from the former Soviet Empire, I focused on what I believed to be the fundamental long-range threat to the newly emerging European security order. And my study, backed by visits to the region, focused on the corridor states ranging from Turkey through the Black Sea to Ukraine, to Belarus and the Baltic States.

These states had an uncertain future with Europe and represented key players for the Russian rump state. What this means in blunt terms, is that there is much uncertainty about the future of Russia and the European order generated by states which have never been within the settled order except by inclusion in the empires which have flowed throughout Russian and European history.

A key response of the Nordics since the very evident breaking of the post-Cold War order by the Russian seizure of Crimea, has been enhanced by cooperation among them despite two states being in NATO and two not. Finland is really a key state affecting how the Russians play the game deep into the corridor which astride Europe and Russia. My travels to Finland and continuing discussions with Finns have taught me much about how they look at the evolving strategic situation and when one looks back at the history immediately after the collapse of the Soviet Empire, one sees a key initial fighter decision which occurred at a key inflection point: Wither Russia and Europe with the collapse of the Soviet Empire?

This what I wrote during my 2018 visit to Finland, I looked back at the acquisition decision made shortly after the collapse of the Soviet Union and how that was linked to what would become the F-35 decision. "The Finnish government is set to acquire 64 new fighter jets for its air force. This is occurring as Nordic defense is being reworked, and the Northern European states are sorting out how to deal with what the Finnish Defense Minister Jussi Niinistö has referred to as the "new normal" in Russian behavior. "It's important that our armed forces have the equipment that they need to fulfill all of their fundamental roles," said Niinistö.

"Niinistö has described Russia's more unpredictable behavior in the greater Baltic Sea region, particularly in the areas of political influencing methods and security policies, as the "new normal". "Changes in the security environment and the multi-purpose use or threat of power have become a new normal. Russia has shown in Ukraine and Syria that it possesses both the capacity and the will to use military power to push its goals.

"The new combat aircraft will be part of an integrated Finnish defense force in the evolving strategic environment of the 2020's. It is important to remember that the last major acquisition also occurred in a significant period of change for Finland in its strategic neighborhood.

"With the collapse of the Soviet Union, and the dynamics of change in the new Russian republic, Finland was able to negotiate its way out of the Cold War agreement with Russia in which Finland was committed to cooperate with Russia militarily in the case that an aggressor was threatening to use Finnish territory to attack the Soviet Union. The agreement required mutual affirmation of the threat and the engagement but nonetheless was a major curb on Finnish military independence.

"With the end of this agreement, and then the unification of Germany, and the opening of a new chapter in the development the European Union, Finland positioned itself for membership in the European Union in 1995. The EU treaty contains a mutual security agreement for all of the members as well. It was in this period of dynamic change, that Finland acquired new fighters for its air force, F-18 Hornet aircraft.

"In 1992, the Finnish government placed an order for 64 McDonnell Douglas aircraft. And at the time of the sale a Finnish diplomat explained the deal this way: "Until now, Finland's neutrality made defense procurement difficult. But from now on, Finland will defend herself by her own means."

"In other words, much like new fighter aircraft will be purchased in a new strategic context of the 2020's, the first big modernization of the Finnish Air Force in the post-cold war period occurred in a period of significant strategic change.

"Buying fighter aircraft for Finland is a challenge but clearly connected to a broader strategic context. This was well summed up by the distinguished Finnish historian, Henrik Meinander, in his 2013 book on the history of Finland as follows: "The government emphatically denied that there were any security policy considerations behind the purchase of the Hornet, but everything points to the contrary. The acquisition of modern defense technology has always had a political dimension since the supply and maintenance of equipment necessities continuing collaboration with the foreign manufacturer. This aircraft meant that Finland's air defenses became compatible with NATO almost immediately. It was only two months earlier that Finland had submitted its application to the EC/EUU, and it was doing all that it could to show that it was a country whose defense and security policy would not be a burden for the EU. The pilots were sent to the USA for training, and the first jet planes were flown across the Atlantic in 1995. Cooperation increased in the period 1996-2000 as 56 of the jets were assembled in Finland and gradually connected to the NATO satellite system and other technical infrastructure."[13]

During my visit to Helsinki in February 2018, this is what one Finnish analyst had to say about the challenge in acquiring the Hornets, but also the significance of the acquisition:

"It was a very bold move in the early 1990s. With the collapse of the Soviet Union, we lost a significant market, and we had a huge recession with unemployment rising significantly. Timing was everything. If the decision had been delayed, it would not have been made. The purchase of the Hornets expanded dramatically

---

13 *Henrik* Meinander, *A History of Finland* (Oxford University Press, 2013), 195.

the cooperation with the United States and other members of NATO and allowed cooperation to become real. At first, there was skepticism about the potential quality of the Finnish pilots but soon the U.S. realized that Finnish pilots are first rate. And this also laid the foundation in the United States, that Finland is a credible regional partner. We do what we promise and by providing advanced weapon systems to Finland, it's a stabilizing factor for the region as well."

"In short, understanding how the Finns see the evolving strategic situation is crucial to understand how they will address not only defense modernization, but integration of their forces nationally and with core coalition partners."[14]

Now that the Finns have made their F-35 decision, we can address this decision as a second key inflection point. The first was a decision which underwrote enhanced Finnish sovereignty in a post-Soviet world. The second is part of enhancing that sovereignty by working more closely with key strategic allies to deflect Putin's efforts to go back to a world in which Finlandization was a word.

Finland has been working cross-border airpower training for several years with Norway and Sweden. Now Finland and Norway will fly the same aircraft. They will be integrated with other F-35 partners in the region, Denmark and Poland and the Netherlands and Belgium.

This means that when the Finns fly their aircraft, they will be part of a significant ISR belt looking deep into areas of Russian interest and can provide C^2 links to create a more integrated force response dependent upon national decisions. As I have written for years, the F-35 is NOT a traditional fighter aircraft; it is a flying combat system which is integratable across a coalition of F-35 fighters.

This means that Putin now faces a much more integrated and lethal force which can engage across the spectrum of conflict. As he contemplates

---

14 Robbin Laird, "Finland and New Combat Aircraft: Looking Back at the Hornet Acquisition," *Second Line of Defense* (February 16, 2018), https://sldinfo.com/2018/02/finland-and-new-combat-aircraft-looking-back-at-the-hornet-acquisition/.

how to regain lost strategic space, some areas which he might have contemplated as areas of relatively low hanging fruit, clearly are not.

And much like President Xi has now generated generational opposition to China in Australia, the Russians have skillful generated Nordic defense collaboration and much closer working relationships with the Balts and Poland as well. This then leaves the impact of the de-facto inclusion of Belarus within Putin's strategic arsenal as having significant impact the fate and future of Ukraine.

As the Nordic cooperation coupled with Baltic defense and Polish efforts create a more formidable defense zone against Putin's aspirations, and with expansion of Muscovy through to Minsk, this leaves the zone from Ukraine through the Black Sea and Turkey in play. How best to address to warfighting and deterrence in this area? Much more than Presidential video conferences are crucial to shape credible polices going forward for this region.

And to finish with the fighter decision at two inflection points issue. The first decision was made right after the collapse of the Soviet Union. The second decision was made at the point where the 30-year mark for the collapse of the Soviet Union was being noted in Russia.

Working With the United Arab Emirates

By James Durso
December 20, 2021

The United Arab Emirates (UAE) recently made two significant military procurement decisions: it would buy the French-made Rafale fighter jet, its weapons, and a dozen Airbus H225M Caracal helicopters for combat search and rescue and anti-ship missions; and, it was suspending discussions with the U.S. for the purchase of the F-35 Lightning II fighter, MQ-9B Reaper drones, and air-to-air and air-to-ground weapons due to "technical requirements, sovereign operational restrictions, and cost/benefit analysis."

Despite the Dear John letter, the emirate said we can still be friends: "The U.S. remains the UAE's preferred provider for advanced defense requirements and discussions for the F-35 may be re-opened in the future."

U.S. Secretary of State Antony Blinken replied: "We remain prepared to move forward with both [fighter aircraft and drones] if that is what the Emiratis are interested in doing."

The *Wall Street Journal* reported the U.S.-UAE discussions foundered over U.S. concerns the UAE would allow China access to the F-35's technology, though the Emiratis previously argued they have a perfect record of protecting U.S. technology.

The UAE won't be allowed to make any modifications to the F-35, but French president Emmanuel Macron directed Thales, the builder of the Rafale's electronics to give the UAE access to all the black boxes. Another Middle Eastern country refused to buy U.S. aircraft after Washington demanded information on every sortie, said it would install spyware on the aircraft, and expected the customer to pay the cost of its snap inspections.

The U.S. been concerned about the UAE-China relationship for some time. Washington is worried about the deployment of Huawei 5G wireless technology in the emirate and other members of the Gulf Cooperation Council. The emirate no doubt feels 5G is critical to its competitiveness as a global business hub and tourism destination; the U.S. likely thinks Chinese 5G will give Beijing access to business, military, and political information in the emirate, an operating and transit site for U.S. military forces in the region.

Recently, the UAE, after a U.S. demand, terminated a Chinese-funded $1 billion project in the Khalifa Port Free Trade Zone the U.S. said had military applications. U.S. President Joe Biden spoke about the project to Abu Dhabi Crown Prince Mohammed bin Zayed who said he heard Biden "loud and clear," though the emirate later declared, "our position remains the same, that the facilities were not military facilities."

This must seem like Groundhog Day for the UAE. In 2006, Dubai-owned DP World was forced to back out of an approved purchase of port management contracts at six major U.S. seaports after the U.S. Congress opposed the deal. Fifteen years later the UAE is learning it can't even conclude a seaport project at home without a U.S. intervention.

As a result of the U.S. arm twisting, the UAE may have to make an offsetting accommodation to China that the U.S. will like even less, a prime example of "it seemed like a good idea at the time."

And it's not just UAE-China ties. Washington is looking askance at attempts by the UAE, Iran's third-largest trade partner (behind China and the European Union), to improve relations with Tehran, despite the occasional hiccup like Iranian threats after the UAE normalized relations with Israel. Recently a U.S. delegation visited Abu Dhabi and warned the Emiratis the U.S. has "visibility on transactions [with Iran] that are not compliant with [U.S.] sanctions," and "Those banks and firms face extreme risk if this continues."

Why is the U.S. taking a hard line with the UAE over trading with a large, consequential neighbor (Iran) or an emerging technology leader and investor (China)? The U.S. administration says – and this time it means it! - it is pivoting to Asia. Washington may or may not succeed but is loath that another regional or global power will fill the vacuum it creates by vacating the region, especially if the new guy is welcomed by the locals, as China seems to be.

How might the UAE see it?

The leaders of the UAE (and Middle East) were likely appalled by the livestreamed rout of U.S. forces in Afghanistan. Did they wonder: if the U.S. will walk away from an effort of two decades and over $2 trillion dollars, do their more modest engagements with Washington matter, regardless of what all those visiting officials say?

As to Iran, there is a large Iranian business presence in the UAE and, if Iran normalizes relations with the rest of the world, the emirate is in the prime location. The U.S. has levied sanctions on Iran since its client, the Shah, fled in 1979 and, in the UAE, that is 42 years of foregone business, all in the name of making the Americans happy. To the UAE, it makes as much sense as the U.S. not trading with Mexico.

And accommodating the U.S. may eventually hurt the UAE, which allows U.S. forces to attack Afghan targets from its bases. The emirate will be a handy target if Al-Qaeda or the Islamic State decide to retaliate for a U.S. strike.

Regarding China, the UAE "has emerged as China's primary economic partner in the Gulf" and there are more than 4,000 Chinese companies operating in the UAE. The UAE and China are partners in energy, e-commerce, and transportation, and the emirate wants cooperative relationships with Chinese universities to bring technology R&D to the Gulf.

A significant Chinese presence in the UAE would be a boost to Beijing's project to build strategic strongpoints, ports with "dual-use commercial-military capabilities," as part of the Maritime Silk Road. The strongpoints are less visible than naval bases, and easier to negotiate than a full-up foreign military base. But, except for specialized weapons-handling facilities, civil and military port facilities are identical, so it is possible the "information" the U.S. gave the UAE about the Khalifa port project was really disinformation to disrupt the growing Chinese-UAE relationship?

China dominates the commercial maritime sector while the U.S. role is seriously diminished. For example, China leads the U.S. in bulk carriers, container ships, oil tankers, natural gas carriers, and chemical tankers. China is the leading manufacturer of shipping equipment, is invested in 100 ports in 60 countries, and is home to seven of the ten busiest ports in the world.

Compensating for unfortunate maritime policy choices by using third parties to check China's growth may work in the short term but won't change the underpinnings of China's maritime strategy, and those third parties will weary of being press-ganged into Washington's war on Beijing.

International business travelers appreciate the UAE's location, amenities, and business friendly environment. So too do traveling American security service officials who will be rapidly identified and cataloged if the UAE adopts China's surveillance technology. It's no joke: the Dubai police rapidly identified the members of the Israeli hit team that killed Hamas official Mahmoud al-Mabhouh and that was using 2010 gear. The U.S. intent may be to displace China as a surveillance technology supplier and, instead of a backdoor to Beijing, the backdoor will be to Washington.

The government of Iran doubled the budget of the Islamic Revolutionary Guard Corps (IRGC) for 2022. Some that money will fund the ongoing expansion of the IRGC's naval force which regularly exercises keeping foreign navies out of the Gulf by blocking the Strait of Hormuz, which sees a daily flow of "about 21% of global petroleum liquids consumption."

The UAE would have found those F-35s and drones useful to counter Iranian naval pressure, but operational restrictions that limit their use to U.S.-approved scenarios will make the UAE military an arm of the U.S. and limit its local freedom of action if that would conflict with U.S. goals wherever else Iran is active, such as Lebanon. So much for a U.S. Middle East policy to "…work with our regional partners to deter Iranian aggression and threats to sovereignty and territorial integrity…"

The UAE's ruling families enjoy public support to the extent they focus on economic fundamentals. The Emirates' leaders may be ready to adjust aspects of their strategy and tactics to cooperate with the U.S., but Washington appears to be oblivious to – or maybe it just doesn't care – if its preferences negatively affect the economies of its friends.

Given the meaningless successes Washington scored against the UAE's sovereignty there's one question: Was the "cost/benefit analysis" the UAE referred to about its wider relationship with America or just the F-35?

CHAPTER FOUR:

THE COMING OF
AUTONOMOUS SYSTEMS

The Past and the Way Ahead

In a meeting with George Galdorisi, Director of Strategic Assessments and Technical Futures at the Navy's Command and Control Center of Excellence in San Diego, California, Naval Information Warfare Center, Pacific, during a visit to San Diego in July 2020, he provided a look back to how the U.S. Navy has worked maritime autonomous systems in the past.

He noted that the U.S. Navy has been interested for a long time in having maritime autonomous systems which could support the fleet. The challenge has been that the technology has not been mature enough to do the core missions the Navy has looked for from this class of air and sea vehicles.

He discussed the infamous DASH system which he noted "failed spectacularly because the technology wasn't robust enough." Then as the XO of the USS New Orleans, he had experience with the Pioneer UAV which they launched from the ship.

> "We actually put small arresting wires on the deck and our commanding officer, who was a Vietnam-era A7 pilot, and had one goal that week. His goal was that we left the pier on Monday morning with three Pioneers, and he wanted to come back Friday afternoon with three Pioneers. We came back with one."

But after a decade-and-a-half of widespread use of unmanned systems by U.S. and allied forces in the land wars, this experience has clearly reshaped the U.S. Navy's approach shaping a way ahead for the use of remote technologies in the fleet. And for the U.S. Navy, the missions which they envisage for such vehicles are the dull, dirty, and dangerous work where you are putting Sailors or Marines in harm's way and would wish to outsource these missions to autonomous systems.

The Navy and Marine Corps have been using such systems in a wide range of exercises to shape proof of concept efforts to sort through what will most effectively meet their needs. For example, Galdorisi noted, regarding the MANTAS system, it has been used by the Navy/Marine Corps team to do "intelligence preparation of the battlefield," where they have gone into the surf zone to use sonars to see obstacles such as mines, as well as other obstacles that could thwart an amphibious landing.

> "In Valiant Shield, they used the MANTAS to bring supplies to the beachhead because once the Marines were on the beach, they had to fight their way inland. As tough as the landing is, the tougher part is resupplying Marines as they work to push off the beach because they use massive amounts of ammunition, fuel, and food."

> "They demonstrated that they could resupply a beachhead with autonomous vehicles and not put Sailors and Marines in harm's way just to deliver materiel to the beach. What you saw yesterday when you rode on the larger MANTAS vehicle and saw other USVs and UUVs was the next step in having autonomous vehicles do the dull, dirty, and dangerous work that Sailors have had to do in the past to execute the mine countermeasures mission (MCM).

> "There is an urgency to provide the MCM capability to the Navy. Legacy capabilities now in use employ a 25-30-year-old fleet of Avenger class MCM vessels and equally old MH-53E Sea Dragon helicopters. Littoral Combat Ship MCM Mission Modules currently under development are leaving an unacceptably

narrow margin between obsolescence of legacy capability and transition to Full Operational Capability (FOC) of the new Mission Modules.

"What industry is proposing is a mine countermeasure system built completely with commercial off the shelf technology. And in this case, they've used the 38-foot MANTAS USV. They have used the Kraken side scan sonar. And they've used the Pluto ROV mine neutralization system. And they have demonstrated these over the past several weeks in various exercises.

"What industry is proposing is a parallel path solution. They are not saying that the Navy shouldn't build another minesweeper. They are not saying the Navy shouldn't have the H-60 helicopter do the AMCM mission. They are saying, 'The COTS technology is available now. Why don't we offer a parallel path solution to again take the Sailor out of the minefield and make it a single sortie to engage?'"

"What this means in practice is that one would send the MANTAS USV autonomous vehicle out in an area where mines are suspected. The MANTAS sonar coupled with the Kraken UUV searches for the mines. The Kraken comes back to the MANTAS once it surveys the area, then the Pluto goes out fine tunes exactly where the mine is and then drops an explosive charge next to it.

"The Pluto backs away, it comes back to the MANTAS and can either explode that mine right then or put explosive charges on several mines and then detonate them at a predetermined time. Importantly, you don't have to blow up every mine in the minefield; you just need a safe path for either the ships or the landing craft to go through."

We then discussed how the U.S. Navy is looking at the various classes of unmanned surface ships to meet various needs for the fleet. Galdorisi underscored that "At the high end are the large USVs, which basically are going to be, in my view, a truck. They will bring smaller USVs to the operational area. The medium USVs will do a lot of the work, whether it's ISR, or mine countermeasures, or other missions. The smaller USVs could do tasks like counter-swarm

> "My professional interest is currently on the medium ones, and there are several medium USVs out there that the Navy is experimenting with. One of the better-known ones in this class is the Sea Hunter, and of course MANTAS, which you saw yesterday. With these ships you can perform a variety of missions, you saw the counter-mine one yesterday. But another mission would be ISR. If you can't see ahead of your ship and you want to know what's going on out there, you can send a USV armed with radar, sonar, FLIR and other sensors out ahead of the task force to do scouting in much the same was as we used to do scouting back in World War II with aircraft."

We then discussed the challenge of bringing together data streams generated by various platforms and their sensor networks and making that data useful to the operators and to the fleet.

Obviously, part of the challenge is working with wave forms that can communicate securely and effectively. It is crucial to ensure that the data streams come back to a single screen allowing the operators to make correlations among those data streams, aided by autonomous systems, but really allowing the man-in-the-loop to make the intelligent judgments and decisions which allows the operator to not be in a stove-piped data stream situation.

He discussed an historical parallel that in his mind is suggestive of the way ahead, "The LAMPS MK III was designed with an elegant concept. Think of it as disassembling a P-3, where you cut off the front end and put that up in the air and took the back end and put it on the ship. And why did you do that? You put the front end up in the air because it has a radar and an EW system and sonobuoys. And you put the back end on the ship because the ship is more stable and has more computing power and more people and more power onboard the ship to work the data.

"In theory, it was great. And all the pilots were supposed to do in the aircraft was keep the helicopter out of the water. They were just driving the sensors around. All the pilots had between them was a small screen about as big as an iPad where they could look at tracks and other information. On the ship you had five people just like the back of a P-3 interested in what the helicopter was picking up in terms of data. And onboard the ship, one had the REMRO, the radar guy, the ESMO, the ESM guy, the ASMO, the ASW guy, and then you had the ATACO who was watching the whole picture, all the dots on the screen. And then you had the CIC watch officer. And they were the bosses. All the pilots were supposed to do in the air was keep the helicopter out of the water.

"But guess who had the best situational awareness? The aircrew had all the data displayed on their screen, the radar picture, the ESM picture and the tracks from the sonobuoys. All of those things were on the same screen where they could go, 'Oh, that one is associated with that one. And that must be the Soviet ship that way, because we're getting the radar, we're getting the ESM spike.'

"In contrast, the guys on the ship were stove piped in their individual roles. In many command centers today there many, many individual screens with lots of people doing individual things. To me, the art of it is bringing all those things together. And that art is what we need to take forward to make best use of the data streams which autonomous systems can provide. The data needs to go to a centralized location whether on a ship or in the air where it is correlated and made sense of."

This is the area where clearly the discipline of human factors engineering, and human system integration comes in and plays a key role in shaping how best to do the convergence or correlation effort and capability which is central to the way ahead. Clearly, artificial intelligence will contribute to providing decision aids, but in Galdorisi's view, to maximize fully unmanned platforms, we need to move from the current paradigm where many people manage a single unmanned platform, to a new concept of operations where a single operator can manage a force package of maritime USVs with different sensors on each. This way, one can make the best use of what the sensors or capabilities deployed on those systems can do for the fleet. This is a major challenge, but clearly a key way ahead.

Manned-Unmanned Collaboration

February 8, 2021

With the shift from land wars to conflicts in contested air and sea spaces, new concepts of operations and systems are developing. The terms anti-access and area denial have been coined to describe how certain competitors (notably Russia and China), are shaping their capabilities to ensure combat dominance in times of direct conflict, but also to underwrite other forms of combat operations, such as "gray zone" operations or hybrid-war concepts of operations.

The core military challenge for liberal democracies is to operate decisively in a contested combat environment to protect their interests – and not allow the 21st century authoritarian powers to rewrite the rules of the game. As Admiral Gilday, the Chief of Naval Operations, recently put it in testimony before the U.S. Senate:

> "Despite benefiting from decades of peace and stability, China and Russia are now using all elements of their national power to undermine the international order at sea. Both attempt to unfairly control access to rich sea-based resources outside their home waters. Both intimidate their neighbors and enforce unlawful claims with the threat of force. Both have constructed sophisticated networks of sensors and long-range missiles to hold important waterways at risk. And China is building a Navy to rival our own."[15]

---

15 Admiral Michael M. Gilday, "Statement before Senate Armed Services Committee, Subcommittee on Readiness," (December 2, 2020), https://www.armed-services.senate.gov/imo/media/doc/Gilday_12-02-20.pdf.

A number of new platforms and capabilities have already been introduced by the United States and core allies and partners to reshape approaches and training for new concepts of operations to deal with the new challenges. New maritime patrol capabilities, surface and sub-surface platforms, missile defense and strike missile systems, and new combat aircraft are all coming into the forces. Along with those new capabilities, new multi-domain training approaches are being introduced as well.

But figuring out the best ways to leverage autonomous systems in combat operations is clearly a work in progress, and lessons learned with initially deployed systems will provide a path to shaping a way ahead. The challenge is not just to build and use autonomous systems, but how to communicate and use the data they gather for proper combat effect. Indeed, one way to look at the impact of such systems is upon the challenges they pose to the networks through which such systems would be managed.

In this assessment, I will draw upon two different systems that highlight both the potential and the challenges for shaping a way ahead for manned-unmanned teaming or collaboration. The first is about Triton and the second is related to counter-mine operations at sea.

The Case of the Triton

There is an expectation that unmanned or remote systems are part of how the U.S. and the allies will shape effective forces going forward. At the heart of that effort will be an expanded leveraging of these systems and shaping ways for manned and unmanned systems to collaborate.

A key area in which the U.S. Navy is already doing this, is anti-submarine and anti-surface warfare. Here, the key element has been the introduction of the Triton unmanned system working with the manned, fixed-wing P-8 maritime patrol aircraft (MPA) and the Romeo helicopter.

During 2020, I visited Norfolk, Jacksonville, Florida, San Diego, and Fallon Naval Air Station, the home of the Naval Aviation Warfighting Center or NAWDC. During those visits I had significant opportunities to talk with senior Naval officers, operators of both P-8s and Tritons, as well as the other key assets in maritime warfare that are most central to shaping a way ahead with the ISR/C² enabled air combat force. This effort included visiting the USS Gerard R. Ford in October and November 2020, where the new carrier will be incorporating data from the maritime patrol community, including Triton, to shape its way ahead in conducting 21st century ISR-enabled combat.

The U.S. Navy's approach to working maritime patrol functions relies on the new manned aircraft, the P-8 MPA; the Romeo variant of the Sea Hawk helicopter; and the unmanned Triton. With these three systems, the Navy is working through how to handle the data necessary to make timely decisions to execute the anti-submarine and anti-surface warfare missions.

The USAF remote piloted operating community is isolated from the manned pilots, whereas the P-8 and Triton operational community is unique in the U.S. military in that personnel rotate between the two platforms. This has led to the formation of a new generation of operators who cross-train for both manned and unmanned IRS platforms. What is being shaped are coordinated operations between the two, where the Triton can sweep the field of operations to identify targets and allow the P-8s to focus directly on those targets – where they need to go, and what they need to do.

While the P-8 can operate with autonomy and networkability, the Triton is a network-generating, network-enabling asset. The vast amounts of data provided by Triton is requiring the Navy and the joint force to rework how to handle data flows from the unmanned asset to gain combat advantages. Put another way, traditional methods of handling data are not adequate to properly manage such massive amounts of information. In fact, learning how to manage data from Triton has been a key driver for change in how to redesign the ISR to C² empowerment systems, which the U.S. Navy seeks to execute distributed maritime operations.

The unmanned asset operates differently from the P-8 or the Romeo in a way that is also leading to adjustments. For instance, both the P-8 and Romeo sortie into an operational area, operate for a period of time and land (either on land in the case of the P-8 or on a ship in the case of the Romeo helicopter). The concept of operations for the Triton, however, is very different. Triton provides the U.S. Navy with a whole new level of situational awareness that the Navy would attain no other way. With 24/7 coverage of the area, and in continuous orbit at 3000km, the Triton can provide domain awareness knowledge crucial to informing the threat and opportunity calculus for the area of operations.

The Triton/P-8 dyad then, poses a significant challenge to reworking the C^2/ISR enabled force. Without enhancing the data management network side of the challenge, the ability to leverage the data generated by Triton will not be maximized.

The data backbone for Triton is not yet completely there. But by deploying Triton, the Navy and the Air Force are moving forward with new ways for data management and to flow ISR more effectively into decision making systems. But again, this is being driven by operational experience of the Triton and other new air systems, and adaptation is based on real world experience, not an abstract science project.

There is clearly a cultural learning process as well. The MPA community has operated throughout its history based on a concept of operations driven by air platform sortie operations. The Triton is based on a multi-aircraft orbit concept of operations which yields a very different data stream than one gets from an air sortied aircraft – somewhere between what space systems deliver and what the sortied air collection platforms can deliver.

And given that the Triton is engaged in tasking, collecting, processing, exploitation, and dissemination of information in real time, learning how to do this for the fleet is a crucial challenge facing the future of a kill web enabled force.

As Triton gains multi-INT or multi-intelligence capabilities, it will become a more effective platform to contribute to the collaborative effort where multiple sensors can be cross-referenced to provide greater fidelity on targeting, and notably when it comes to smaller vessels of interest as well.

What the Triton experience has demonstrated, without a doubt, are the challenges that unmanned or remote systems pose to the C^2 and ISR networks. By navigating effective ways ahead with regard to network and C^2 innovations, the role of autonomous systems will be reduced and their contributions more limited than might otherwise be the case.

Again, the Chief of Naval Operations has highlighted how to look at the challenge. Referring to maritime autonomous systems, he had this to say:

"Those vessels are useless unless we can command and control them with a very high degree of precision and reliability. And so that's where we start talking about the Navy's Project Overmatch, that falls underneath, or nests underneath JADC-2. And so there are four big pieces to that. It's the networks. It's the infrastructure. It's the data standards.

"And then finally, it's the capabilities, whether they're battle management aids or whether they're artificial intelligence and machine learning capabilities that we apply to that data that allow us to decide and act faster than the bad guy, and then deliver ordnance faster out of these unmanned platforms."[16]

An Approach to Counter-Mine Warfare

An alternative approach to leveraging maritime remotes is to work with them within the realm of the operational space of a ship, and then to deliver information from the ship to the relevant members of the operational fleet. During a visit to San Diego in July 2020, I had a chance to look at a demonstration of how this might work with a new counter-mine system featured at Trident Warrior 2020 which was held in San Diego from 13-16 July 2020. There is a compelling need creatively to apply new, innovative technologies to address the operational and tactical challenges posed by mines, as well as the need to expand the use of unmanned systems to tackle Mine Countermeasure Mission (MCM) challenges.

Meeting this demand with COTS hardware and software – and not wagering on emerging technologies that will take years to develop, mature and field—should be a priority for Navy and Marine Corps planners. Rear Admiral Casey Moton, Program Executive Officer, Unmanned and Small Combatants (PEO USC), has stated that one of the functions of his office is to ensure that unmanned systems the Navy seeks to buy have the right

---

16   Megan Eckstein, "Pentagon Ghost Fleet Ship Makes Record-Breaking Trip from Mobile to California," *USNI News* (November 10, 2020).

level of technical maturity, especially in the most basic hull, mechanical and electrical (HME) attributes.

This strongly suggests that the Navy would be well-served to move forward by focusing on COTS technologies that have been wrung out in Navy and Marine Corps exercises, experiments, and demonstrations. This will ensure that these systems have the requisite HME attributes and maturity to succeed.

What I saw in San Diego were all the component parts of what several industry representatives, led by Teledyne Brown Engineering Inc, brought together to demonstrate an autonomous MCM solution that takes the Sailor out of the minefield. It is important to emphasize that every component part of this solution has been in the water and tested in the operational environment.

I witnessed what each individual component could do and received a briefing on how Teledyne Brown has an integrated solution—dubbed "Clear-Sea" – to pull all these components together and achieve a single-sortie detect-to-engage MCM capability. The "mother ship" for all the components of this Clear-Sea MCM capability demonstrated in San Diego was the T38E (38-foot extended) MANTAS high-speed catamaran. Earlier versions of the MANTAS have been proven in numerous Navy and Marine Corps exercises, experiments, and demonstrations.

I rode on the MANTAS and noted how the catamaran hull allows the boat to slice through choppy waters and provide a smooth ride that monohulls cannot. I also noted how the size of the vessel can easily accommodate the mine-hunting and mine neutralizing systems that complete the system.

The planned production T38 is similar in size to an eleven-meter RHIB carried by many U.S. Navy ships and thus can be easily integrated aboard most U.S. Navy warships. In comparison to an eleven-meter RHIB, the T38 is two feet longer, five inches wider, drafts 17 inches shallower at max displacement, and includes a cross-section height over eight feet lower, making it extraordinarily hard to detect. The T38 can operate in up to sea state five, has a cruise speed equal to, and a maximum speed twice that of an eleven-meter RHIB.

The first component that I saw – and that will be carried by the T38 – is the ThayerMahan Sea Scout subsea imaging system. The Sea Scout is specifically designed for missions such as mine hunting. The Sea Scout system is founded on the in-production COTS system Kraken Robotics Katfish-180 tow-body mounted Synthetic Aperture Sonar. The system is designed to search for mine-like objects (MLOs) and is integrated by ThayerMahan's remote operations and communications system.

I learned that this system could survey up to three and a half kilometers per hour at a resolution sufficient for MLO classification, and is programmable for bottom following, terrain referencing, obstacle avoidance, and "flies" at a pre-programmed depth. Automatic Target Recognition identifies likely MLO anomalies, which are then presented in near-real-time to the man–in-the-loop for verification as an MLO. Verified MLOs are added as a waypoint for validation, while invalid MLOs are discarded or passed to the navigation database as a hazard to navigation. Verified MLOs are continuously updated to a recommended route for the Mine Neutralization System (MNS) Remotely Operated Vehicle (ROV).

The Pluto ROV mine neutralization system pictured during the MANTAS-led countermine exercise as part of a wider U.S. Navy unmanned systems event in San Diego in July 2020. Credit Photo: *Second Line of Defense*.

The next component I saw was the Idrobotica Pluto Plus MNS ROV which executes the "dull, dirty and dangerous" work previously conducted by classes of U.S. Navy ships by providing real-time HD video validation of mine-like objects. It too will be carried by the T38. I was briefed on how this

MNS ROV autonomously executes the MLO route for final classification and man-on-the-loop validation of each MLO while the T38 shadows and supports it as an over-the-horizon communications link and countermine charge supply link. Once the operator identifies a validated MLO as a likely mine that must be destroyed, an explosive charge is placed on the mine.

The MNS ROV then clears the area. The classification, validation and engagement processes are then repeated until the field is cleared. The countermine charge detonation sequencing may be altered to detonate in any order and at any time desired. I was able to see what these sensors found during their several-week operation from the Idrobotica Pilota Watch-Stander Station.

I was struck by the fact that this watch station is manned by a single individual. This system and its software architecture accommodate integration of variable depth sonar or hull mounted sonar, AUV and ROV functions, auto-pilot control and propelled variable depth sonar. I noted that the fidelity of the images displayed on this watch station left little doubt as to the identity of what was observed.

While each component in this system was impressive, that is not enough – not by a long shot. These individual components must be fully integrated in order to deliver the subsystems as a cohesive turn key unmanned MCM solution that is easy to operate and easy to maintain. Teledyne Brown Engineering has a deliberate plan to do just this and is prepared to demonstrate incrementally more integrated versions of what I observed in San Diego.

Importantly, from my point of view, among all the MCM solutions I have examined in my years following (and writing about) this mission area, this one stands out as a very capable single-sortie detect-to-engage MCM capability solution.

Regarding manned-unmanned collaboration, this kind of solution allows for the data that is collected onboard the vessel, gets interpreted for the anomalies back to the professionals onboard the fleet. This means that one does not need a wide area network to deliver the desired mission effect, but one tied back to the operating ship, which can then use a variety of communication tools to provide data regarding the mine threat and the results from the counter-mine operations.

In other words, Triton highlights the broader opportunities which remotes can deliver to the wide area network; and counter-mine case highlights how networks can be focused on a core mission without the need to rely on a broader network. Progress on both sides will be key to sorting through the opportunities which unmanned or remote systems can provide the operating forces.

Conceptualizing Next Generation Autonomous Systems
April 15, 2021

The April 2021 Williams Foundation Seminar on Next Generation Autonomous Systems (NGAS) provided insights regarding a number of key issues concerning the way ahead with such systems. A key consideration is how will they enter the force, how will they be part of force transformation and how best to understand how the manned-unmanned force mix might evolve.

My own focus has been upon the evolution of U.S. and allied forces in a direction of shaping a distributed but integratable force able to operate in contested environments. And NGAS are clearly part of the future of how distributed forces will operate in the future. For example, the core change already seen regarding how the U.S. Navy and USMC are shaping ways to distribute the force more effectively and this evolving template clearly anticipates a growing role for NGAS.

The presentation by Marcus Hellyer, a well-known and regarded defense analyst at the Australian Strategic Policy Institute, provided a particularly insightful look at how one might consider the way ahead for the entry of NGAS into the force as well as how the overall force might be calibrated for the future fight.

Hellyer looked at the broader topography of the forces and asked the question, where might autonomous systems fit into where we need to drive our force structure? The force is moving in the direction of being more disaggregated and autonomous systems will be useful in that process.

How do we manage disaggregation and what might be the role of NGAS in that process as well as providing more cost-effective options as well?

In my follow-up interview with Hellyer we discussed his approach.

Question: Is that a fair way to summarize your argument?

Hellyer: It is. I, like you, get a little frustrated when we get bogged down in endless debates about hypothetical futures for AI or the legal and moral and ethical aspects of autonomy. I'm not really after autonomy for its own sake. Autonomy is a tool, not an end in itself. Like you, I'm very interested in moving towards distributed concepts, whether you want to call them the distributed kill web or mosaic warfare or whatever the term is that you want to use, I think that's where we need to be going.

In part, it is also about cost-effectiveness as well. To paraphrase recent U.S. Navy CNO comments: Can we continue to build $3 billion ships to carry 32 VLS cells? We need to start harnessing the disruptive potential of disaggregated systems. To get out of that kind of cost death spiral, we need to disaggregate capability. Simple things are faster to build, and so you can build a lot more of them. To do that, you have to disaggregate capabilities off three-billion-dollar ships into smaller entities. But to make those entities relevant, you then need to link them together so they can talk with each other and work together. But to me, you need to disaggregate simply so you can get more sensors and more weapons into the air or into the water, and to shape a more resilient system.

In my presentation to the Williams Foundation, I spent quite a bit of time looking at a kind of analogous transition. I did that to make a couple of points. The first one is that really disruptive transitions can sneak up on you quite quickly. If you're not prepared for them, you will be taken by surprise. And we have a really good example of a complex system of systems using disaggregated components that is evolving in front of us. The example I used was Australia's electricity sector. Our electricity sector has dramatically transformed in a very small period of time.

I highlighted a screen grab from an app that shows at any point in time where Australia's electricity supply is coming from. A couple of weeks ago, we hit a point where over half of our electricity supply was coming from renewable sources. So that transition to renewables has actually progressed quite a distance. We've reached a tipping point. I know tipping point is a cliché but we're there, not because renewables now provide all of our electricity or even most of it. That 50% point was obviously one moment in time when the wind was blowing, and the sun was shining. It's not hitting close to 50% all the time. But last year, about 28% of our electricity came from renewables.

We've reached a tipping point in the sense that the commercial sectors do not want to invest their own money in traditional forms of generation; no business wants to build a coal-fired power plant. No business really wants to build a natural gas power plant. Only the government is considering whether it will pay to do that. We've reached that kind of tipping point where business thinks that it's not economically viable to keep investing in fossil fuel powered generation. A transition has occurred; it's just that our thinking hasn't really caught up with it in some ways.

And this analogy also speaks to the distributed issue with regards to defense. The new electricity grid is not based on a small number of very large generators. It's based on a large number of generators that range from small to larger. Australia has one of the highest take ups of rooftop solar panels in the world. You have private houses around Australia who are now feeding electricity into our electricity grid. The result is that we range from individual households up to very large generators. We still do have some coal-fired power plants, but out in the countryside, we now have very, very large commercial-scale solar and, as in America, very large wind farms.

But that's a different kind of grid. You've got lots of contributors switching on and off, feeding in at different times, turning on in response to the market, turning off when the wind doesn't blow, or the sun doesn't shine. It requires a much more flexible, agile kind of grid and requires some of the kinds of autonomous brainpower that a military-distributed kill web would require.

I talked about that because I think it's a really nice example of a transition that's occurring in front of our eyes, but it's also a transition that I think has some really nice relevant analogies for the military in terms of a more distributed grid suggesting what force distribution can provide as well.

Question: What you are describing is the emergence of a mixed power system, where clearly fossil fuel remains crucial in many ways and funding to generate such capabilities is crucial to Australia's ability to have security of supply as well. It's a different mix, but the mix is being driven by introducing new capabilities and new approaches. To your point, it also allows you to think about a more viable grid in terms of not being so dependent on a small number of larger generating plants and transmission belts.

In a way, this is an analogy to a distributed military kill web where you are shaping multiple ways to generate the combat effect one wants rather than relying on single point of failure large systems. Is that a fair characterization of your argument?

Hellyer: It is. I think one useful kind of observation from the electricity sector is that rather than focusing on the capability of the individual generator we need to look at the resilience of the entire system. Renewables will always look poor compared to a really big traditional generator, whether it's gas or coal or nuclear because a single facility generates less power. But we need to look at their contribution to the resilience of the entire system. In that regard, a renewable grid or a combination grid is much more resilient in many ways.

If you look at the electricity sector, don't look at the new technology as a like for like replacement for the old technology. We were talking earlier about the Osprey. If you look at the Osprey as simply a fast helicopter, you are kind of missing the point.

So in the electricity grid, large-scale batteries are not really there to replace coal-fired power plants. If you look at them in that regard, they'll look like very poor replacements. What batteries do is they can stabilize the grid because they can switch it on and off instantaneously in response to demand. And because they can switch on and off so quickly, they completely outperform traditional generators in response to the spot market in the electricity sector.

They actually have a different kind of capability and one that lets them really outcompete the traditional generators. They are smaller but to use a military term, "they are much more agile". They play a different role, but a complimentary one with the larger, traditional power generators. The challenge when we're looking at new technologies is not to look at them as like for like replacements of what we have now, but to actually see what they do differently—that seems to be a particular challenge for militaries where the continual, daily competition of the marketplace isn't at work.

Another useful analogy between the electricity sector and the military is the issue of sunk cost and how to avoid 'stranded assets'. Whether we're talking about an LHD (Landing Helicopter Deck) or a coal-fired power plant, if it's in service, we've put so much money into it that we're going to keep using it so we'll need to find ways to adapt it and find a way to use it purposefully in that web or mix of technologies.

If we use a private sector analogy for the military, what we need to focus on is shaping a balanced portfolio. NGAS will enter the force to provide a balanced portfolio. And one of the potential advantages with NGAS is an ability to put them into play much more rapidly than you can with large platforms, capabilities which enhance the force. They offer you the ability to keep your big, traditional investments relevant.

The big question, and one we probably can't answer yet is how much money do you keep committing to build those exquisitely capable yet extremely expensive traditional platforms like frigates and submarines? When do you turn that off? And how much do you put into the newer autonomous technologies, which to some degree are riskier because we don't know exactly what's going to become of them. We don't know exactly how to use them. We don't know exactly how to integrate them together and how all the command-and-control networks are going to work.

But as another speaker at the Williams Foundation conference said, we need to have 'a bias toward action'. That is, we can't solve all the issues around autonomy in the abstract. We need to experiment and invest and solve as we go. Again, the electricity sector offers a nice analogy. Initially, we started out with a few people putting some solar panels on their roof.

That only grew slowly at first and very few people thought then that they could drive our power grid, yet here we are today with nobody wanting to put new money into the old technology.

The Quest for Next Generation Autonomous Systems
May 25, 2021

At the Williams Foundation Seminar on Next Generation Autonomous systems, held on April 8, 2021, the moderator was WGCDR Keirin Joyce. I had met Joyce at an earlier Williams Foundation presentation on unmanned systems and had a chance to follow up on his take on the issues discussed at the seminar in a phone interview on May 14, 2021.

When I first met Joyce, he was in the Army working on unmanned systems; now he is working Triton and Sky Guardian. He has served for 24 years in the Australian Army, where he last served as Program Manager of Unmanned Aerial Systems from December 2016-January 2020. Since then, he is serving in the Royal Australian Air Force as Chief Engineer for Royal Australian Air Force Remotely Piloted Aircraft Systems / Unmanned Aerial Systems at ISR Systems Program Office, including MQ-4C Triton under Air 7000-1B and MQ-9B SkyGuardian under Air 7003.

Precisely because he has been involved with two services and is knowledgeable regarding the civilian side of artificial intelligence and robotics, he was the perfect choice to be the seminar moderator.

During the seminar, he highlighted an example of how current forces can use new unmanned technologies to support the evolving kill web, in which a small team with ISR and C2 capability can inform a firing solution by a virtual task force firing solution provider. WGCDR Joyce noted that in an Exercise Hamel held in 2018, a two-man Army team using a Black Hornet Nano UAV was able to identify a tank formation, and then with their radio able to pass that information on to the Royal Australian Air Force (RAAF) for a strike opportunity against that tank formation.

This example highlights certainly one role which unmanned systems can play in providing ISR better labeled as information than intelligence surveillance reconnaissance because in this case you have the two-man team inside the Weapons Engagement Zone providing inputs to an external provider for a firing solution.

The first issue we discussed was the importance of understanding the challenge of generating innovation associated with autonomous systems into the operational military. The military as an organization is often described as risk averse, but since the military must be prepared to fight tonight, disruptive change for its own purpose can degrade military capabilities rather than enhancing them.

The ADF has been described through Williams Foundation seminars since 2014 as building a fifth-generation force. In my own words, I see this as shaping an integrated distributed force through which kill webs can operate to provide for a scalable combat force. With such a template, the role of next generation autonomous systems can enable either enhanced mass to modular task forces, or enhanced decision-making capability either at the tactical edge or at the wider tactical or strategic decision-making levels. As Joyce put it:

> "We know that we have to go to war with what we've got. When you go to the next big thing in defense, you proceed from what you already have."

The second issue was the key role in which Australia finds itself with regard to working next generation autonomous systems. As Joyce noted:

> "We are recognized as a global leader in autonomy in the mining and resource sector, both ground and aerial survey autonomy. I think a lot of that technology is able to be brought across to defense or upscaled towards defense applications."

Australian innovations have a wider market for both development and deployment. Australia also can draw upon innovations being shaped by the other five eyes members, and as Canada, the UK, and the U.S. particularly do not have the same geographical defense needs, there will clearly be different approaches to incorporating next generation autonomous systems into their forces. As Joyce underscored:

"I think there is a melting pot of technology built in Australia that we're good at and we have a lot of potential to contribute on a global scale."

The third issue is the cross between the first and second points: Australia is already building a fifth-generation force which enables further innovation as well. Regarding the fifth-generation force, the core role of software has clearly emerged as a key element of change. As forces get more familiar with how to manage software upgradeability in current platforms, a learning cycle is being shaped whereby systems which are built primarily around software—the next generation autonomous systems—will become key elements for force transformation.

WGCDR Keirin Joyce.

With the shift to the digital native generation of warriors, innovation processes are changing as well. WGCDR Joyce used the example of the potential impact of drone racers on military innovation.

"The Drone Racing Teams of the Army, Navy, and Air Force are a key force for change. These are kids that have decided to take up drone racing in their spare time. None of them are employed to do this full-time. They have taken it off as a hobby and not through university, not through technical college, but off You Tube videos and collaborative communities that have taught themselves all the skills on how to build a UAV. They literally learn it all on You Tube, and they have this amazing skill set that sits at a peer level and in some cases in advance of our socially qualified engineers.

"In Australia, we've used these drone racing pilots in support of our weapons' technical investigations and intelligence, in support of rapid prototyping, assisting with ground autonomy trials, and all of these soldiers and aviators are doing this in their spare time. I think it's something that we need to tap more and to develop deployable rapid prototyping labs, or deployable space labs. In the future, it's plausible that when we are confronted with the next asymmetric threat that our opposition force comes up with, there is absolutely the possibility that we can design, prototype and manufacture solutions, not by engineers, but by people who just know how to do it and have taught themselves how to do it because it's fun. I think that is a real skill set that we should be focusing on and tapping: it is an opportunity that costs next to nothing.

"Perhaps we should be setting up structures in our organizations where we let these people do their day job one posting, and then on the next posting their whole job is just running or contributing to innovation labs. And then they go back to their job, and then they go back to the innovation lab. We could really foster those skill sets and thought processes and innovative approaches to whatever sixth gen is, because when we take our Fifth-Gen Force to the next battle, we go with what we've got. And if we want rapidly to uptake that force to a Generation 5.1, or a Generation 6 application, then we are going to need skills to do that. Most of the skills needed are in code, in electronics, software, and in data: drone racers."

The fourth issue is the relationship between the broader ecosystem for robots, AI and autonomy and finding ways for the military to tap into that broader ecosystem. WGCDR Joyce underscored how important being able to do so was for the Australian military and he provided an example of such a case.

"One case study in particular is prototyping an aircraft for the Electric Vertical Take-off and Landing (eVTOL) market for unmanned aerial taxis. There's a company out of Sydney called AMSL. They're doing it for the commercial market. But they have partnered with Defense to take the five-passenger seats out and design a configuration for us to do 500 to 600 kilograms worth of combat resupply. We have also asked them to do the design work so that when the airplane is otherwise coming back empty from doing a resupply, we could also put in up to two stretchers for casualty evacuations. They are already doing the collaborative research with telemedicine and automated monitoring of stretcher-bound patients.

"All of that technology is coming in from the medical tech field, and that's being underpinned not necessarily by defense or even the medical field, it's by our civilian medical evacuation helicopter providers—people like CareFlight, who provide some of our emergency response helicopters for our ambulance services."

The fifth point is determining where the quest for next generation autonomous systems fits into the evolution of the art of warfare. This can be looked at in two different ways: one the specific defense geography of Australia, and secondly, the strategic shift from the Middle Eastern land wars to operating in conflicts with peer competitors.

This first revolves around shaping the distributed integratable force in which combat clusters can operate at the tactical edge with enough capability to achieve their tasks as allocated by mission command requirements. Distribution is about working multi-domain warfighting packages. Next generation autonomous systems can provide increased mass for each combat cluster notably with ISR payloads already on the way.

The second revolves around the geography of Australia. Given the importance of Western to Northern Australia to the first island chain of the Solomon Islands, there are several ways next generation autonomous systems can provide for capabilities throughout the distributed operational space. For example, port security at a distance is a crucial requirement. Already, autonomous maritime USVs exist with the relevant ISR systems to provide significant inputs to meeting this mission.[17]

As the ADF works through how best to build a defense grid over this region for its operations, it makes a great deal of sense to build in new autonomous systems as players in that defense grid. This solves a key problem, which is where to add new capabilities without degrading extant capabilities, for as you build out a new approach to an operational area building in new platforms and systems can be done with realism in terms of delivering a desired combat capability, rather than just building prototypes or briefing slides, more likely to put your audience asleep than building capabilities which deter an adversary.

And finally, we discussed Triton. WGCDR Joyce has Triton in his portfolio, and I have visited Jax Navy several times as well as RAAF Base Edinburgh where the P-8s and Tritons will be operated from. The point can be made simply: This is a U.S. Navy-led effort on manned-unmanned teaming NOW and lessons learned from such teaming clearly inform a way ahead for next generation autonomous systems.

In short, next generation autonomous systems are clearly on the way. As WGCDR Joyce underscored: "All of the services see robotic autonomous systems as a significant part of the road ahead. It's just that the services are getting after them differently."

---

17 George Galorisi, "Employing Unmanned Surface Vehicles to Enhance Port and Harbor Security," *Second Line of Defense* (April 3, 2020), https://sldinfo.com/2020/04/employing-unmanned-surface-vehicles-to-enhance-port-and-harbor-security/.

The Eco-system for Next-Gen Autonomous Systems

June 3, 2021

At the Williams Foundation seminar on Next Generation Autonomous Systems, April 8, 2021, an important consideration was how the ADF could leverage a broader ecosystem of change in the commercial sector where robotics and artificial intelligence were playing key roles. An important presentation at the seminar was by Professor Jason Scholz, CEO of the Trusted Autonomous Systems Defence Cooperation Centre. He is also a tenured Innovation Professor at RMIT University in Melbourne.

The broader Australian effort regarding autonomous systems provides an opportunity for the ADF to shape sovereign defense capabilities in this area as well as working more effectively with relevant global partners in this area. And it is not simply a question of equipment; it is about working ADF concepts of operations interactively with core allies. As the ADF works its way ahead with regard to building out its fifth-generation force to enable integrated distributed operations, selective autonomous systems will enable the force to become more effective, more lethal, and more survivable.

This is how Scholz described the challenge and the way ahead for the ADF in the autonomous systems area:

> "Autonomous systems for air, land, sea, space, cyber, electro-magnetic, and information environments offers huge potential to enhance Australia's critical and scarce manned platforms and soldiers, and realizing this now and into the future requires leadership in defense, in industry, in science and technology and academia with an ambition and an appetite for risk in effecting high-impact and disruptive change."

He underscored the crucial importance of leveraging the broader commercial developments and uses already underway.

> "We need a diversity of means to make this work. And it happened into the future. This is an initiative of defense and Defence Science and Technology (DST) group. It leverages

strong commercial technology drivers to solve these long-term challenges experienced by the department."

The Centre takes an approach which is "defense needs-driven," with every project clearly having to show how it can be a "game changer for the ADF to fight and win." Projects are "industry-led" often with smaller firms, to ensure new technologies get through the "valley of death." All projects are "research supported," which includes subcontracting government researchers and academics to industry—a novel approach.

I had a chance to discuss with Jason, to understand the nature of the way ahead in practical terms during a phone interview on May 27, 2021. The focus of that conversation was very much on how to get these innovations into the hands of the ADF.

Trusted Autonomous Systems CEO, Professor Jason Scholz was awarded the 2020 McNeil Prize in December 2020 by Chief of Navy, Vice Admiral Michael Noonan, AO in a virtual ceremony.

What the ADF refers to as building a fifth-generation force can also be labeled as building a distributed and human-machine-team integrated force. This is clearly underway with the platforms and systems, which the ADF is already acquiring, but what next generation autonomous systems can do is accelerate the transition and build out greater mass for a distributed force. And as autonomous systems are leveraged, the way new capabilities will be added, and supported will change, including in terms of the industrial model supporting the force as well. For example, the ADF is operating several software upgradeable systems already, with the Wedgetail being the first platform introduced into the force which is built around software upgradeability.

With a manned system, obviously there is concern for the safety and security of the manned elements crewing the platform, so that software redesign needs to be done in regard to these key considerations. But as Scholz put it in our interview, with the Centre's focus on the "smart, the small and the many," compared with traditional "complex, large and few" manned systems, code rewriting can be much faster.

It is also the case that digital engineering and digital twins are changing how all platforms are designed and supported. But in the case of next generation autonomous systems, the entire life cycle of these "smart, small and many" systems is very different. "They will be attritable; there will be no need to develop and maintain 30 years of systems engineering documentation—some of these might be used only once or a few times before disposal. When you need to adapt to the threat, digital engineering supports fast redesign and T&E in the virtual, and to add a new capability, you just download it as software," Scholz says.

And the question of how to handle the requirements process is very different. This is already true for software upgradable platforms like Triton, but it has been VERY difficult for acquisition systems to recognize how software upgradeability simply blows up the traditional requirements setting process. Next generation autonomous systems are built around software and digital life cycles; this means that how they are validated and introduced requires a clearly modified acquisition approach.

I remember how difficult it was to introduce the Osprey into the USMC and then into the force. I interviewed a Marine in the early days of introduction, and he referred to the challenge of transitioning from being a "bar act" to becoming a core combat capability, which significantly transformed the force. Autonomous systems face the problem of moving from being a "bar act."[18]

So where might these systems be introduced in the near term, gain operator's confidence, and contribute in the short to mid-term to a more effective ADF? The shortest path to escaping the "bar act" phase is in infrastructure defense. Maritime autonomous systems certainly could provide a significant contribution in the relatively short-term to something as crucial as extended port security and defense.

Indeed, Scholz worked with CMDR Paul Hornsby in the 2018 Autonomous Warrior exercise.[19] According to Scholz:

"This was the biggest trial of autonomous systems, which the Royal Australian Navy has done to date. We had 45 companies actively participating with live demonstrations, as well as hosting the final demonstration of the Five Eyes nations Autonomy Strategic Challenge, which was an initiative of The Technical Cooperation Program (TTCP). During the exercise, we were able to control 13 separate semi-autonomous vehicles, in the air, on the surface, underwater, and on land simultaneously from a single operator at a workstation. One of the vignettes was littoral base defense."

He argued that for the ADF, a "human-centered, AI-enabled, internet of things" approach is a way to think of it. From our work with Second Fleet, VADM Lewis and his team are rebuilding their approach around mission command for a distributed force. This is the strategic direction already underway.

Scholz sees autonomous systems as providing mass to the distributed force.

18 "The Evolution of the Osprey: "We are No Longer a Bar Act," *Second Line of Defense* (September 9, 2012), https://sldinfo.com/2012/09/the-evolution-of-the-osprey-we-are-no-longer-a-bar-act/.

19 Robbin Laird, "The Australian Approach to Developing and Deploying Remotes in the Maritime Environment," (October 12, 2019), *Second Line of Defense*, https://sldinfo.com/2019/10/the-australian-approach-to-developing-and-deploying-remotes-systems-in-the-maritime-environment-the-perspective-of-cmdr-paul-hornsby/

"Humans express mission command goals to machines, machines express to the operator what actions they can take to achieve that, and a contract agreement is formed. Within the commander's intent, machines then subcontract to other machines and so on, dynamically adapting as the battle evolves to build that Mosaic."

In both his presentation and our discussion, he highlighted a capability on which they are working now that can provide for sensors and communications capabilities to support the force which complements manned assets to provide for Information, Reconnaissance, and Intelligence. In other words, autonomous systems can provide for sensor networks, which can be part of the effort to leverage information systems to deliver more timely and effective decisions.

"For example, high-altitude balloons can operate at 50,000 to 70,000 feet, above manned aircraft—largely solving the detect and avoid airspace problem. The endurance of these are a few days to weeks with the potential to station-keep or track surface targets with edge intelligence. The cost of these are a few thousand dollars each.

"They are reusable maybe six times and can carry comms and ISR. Launch them in hours not like the months for cube sats. They are attractable, so you can put them in places you wouldn't put other assets. They can assist first responders or offer support to war fighters."

In short, the ADF is already undergoing a transition to shape a distributed integrated force. Next Generation Autonomous Systems can provide a further set of capabilities for a more effective, dense, survivable, and capable ADF as it builds out for operations in the Indo-Pacific region and enhances its defense of the Australian continent.

Maritime Autonomous Systems

May 29, 2021

At the recent Williams Foundation seminar on Next Generation Autonomous Systems, Vice Admiral Noonan, Chief of the Royal Australian Navy, provided his perspective on the way ahead for maritime autonomous systems in the build out and evolution of the Royal Australian Navy. At the heart of his presentation was an opportunity to discuss the Navy's new Remote Autonomous Systems-AI 2040 strategy.

As he put it:

> "Our Navy has already begun a journey to shape the maritime environment. To deter actions against our national interests. To respond with credible Naval power. To use robotics, autonomy, and artificial intelligence. Employing ever more reliable, robust, and repeatable systems.

> "We will continue to drive our edge to help keep our people safe. To create mass, tempo and reach at sea and in all the lanes to enhance the joint force and strengthen our coalition with human command and trusted machine control. Our technologies are enabling our people to thrive. Our people, using technologies, are able to make smarter systems and better decisions."

The RAS-AI strategy is focused on enhancing the fleet, not supplanting it. And he underscored that the Royal Australian Navy is working currently to introduce these technologies into the fleet.

I have argued elsewhere that that shift in manned platforms to relying on software upgradeability as a key driver for ongoing modernization clearly becomes a central piece in understanding how to build out RAS-AI capabilities for the maritime autonomous systems platforms or assets.

The Vice Admiral introduced a very useful term, which covers the way ahead for thinking about integratability across the crewed and uncrewed assets in the force. As he put it:

"Evergreen, I think is the new term for spiral development. That's the way I look at it. It's about ensuring that we have systems that remain contemporary, and I am challenged daily about capability gaps and about deficiencies in the long lead times that require us in the shipbuilding space.

"It takes about 10 years to build a submarine, or five years to build a frigate. And are we incorporating old technologies? The bottom-line is no, in that we are designing future and evergreen in growth into our platforms. And I think that's a very important concept that we have not always fully grasped."

I had a chance to further discuss how to think about the way ahead for maritime autonomous systems within the fleet with Vice Admiral (Retired) Tim Barrett. I have been in an ongoing discussion about maritime matters with Barrett ever since I first met him in 2015, and as a key architect for shaping the build out of the 21st century Royal Australian Navy, I wanted to focus on the interaction between the new build strategy for the Navy's surface and subsurface platforms and the introduction of autonomous systems into the fleet. Vice Admiral (Retired) Barrett is currently on the board of TAS, the organization headed by Jason Scholz.

Vice Admiral Barrett presenting at the Williams Foundation seminar on air-land integration in March 2016. Credit: *Second Line of Defense*

This means that Barrett brings to the discussion a deep understanding of the challenges of building out the RAN's surface and subsurface fleet with the coming of new autonomous technologies. The challenge, of course, is to shape an approach which allows for their integration and dynamic processes of change over time.

The core point which Barrett drove home in our conversation was the key challenge of building out the integrated distributed force with an open aperture to inclusion of the force enhancement capabilities, which maturing autonomous systems can provide. He argued that at TAS the focus was not just on the next big thing as how what developers can bring to the party which can enhance the capabilities of the force.

As he put it:

"The new technologies need to be fitted into a broader operational environment. The force has to fight tonight; how can we shape ways ahead which lead to force enhancement?"

In focusing on the subsurface domain, he argued that the context for submarines was changing significantly. They are increasingly operating in a broader kill web environment and need to be able to tap into trusted data to aid their operations and focus their efforts.

Clearly, autonomous systems can play an increasingly big role in mapping and tracking the undersea domain, and the manned assets become much more capable as trusted data networks can be tapped into. As he noted:

> "Submarines are part of the undersea domain battle. They are key contributors, but they have to work within an integrated and distributed mode, which provides them with the information and context in which they can best operate and enhance the operational outcome."

Evolving autonomous systems will be able to provide enhanced undersea domain awareness, which will then enhance the capability of the force to execute their operational plans more effectively. But this leads as well to reinforcing the broader challenge facing the force: How do you manage and distribute the data being generated to provide information for tactical decision making at the edge and for broader tactical theater wide decision making?

And this leads Barrett to his version of Occom's razor when assessing what a particular autonomous system might contribute to the force:

> "I'm less interested in what the particular device being proposed—whether it is a swarming device, an undersea array or a sea glider—but I'm more interested in how your device obtains data, and how reliable it is and how to distribute it and how relevant it is or is not to the commander fighting the battle in operational space in which he is operating."

Notably, how do autonomous systems close gaps in the information-decision dynamic within which forces can operate as an effective kill web?

The Impact on Logistics Capabilities

April 23, 2021

At the recent Williams Foundation Conference on Next Generation Autonomous Systems, Col. Beaumont, Director of the be Australian Army Research Centre (AARC), focused on the intersection between logistics and support innovation and automation and autonomous systems. It was clear from looking at his presentation that Beaumont highlighted the role of better information systems and the internet of things as a core way ahead to shape a more effective logistics support system.

During our discussion, this is how Beaumont started:

> "The new automation and autonomous systems technologies offer great promise and provide valuable tools, which will be adopted more widely over time. You don't want to get seduced by technology to the point that you're taken down some rabbit warrens that create risks in themselves. I see automated tools as providing for serious strategy change in a relatively short period of time, rather than overemphasizing what autonomous platforms can quickly provide."

By shaping more capability to use information tools, automation tools associated with the Internet of Things allows for reshaping the template for logistics support. As that template is worked, the ecosystem is created within which further ability to leverage next generation automated systems is enhanced. It is a question in some ways of putting the cart before the horse.

Beaumont highlighted that "even as simple an effort to implement enterprise business tools but to do so within a deployable system is a key advancement which allows us to shape a more effective way ahead. In large part, it is about building sensor networks within an overall logistics system and finding ways to tap into those networks to provide for more effective decision support and for these new systems to enable better domain knowledge throughout the logistics enterprise." It is about taking those sensor networks and having the computing tools which enable you to be able to rapidly predict or act without direct human intervention to enable decisions with regard to doing the right thing in the right place at the right time to support the force from a logistics point of view."

His focus clearly is upon shaping a logistics enterprise system, which can use automation and information more effectively to drive better tactical and strategic decision making with regard to logistical support. What we have already seen in practice is the challenge of overcoming cultural and organizational barriers to do so. We have seen in some militaries over-reliance on commercial IT systems, which leaves their logistics system vulnerable to adversary cyberattacks.

We have seen in the case of a new enterprise support system like the F-35 resistance to change in order to use the information generated by the enterprise system to change the configuration of logistics support itself.

As Beaumont put it:

> "To use a new system effectively, you have to develop the processes that truly can leverage the new system. One has to combine all sorts of different organizational factors to get the innovation which new technologies for support can provide, whether that be organizational redesign, or making sure the right people are trained to do it, and different specialties may be required as well to leverage the new technologies."

Lt. Col. (Now) Colonel David Beaumont presenting at the April 2019 Williams Foundation Seminar. Credit *Second Line of Defense.*

New technology is not a bromide that solves anything. You actually have to think about usability to the force. You have to think about finding ways that technology actually empowers the force rather than just simply disrupts it. It is often called disruptive technology, but that's not a positive thing if it's so disrupting that you actually reduce the capability of the force to fight. That's hardly innovation.

We then turned to the question of how autonomous systems could be introduced into the Australian Army with a real benefit for the force and expanding its operational capabilities.

From the logistics side, the challenge is two-sided—how do you bring these assets into an operational environment? How do you service them? How do they help rather than burden the force? How can they provide logistical support for a deployed force most effectively?

The Australian Army is certainly experimenting with several autonomous systems, but the logistics side of this is a key part of shaping the way ahead, both in terms of enhancing the demand for logistical support and providing for logistical support.

We discussed one area where it might make a great deal of sense to get the kind of operational experience where such systems could be introduced and supported without introducing excessive risk to the combat force, namely, in support of HADR missions. A HADR mission involves moving significant support forward from either an air or sea-delivered force. How might autonomous systems be used to assist in moving relief supplies to the right point and the right time? How might deployable "internet of things" automated information systems be set up to manage the flow of supplies to the right place and at the right time?

Beaumont noted that at the Williams Foundation Seminar "there seemed to be a wide consensus upon the importance of experimenting with these new systems to determine how best to use them."

In short, Beaumont highlighted the near-term opportunities to use new enterprise system approaches and technologies to reshape the logistics enterprise system and in so doing shape the kind of template conducive to further changes, which autonomous systems could introduce.

A New Generation of Military Unmanned Vehicles

By George Galdorisi
September 18, 2021

At the highest levels of U.S. intelligence and military policy documents, there is universal agreement that the United States remains at war, even as the conflicts in Iraq and Afghanistan conclude. As the cost of capital platforms—especially ships and aircraft—continues to rise, the Department of Defense is increasingly looking to procure comparatively inexpensive unmanned systems as important assets to supplement the Joint Force.

As the United States builds a force structure to contend with high-end threats, both the DoD and the Department of the Navy (DoN) envision a future force with large numbers of unmanned systems complementing manned platforms. The conflicts in Iraq and Afghanistan have spurred the development of unmanned air vehicles and unmanned ground vehicles to meet urgent operational needs. As a result, the lion's share of previous year's DoD funding for unmanned systems has gone to air and ground systems, while funding for unmanned maritime systems (Unmanned Surface Vehicles (USV) and unmanned underwater vehicles) has lagged.

However, this balance is shifting, as increasingly, warfighters recognize the need for unmanned maritime systems in the fight against high-end adversaries, as well as against nations or groups to whom these adversaries export their weapons systems. Like their air and ground counterparts, these unmanned maritime systems are valued because of their ability to reduce the risk to human life in high threat areas, to deliver persistent surveillance over areas of interest, and to provide options to warfighters that derive from the inherent advantages of unmanned technologies.

A Department of the Navy Perspective

Operating as it does in five domains (air, surface, subsurface, ground, and cyber) the Navy and Marine Corps recognize the potential and the promise of unmanned systems to deliver asymmetric advantages to U.S. forces, especially in areas where adversaries have extensive anti-access and area denial capabilities.

In January 2021, the Chief of Naval Operations issued CNO NAVPLAN (Navigation Plan) designed to chart the course for how the Navy will execute the Tri-Service Maritime Strategy Advantage at Sea. Not surprisingly, this short (18-page) document identifies unmanned systems as an important part of the Navy's future plans, noting, in part:

> "Advances in autonomous systems have shown promise for an effective and affordable way for the Navy to fight and win in contested spaces. We will modernize the fleet to harness these technologies and maintain our advantage at sea... Objective analysis confirms that America needs a larger, more lethal fleet. The Navy requires greater numbers of submarines, smaller and more numerous surface combatants, more lethal offensive capabilities, a host of integrated unmanned platforms—under, on, and above the sea.

> "Unmanned platforms play a vital role in our future fleet. Successfully integrating unmanned platforms gives our commanders better options to fight and win in contested spaces. They will expand our intelligence, surveillance, and reconnaissance advantage, add depth to our missile magazines, and provide additional means to keep our distributed force provisioned... By the end of this decade, our sailors must have a high degree of confidence and skill operating alongside proven unmanned platforms at sea."

The Chief of Naval Operations announced the issuance of the CNO NAVPLAN at the January 2021 Surface Navy Association Virtual Symposium. In his remarks, he highlighted the importance of unmanned systems, and announced the impending release of a new Navy campaign plan focused on developing unmanned systems, noting, in part:

> "Unmanned vessels also provide the service with affordable solutions as it works to grow its fleet... We need a hybrid fleet of manned and unmanned systems capable of projecting larger volumes of kinetic and non-kinetic effects across all

domains… Additionally, the service will need its sailors to be adequately trained to operate confidently alongside unmanned sea platforms."

There is little doubt that the U.S. Navy is committed to making unmanned systems of various types and capabilities an important part of the Navy Fleet in the near mid- and especially long-term. As one indication of this commitment that the industry is ramping up to deliver these capabilities, witness America's largest shipbuilder, Huntington Ingalls Industries' purchase of Spatial Integrated Systems Inc., a leader in autonomous technology, in December 2020.

In March 2021, the Department of the Navy published its long-awaited Unmanned Campaign Framework. Designed to coordinate unmanned systems efforts across the Department, the document lists ambitious goals designed to help make unmanned systems an increasingly important part of the Navy's platform inventory.

The framework has five goals:

- Advance manned-unmanned teaming effects within the full range of naval and joint operations.

- Build a digital infrastructure that integrates and adopts unmanned capabilities at speed and scale.

- Incentivize rapid incremental development and testing cycles for unmanned systems.

- Disaggregate common problems, solve once, and scale solutions across platforms and domains.

- Create a capability-centric approach for unmanned contributions (platforms, systems, subsystems) to the force.

The Unmanned Campaign Framework met with some Congressional criticism for being short on details and measurable goals. That said, the 38-page report does provide an organizing impulse and guide for how the Department of the Navy intends to shepherd unmanned systems into the Fleet and Fleet Marine Forces.

Running into Barriers

The DoD, and especially the DoN, have lofty goals for the extensive use of unmanned systems to support the Joint Force. However, these goals are constrained by the sheer physics of the ways in which current unmanned systems are designed. For the most part, developers of today's systems began with the objective to "take the operator out of the machine." This means that they started with a current aircraft of ship hull, and then attempted to operate it either remotely or autonomously.

This approach has many merits, especially in cutting costs by using existing platforms that have undergone years—or even decades—of research, development, fielding and operating. And these platforms have the additional benefit of being familiar to those working in the S&T, R&D, and acquisition communities, and of course, being immediately available to developers. This has enabled a great deal of progress—up to a point.

This way of doing business represents a somewhat limited and less-than-innovative approach, but it has delivered a robust first generation of unmanned systems to warfighters. This has, in turn, resulted in valuable operator feedback as to what capabilities are desired in the next generation of unmanned systems. In many cases, operators have asked for UxS that can operate beyond human capability.

A New Paradigm for Unmanned Systems Development

While the current methodology of developing unmanned systems has some merits, it does have one major flaw. Those creating these UxS are constrained by the physics of those platforms they are modifying in that all of these aircraft or ships once had a crew onboard, and therefore could only be operated to the limits of human capability of the pilot in the cockpit or the mariner on the bridge.

As one small example of the limits of human capability, both versions of the U.S. Navy's Littoral Combat Ship (LCS) can travel in excess of forty knots. In a Navy that has centuries of a tradition of bridge watch standers actually standing for the entirety of their watch rotation, due to the high speed and the way it pounds the seas, watch standers on the LCS must be buckled into their chairs to survive their watches.

The U.S. Navy is beginning to see the benefits of designing and fielding unmanned systems that can operate "beyond human capability." This paradigm shift is important for a number of reasons. In the surface domain, it enables the use of unmanned maritime systems that can travel at a higher speed than humans can long endure, operate in higher sea states than conventional vessels, and make turns with G-forces that would not be tolerable by humans.

The benefits of such systems are clear. They can travel at high speeds to an operating area to complete a mission in far less time, outrun any manned surface vessels seeking to attack them, and in any conflict, outmaneuver adversary platforms through high G-turns. These attributes open up concepts-of-operations that give commanders options that they never had—or might not have even thought of—before.

As one example of how industry is now developing and fielding unmanned systems that operate beyond human capability, one Florida-based corporation, Maritime Tactical Systems, Inc. (MARTAC), demonstrated such a system in an international high-speed run. By way of background, MARTAC's family of unmanned maritime vehicles evolved from a long line of catamaran-hulled racing boats that had achieved speeds of over 250 miles per hour and operated at high-Gs. Stepping down the size of these racing boats was an evolutionary—and revolutionary—process that has garnered the intense interest of U.S. Navy officials.

Secretary of Defense Lloyd J. Austin III speaks with Cmdr. Tom McAndrew, Deputy Commodore Task Force 59, Unmanned & Artificial Intelligence (A.I.) Integration in Bahrain, Nov. 21, 2021. MARTAC's Devil Ray is seen in the background. Photo by Chad McNeeley, Office of the Secretary of Defense Public Affairs.

As one demonstration of this capability, this summer, MARTAC launched its Devil Ray T38 USV from Palm Beach, Florida Inlet, with the goal of performing a fully autonomous run across the Florida Straits to West Bank, Bahamas, in less than one hour, and then returning in the same time window.

During this demonstration, the Devil Ray T38 acquired its first alignment waypoint outside of the Palm Beach Inlet, Florida, and began its high-speed run across the straits. The Devil Ray arrived at the Bahamas waypoint for a total run time of 57 minutes. During the transit, the Devil Ray achieved a top speed of 82 miles per hour, which included a four-minute stop to avoid shipping traffic in the straits.

The return trip from West End, Bahamas to Palm Beach Inlet, Florida followed a similar track with a total transit time of 59 minutes including a six-minute stop to avoid fishing boat traffic. During each round-trip run, the Devil Ray maintained an average cruise speed of 70 miles per hour.

Importantly, in an environment where Congress is questioning the Navy's ability to field unmanned systems that not only have strong operational capabilities, but also reliable basic mechanical and navigational systems, during these tracks the Devil Ray achieved an average tracking accuracy of +/- 1.3 degrees and a steady state cross track error of +/-3 m.

Here is how Bruce Hanson, MARTAC's CEO, described this high-speed run:

"We are excited that our Expeditionary Class Devil Ray T38 is the first USV to fully autonomously perform a high-speed international run. This is a culmination of ten years of product development and thousands of hours testing and running our patented MANTAS-X Class and Expeditionary Devil Ray Class USV systems for reliability and accuracy. This is the first run in a series that will continue to vet and refine our technology to address the needs of our military, scientific and commercial customers' missions, and applications. MARTAC's USV classes simply operate beyond human capability."

A Way Ahead for Unmanned Systems Development

There is a popular quote making the rounds, "If you can imagine it, you can achieve it." While this Bahamas run is just one example of what the next generation of unmanned systems can deliver, the Navy has been forward leaning in inserting such systems in a series of exercises, experiments, and demonstrations as a way to "imagine" how such platforms will support tomorrow's Navy.

For example, the Devil Ray was featured during the summer of 2020 during the U.S. Navy's Trident Warrior exercise in San Diego, as well as in the subsequent Inaugural Unmanned Systems Integrated Battle Problem 21 to showcase these innovative unmanned capabilities. Additionally, Devil Ray's capabilities were demonstrated at this summer's Navy League Sea-Air-Space Symposium.

This approach bodes well for the Navy's efforts to have unmanned systems make up a substantial portion of the Fleet. And it recalls the motto of Admiral Wayne Meyer, the "Father of Aegis:" "Build a little, test a little and learn a lot." The future may well be a U.S. Navy with large numbers of

UxS that can truly operate beyond human capability. The result will provide an asymmetric advantage for U.S. warfighters.

A New Paradigm for Ocean Observation?

By George Galdorisi
January 5, 2022

For two weeks in November 2021, the Glasgow climate change summit dominated national and international headlines. While some perhaps rightly criticize the summit as being long on rhetoric and short on concrete actions, what it *did* accomplish was highlight the potentially disastrous impact of climate change.[20]

When most people think of climate they look to the sky. This is only partially correct, as it is the oceans that sustain the planet. While most climate change activists are energized to prevent pollutants from spewing into the air, they would be well-served to give equal attention to the oceans. Indeed, when most of us look at a globe, we focus on the shape of the seven continents. Rather, we should see the shapes of the seven seas – seas that are increasingly under stress.

Like other navies, the United States Navy plies the oceans and must have in-depth (no pun intended) knowledge of the ocean environment. This is crucial to making optimal decisions regarding naval operations. For decades the U.S. Navy gained its knowledge of the ocean environment by conducting ocean sampling from Navy vessels. This worked – to a point – with a navy of almost six hundred ships. Today, with a ship count of less than three hundred, and with numbers of ships not predicted to increase for some time, the Navy is seeking viable alternatives to sample the ocean environment.

Fortunately, a new pact between the United States Navy and the National Oceanic and Atmospheric Administration (NOAA) has explored the idea of using unmanned surface vehicles equipped with a wide array of sensors to conduct this ocean sampling. This initiative serves two purposes: providing those with stewardship of the environment like NOAA

---

20   John Kerry, "COP26 Prepared the World to Beat Climate Change," *The Wall Street Journal*, November 22, 2021.

with the information needed to make data-driven decisions to help combat climate change, as well as providing the U.S. Navy with timely and relevant information about the oceans which can then be used in tactical and operational situations.

How this partnership evolved, what has happened thus far, and where it can go in the future provides a best-practices example that nations and navies can leverage to provide an effective and efficient way to gain a comprehensive knowledge of the ocean environment.

Background

Beyond the Glasgow Summit, a number of streams have come together in 2021. Collectively, they highlight the continuing importance of comprehensive ocean observation to the Nation and the Navy. Importantly, there are new, innovative ways and means that this real-time cataloging of oceanic phenomena can be conducted reliably and repeatedly and at relatively low cost.

The open and defense media has been well-populated with stories noting the harmful impact of climate change. Other articles have been more explicit in describing how the new administration will instantiate this imperative, noting, for example, that, "The Pentagon will include climate change-related issues in its National Defense Strategy."[21]

The media has been well-populated with stories noting that climate change is now a U.S. national security priority.[22] Other articles have been more explicit in describing how the administration will instantiate this imperative, noting, for example, that, "The Pentagon will include climate change-related issues in its National Defense Strategy."[23] Most recently, a

---

21 Paul Mcleary. "Biden Orders Pentagon To Include Climate Change In New Strategy & War Games," *Breaking Defense*, January 27, 2021.

22 Yaryna Sekez, "Our World in 20 Years," *The New York Times*, January 31, 2021.

23 Paul Mcleary. "Biden Orders Pentagon To Include Climate Change In New Strategy & War Games," *Breaking Defense*, January 27, 2021.

series of reports from the U.S. Government address the security implications of climate change in stark terms.[24]

An important aspect of dealing with climate change has been – and will continue to be – ocean observation. This is one of the reasons that two major oceans stakeholders, the U.S. Navy and NOAA, signed an agreement to collaborate on ocean observation, data collection and analysis and have now moved forward to conduct detailed experimentation to see if their theory that unmanned surface vehicles can provide an effective and efficient means to conduct ocean observation was, indeed, viable.

This U.S. Navy-NOAA initiative includes the plan to jointly expand the development, acquisition, fielding and operation of unmanned maritime systems in the nation's coastal waters as well as in world's ocean waters.[25] This opportunity has only become possible because of the rapid development of unmanned maritime systems that can be fitted with a package of sensors to accurately and comprehensively measure ocean phenomena and then communicate this information to land-based sites.

Taken together, these trends presage a new era in ocean observation that will lead to comprehensive data collection to support Navy operations across the globe. This effort will also enable a wide range of stakeholders to compile the data that is crucial to addressing the national security threat of climate change by enabling scientists to make data-driven decisions based on the health of the oceans and the atmosphere.

The Oceans and National Security

Volumes have been written about the negative impact of climate change and global warming. In 2021, this new shift in addressing climate change,

---

24   Christopher Flavelle et al, Climate Change Poses a Widening Threat to National Security, The New York Times, October 24, 2021, accessed at: https://www.nytimes.com/2021/10/21/climate/climate-change-national-security.html.

25   "NOAA, U.S. Navy Will Increase Nation's Unmanned Maritime Systems Operations," *NOAA Press Release*, accessed at: https://www.noaa.gov/media-release/noaa-us-navy-will-increase-nation-s-unmanned-maritime-systems-operations. See also, "NOAA, U.S. Navy Will Increase Nation's Unmanned Maritime Systems Operations," *Ocean News and Technology*, August 6, 2020, as just two articles heralding this historic – and important – partnership.

not as an abstract issue, but as a clear and present danger, was put this way by Defense Secretary Lloyd Austin: "The Department will immediately take appropriate policy actions to prioritize climate change considerations in our activities and risk assessments to mitigate this driver of insecurity.[26]

In order to address climate change at the national level, a wide array of federal, state and local officials recognize that they must make decisions based on data, not guesswork. Making these data-driven decisions depends on collecting the right data, at the right place, at the right time. This is not a trivial undertaking, and in a budget-constrained environment, having various agencies collect – but fail to share – oceanic data, is a recipe for failure. These gaps lead to an incomplete picture of the ocean's health, and with it, sub-optimal solutions to achieving long-term ocean sustainment, including dealing with climate change.

This U.S. Navy-NOAA partnership is a natural outgrowth of the fact that both organizations must collect and utilize much of the same oceanic data. Add to this the fact that the Navy and NOAA recognize the importance of unmanned maritime systems for a plethora of missions, ocean observation among them.

A Partnership to Leverage Unmanned Surface Vehicles

One of the reasons for this new U.S. Navy-NOAA partnership is that by working together, NOAA will be able to leverage the Navy's expertise, infrastructure, best practices and training to accelerate its science, service and stewardship mission, especially its efforts to address climate change. The Navy's executive agent and key stakeholder in this effort is the Naval Meteorology and Oceanography Command.

The Naval Meteorology and Oceanography Command's mission is to define the physical environment from the bottom of the ocean to the stars to ensure the U.S. Navy has freedom of action to deter aggression, maintain

---

26   Ellen Mitchell, "Pentagon Declares Climate Change a "National Security Issue,' *The Hill*, January 27, 2021.

freedom of the seas and win wars. Additionally, Naval Oceanography has been a global pioneer in the development and use of unmanned systems.[27]

Rear Admiral John Okon, Commander Naval Meteorology and Oceanography Command, emphasized why this partnership is important when he noted, "This agreement lays the foundation for collaboration, engagement, and coordination between NOAA and the U.S. Navy that our nation has never seen before. It will help us take advantage of each other's strengths to advance each of our strategic and operational mission priorities."[28]

NOAA conducts research and gathers data about the global ocean and atmosphere to forecast weather, predict climate, protect the ocean and sustainably manage marine resources. These missions rely on a continuous process of testing and evaluation of new technologies such as unmanned systems to improve data gathering.[29]

Retired Navy Rear Admiral Tim Gallaudet, Assistant Secretary of Commerce for Oceans and Atmosphere and Deputy NOAA administrator, emphasized the importance of this partnership, "With the strengthening of our ongoing partnership with the Navy, NOAA will be better positioned to transition unmanned maritime technologies into operational platforms that will gather critical environmental data."[30]

Shaping a Viable Oceanic Sampling Methodology

One important aspect of the U.S. Navy-NOAA partnership is to enhance the ability of both organizations to conduct data collection. This is critical to

---

27   Naval Meteorology and Oceanography Command website, accessed at: https://www. cnmoc.usff.navy.mil/

28   Naval Meteorology and Oceanography Command press release, August 4, 2020, accessed at: https://www.cnmoc.usff.navy.mil/Press-Room/Press-Releases/Article/2383205/ us-navy-and-noaa-sign-agreement-to-improve-nations-unmanned-maritime-systems-op/

29   NOAA website, accessed at: https://www.noaa.gov/.

30   "NOAA Finalizes Strategy to Enhance Growth of American Blue Economy," *Ocean News*, January 25, 2021

ensuring that the Navy Fleet has the right oceanographic and metrological information at the tactical and operational edge.

Much of this same data collected to support the operating forces is *also* vital to help assess the health and vitality of the world's oceans as well as the ability to make data-driven decisions to combat climate change. For both the Navy and NOAA, a major appeal of unmanned systems is to provide a persistent sensor picture for areas of interest.

One important factor that is driving this move to unmanned maritime systems is the high cost of using manned air or sea craft to conduct these observations. Add to this the dangers of using these vessels in bad weather, in turbulent waters, or at night. Given the totality of these factors, using affordable unmanned surface vehicles to conduct these observations has a strong appeal to a wide array of stakeholders.

The Navy and NOAA agreed to move out rapidly in an effort to experiment with ways to enhance their ability to conduct comprehensive ocean observation. In order to organize an experiment in the near-term, a decision was made to use commercial-off-the-shelf (COTS) technology that was mature and which met the exercise objectives. Based on these criteria, one U.S. corporation, (Maritime Tactical Systems, Inc. (MARTAC)), was invited to demonstrate the use its unmanned surface vehicles to conduct a comprehensive an environmental monitoring evaluation. This month-long endeavor was conducted under the auspices of the Naval Meteorology and Oceanography Command (CNMOC). Under CNMOC's stewardship, an Advanced Naval Training Exercise (ANTX) was conducted in the Gulf of Mexico, south of Gulfport, Mississippi.

Naval Meteorology and Oceanography Command scientists outfitted a COTS MANTAS unmanned surface vehicle with a CNMOC Environmental Monitoring System. These systems and sensors were designed to be carried by this USV to provide a one-vehicle solution to important environmental sensing that was, in the past, conducted by multiple platforms.

CNMOC equipped the MANTAS USV with seven sensors. These included: Teledyne Benthos ATM603 Underwater Modem, FLIR M232 Camera, Teledyne Citadel CTD-NH Conductivity Temperature Depth

Monitor, Teledyne DVL with ADCP Doppler Velocity Log, Norbit iWBMSh-STX Echosounder, Turner C3 Fluorometer, Quanergy M8-1 Plus LIDAR, Airmar WX220 MET, Meteorological Sensor, and SeaView SVS-603 Wave Height Sensor. This sensor data was communicated in real-time to the CNMOC control station.

A second unmanned surface vehicle (another MANTAS USV), this one equipped with a different suite of ocean monitoring systems and sensors, was employed to conduct an additional round of testing. The sensors employed included an iWBMSh-STX and Klein UUV 3500 side scan sonar. As testing continued with both USVs, CNMOC scientists and engineers provided vital feedback and suggested several enhancements to these vessels.

The ocean observations included: wave height, wave frequency, current speed and direction, wind speed and direction, air temperature, barometric pressure, fresh and salt water concentration and bottom bathymetry/contour. All of these measurements are essential components that feed environmental models vital to naval operations and also contribute to important data-driven decisions regarding climate change.

The ability to conduct surveys in higher sea states had thwarted other unmanned surface vehicles in the past but was one of the highlights of this month-long event. The catamaran-hulled MANTAS was able to operate in sea state five conditions. Additionally, the USV has a number of compartments that protected sensor components in heavy weather.

Dealing With Episodic Ocean Events

Beyond the collection of vial ocean data, another area where unmanned surface vehicles can make an important contribution is in response to real-world environmental events. The testing described above occurred in the littorals of the Gulf of Mexico, an area that has more than its share of environmental challenges. Unmanned surface vehicles provide the ideal asset to evaluate the extent of damage as a first step in triaging the problem.

One persistent issue well-known to those familiar with the Gulf of Mexico is the fresh water runoff from the Mississippi River. Periodically, this runoff reaches levels that can damage the near-shore areas on the Gulf.

Additionally, green tides and red tides have a similar negative impact. Every time one of these events happens, it hurts tourism in a local region. Using a solar-powered unmanned surface vehicle that can remain at sea and monitor the environment for up to thirty days at a time can alert communities to the extent of these tides. This enables officials to be more exact in determining which beaches should close and which ones can remain open.

Persistent Oceanic Observation *is* Within Reach

Given the ongoing importance of collecting the right environmental information at the right time at the right place to support the U.S. Navy, as well as help make data-driven decisions to address the national security implications of climate change, finding a cost-effective means to collect this oceanic information autonomously while having humans on-the-loop (as opposed to in-the-loop) is crucial.

The use of commercial-off-the-shelf unmanned surface vehicles successfully employed during this demonstration can be readily scaled-up in USV platform size and thus provide for added oceanographic sensors. This will allow for a further extension of capability within specific oceans, seas, bays, rivers and other waterways, and can also lead the way for enhanced data collection, transmission and evaluation of water conditions and the ocean environment.

U.S. Navy officials have encouraged MARTAC Inc. to scale-up the 12-foot MANTAS used for this CNMOC ANTX effort and produce larger vehicles in order to conduct more comprehensive ocean observation. To this end, a larger 38-foot unmanned surface vehicle, now referred to as the Devil Ray T38 USV was deployed during U.S. Navy exercises Trident Warrior and Integrated Battle Problem. These larger vessels (including 24-foot and 50-foot Devil Ray USVs) could be ideal USVs to conduct extended and more detailed ocean observation with their added ability to carry considerably more sensors and remain at sea for longer periods.

As one example of what this increased size provides vis-à-vis ocean observation, a 24-foot, or 38-foot Devil Ray, using an ocean bottom surveying speed up to fifteen knots, can remain underway for up to seven days until it needs refueling, after which it can again resume its survey mission. Multiple USV craft can be used to perform independent scans within the same area, thereby greatly increasing the amount of total area that can be surveyed.

Leveraging these larger USVs to accomplish these priorities will go a long way toward making data-driven decisions to provide valuable environmental information to Navy and Marine Corps forces, as well as help government agencies make better data-driven decisions to address climate change.

Given the capabilities of USVs to conduct comprehensive oceanic observation, there will likely be an increased demand for unmanned systems prototyping and experimentation to support comprehensive ocean sampling. The vast array of technologies emerging in today's unmanned maritime systems provides a tremendous opportunity to move forward with an effective and affordable oceanic observation taxonomy.

CHAPTER FIVE:

TRAINING AS A WEAPON SYSTEM

Last year, I published a book entitled *Training for the High-end Fight: The Strategic Shift of the 2020s*. That book focused on discussions with warfighters at various training centers central to reshaping U.S. forces for the high-end fight. Those visits were to Norfolk, Virginia; Jacksonville and Mayport, Florida; San Diego, California; and Las Vegas and Reno, Nevada.

I argued in the book that along with C^2 and ISR becoming very different with the strategic shift from the Middle East land wars, training was changing significantly in terms of its focus and what was required to make the strategic shift from the counter-insurgency operations and the land wars. And because the current generation of officers has largely grown up with the land wars, it is as much a strategic shock as a strategic shift. There are a small number of senior officers in the service who served at the end of the Cold War and their memories and training from that period provide a seed corn in the training reset as well.

Or put another way, with a refocus on the high-end fight, the U.S. Navy and the U.S. Air Force need to operate throughout the extended contested battlespace. And with nuclear armed peer competitors, the nuclear dimension weighs over extended conventional operations as well.

As my colleague Ed Timperlake often reminds me, the legendary Admiral Arleigh Burke underscored that training started with the core requirement—know your platform. Training clearly must start with ensuring that the warrior knows how to fight effectively from the ground up with the platform he operates from.

But training today, knowing your platform is clearly not enough. What the U.S. military is shaping is a distributed but integratable force. They are taking their resources, dispersing them, and operating with a mix and match modular task force capability. Learning to fight with a distributed force is part of the new training challenge. Being able to cross-link platforms within evolving task force packages is another part of the challenge.

In a 2020 interview with Lt. Jonathan Gosselin, a P-8 Weapons and Tactics Instructor at the Maritime Patrol Reconnaissance Weapons School, during my visit to Jax Navy, the challenge of learning cross-platform targeting was highlighted as an example of the new training challenge posed by shaping maritime kill webs. When he first deployed, the P-8 was an anomaly. Now it is deployed to all the COCOMS worldwide. The P-8 global fleet provides ISR, ASW, and Surface Warfare products to the combatant commanders. In his current position, he serves as an innovation, cross-functional team lead where he works with innovation experts, defense industry, and the Navy to shape projects which are then generated for implementation by industry. He works as well on process changes where advances in Tactics, Techniques and Procedures (TTPs) can be enabled as well.

For Lt. Gosselin, at the heart of the effort is really understanding, training for and executing third party targeting. He argued that moving from a stove-piped mentality where one is both the sensor and the shooter, to a kill web perspective, where the P-8 could provide the sensors for a firing solution, or whether the P-8 would deliver a weapon provided by another asset to perform the firing solution is at the heart of the change.

In effect, dynamic targeting across a distributed integrated force is the goal. As Lt. Gosselin put it:

> "We're talking about taking targeting data from one domain and quickly shifting to another, just like that. I have killed a target under sea. I am now going to go ahead and work the surface target and be able to understand the weapon-sensor pairing network and to call in fires from different entities using commander's intent to engage the target. That's what we're trying to do. Get our operators to understand that it is not just a one-piece

answer. There may be a time when you have to transfer the action to another shooter."

Lt. Jonathan Gosselin at Jax Navy during *Second Line of Defense* visit in 2020.
Credit: *Second Line of Defense.*

To do so, he is engaging significantly with the Triton squadron as well to shape a way ahead for kill web dynamic targeting. Lt. Gosselin noted:

> "With the P-8 and Triton we are able to expand our envelope of situational awareness (SA). We can take that and now take the baseline concepts from what the P-3 did and apply them to more advanced tactics, techniques, and procedures in the form of integrating with the B-21, the B-1, the F-18s, the F-35 joint strike fighter in a dynamic targeting kill web."

And regarding the cultural shift, this is what he added:

> "It's important to talk not about how I can defeat this target, but really it should be, how can we defeat this target? Let's break ourselves out of this stovepipe and understand that I may not always be the best shooter. I may be the best sensor, but I may not be the best shooter."[31]

---

31   Robbin Laird, *Training for the High-End Fight: The Strategic Shift of the 2020s* (2021).

But distributed operations which can deliver an integrated effect are an art form which requires significant training as well as capabilities to deliver C² at the tactical edge. But they also provide for connectivity among the pieces on the chessboard to provide for the kind of escalation dominance crisis to full spectrum crisis management. With the development of flexible multi-mission platforms, there is an ability to flex between offensive and defensive operations within the distributed battlespace. It is clearly challenging to operate such a force, delegate decision making at the tactical edge, but still be able to ensure strategic and areawide tactical decision-making.

The strategic thrust of integrating modern systems is to create a grid that can operate in an area as a seamless whole, able to strike or defend simultaneously. This is enabled by the evolution of C² and ISR systems. By shaping an evolving ISR enabled C² systems inextricably intertwined with platforms and assets, which provide for kill web integratable forces, an attack and defense enterprise can operate to deter aggressors and adversaries or to conduct successful military operations.

How do you train to do this effectively? Part of the answer is given by training through exercises and then cycling lessons learned from exercises back into the evolving training regime. But the nature of the systems being built and integrated into the force create another problem. Systems like the F-35 outpace and outreach physical training space. And shaping a kill web approach to cross-linking platforms to deliver the desired crisis management or combat effect needs to be part of training as well. How much do you want to show the adversary in exercises? And if you do not do that training in an exercise, where are you doing so?

Air Marshal (Retired) Geoff Brown put that challenge succinctly in an interview I did with him in 2019.

> "Warfighters need to be able to fight as an integrated whole in and through an increasingly contested and complex battlespace saturated by adversary cyber and information operations. But how to do this so that we are shaping our con-ops but not sharing them with an adversary in advance of operations? The battle for information control needs to drive our training needs much

more than it does at the moment. We need to provide warfighters with the right kind of combat learning."

In short, training is becoming redefined as a driver of combat development and platform changes in the context of evolving concepts of operations and tactics. With the new generation of software upgradeable platforms, training driving combat development is part of then rewriting code and determining how platforms can cross-link and operate more effectively as flexible modular task forces.

Brigadier General (Retired) Novotny on Training
August 26, 2021

I first met Brigadier General (Retired) Robert Novotny at RAF Lakenheath in 2016. There we focused on the coming of the F-35 to the base after the Brits would deploy the aircraft onboard their new class of carriers. We discussed the broader implications of being able to integrate F-35s throughout the region as well. After that assignment, he went to Air Combat Command at Langley AFB and then on to his last assignment, which was to command the 57th Wing, Nellis AFB.

In dealing with the post-land wars focus of the USAF, advanced training is a key weapon system. Here is how BG (Retired) Novotny put it:

"I think the good news is that the Air Force does find significant value in training. We find it not only significant in the virtual world, the war gaming world, but in particular, in the live fly scenario. There we put all the relevant assets together in a formation, and we stress the human being component within the combat force. How does the air combat force integrate and operate and communicate in that kind of environment where there's so many platforms and so many weapons systems?"

C^2 is clearly a key weapon system when working complex multi-mission combat integration. Novotny put it this way:

"How do we ensure that the communication architecture can do what we need it to do? How survivable is it when we stress it? Nellis and the 57th Wing are the crown jewel of the USAF for all testing and training. And I think you've seen in the last year, even the last two years, the explosion of the colored flags scenarios to broaden how we train as well."

He then discussed the expansion of the training envelope as seen from the evolution of the training flag exercises.

"Red Flag is a large force training exercise built upon some of our failures in Vietnam and is designed to get that young airman into those stressful situations, communicating mission planning, exercising, communicating debriefing in package formations that we think we might use against a conventional threat. Then we've created Green Flag, which is more focused on air-to-ground integration with our partners at the National Training Center and the Joint Readiness Training Center, both at Fort Irwin and in Fort Polk. But now you see the Orange Flag series of exercises, which is really an operational test integration scenario.

"We've been doing those for a long time. We've just finally put a name to them and where we bring yet to be released capabilities and systems and software and data links. And we put those systems into what we like to call deep end testing. It is a philosophy of throwing the child into the deep end of the pool and seeing if they swim.

"With the Orange Flag approach, we do deep-end Orange Flag scenarios. And then I think most recently you've seen the announcement of Black Flag and Emerald Flag, which again are integrated test and training events really focused on getting after the highly contested environment with new and emerging technologies. Do these technologies work the way we want them to?

"From a training perspective, it helps us look over the glare shield into the future. How are we training today? And with these new tools that are coming to a new toolkit, are we retraining properly for future warfare for future weapon systems, or do we need to change that?"

Bob Tasca III, National Hot Rod Association (NHRA), speaks with Brig.. Gen. Robert Novotny, 57th Wing Commander, and his wife, Dawn Novotny, during the NHRA Nationals at the Las Vegas Motor Speedway, Nevada, Nov. 1, 2019. Photo by Airman 1st Class Christopher Stolze, Nellis AFB Public Affairs.

According to Novotny:

"Nellis has the right mindset and the right vision. The USAF has the right vision. What we lack is consistent funding and an ability to rapidly upgrade those infrastructures. It is also the case that our weapons systems have out outpaced our current infrastructure. For example, I grew up on the Nellis Test and Training Range in the mid-nineties. And the threat we trained to was a North Korean MiG-29, who could only shoot me at about 12 nautical miles.

"Now we're trying to train against what could be a J-20 Bravo low to almost zero RCS threat with an advanced electronic attack with surface air missiles that can shoot you at 400 miles. And we don't have enough space. We don't have enough geography to set up those kinds of scenarios. As a result, we've moved a lot of stuff to Alaska and even Alaska has significant restrictions while it has more room to try to exercise the systems. And you can only really fly up there predictably for about four to six months. Otherwise, the weather becomes problematic, both on the ground and in the air.

"This means that we are migrating a lot more work into the virtual world, which is really good for exercising systems and the data links and the communication portfolio, but unfortunately alleviates all of the stress and pressure and that combat tempo of live training that we tried to create when we started Red Flag. The challenge is to find the best ways to combine the two as we train for the evolving challenges of the high-end fight."

The virtual side of training is becoming important as well to train to the evolving threat envelope, as both the blue and red sides add new capabilities. By modeling a new capability and inserting into the virtual side of live virtual constructive training, the approach is to anticipate how a new red side technological capability changes the combat equation.

We closed by discussing a crucial near to midterm opportunity to ramp up U.S. combat capability. Whether in the North Atlantic fight involving the Russians or the Pacific fight involving the Chinese, Russians, or North Koreans, finding ways to ramp up air-maritime integration is crucial. The U.S. Navy is focusing on ways to fight more effectively as a fleet; the USAF is working on ways to shape a more effective combat force built around fight generation capability.

But why do the U.S. Navy and USAF not train as an integrated force? As Novotny put it, each force faces significant challenges to adapting to the new realities.

"We're consumed by the tyranny of the present. I must create these many pilots, I must create these many wingmen and flight leads, etc. One problem is the constant threat of pilot retention. Then there is the never-ending demand signal from Central Command of deploying forces, reconstituting forces needing our own internal training requirements and more. Therefore, training jointly, which is the way we're going to fight today, and in the future, seems to be the first thing that falls off the plate, which is maddening.

"I can't tell you how many times when we do those training exercises, for example, a Valiant Shield or a Northern Edge exercise, we find out how great those training experiences are because of what we learn. But then we immediately fall back into our comfort level, which is to train internally because our fleet is so inexperienced."

I suggested that one way around the chokepoint of the present is to leverage the coming of the B-21 to the Pacific. Clearly, the B-21 as a weapon system will have its major impact as an air-maritime combat capability. Why not build a training system into the B-21 program now which would shape joint maritime-air operations in the Pacific?

This would not solve all the challenges facing force integration but would be a powerful building block which would drive change immediately when out of the box. And if the new bomber were to operate from Alaska and or Australia then working the Navy's distributed maritime approach with the USAF's approach to agile combat employment would drive significant change from its very first appearances in the Pacific.

Training, Skill Sets, and the High-end Fight
July 21, 2021

Training is focused on TTPs, or the Tactics, Techniques and Procedures, which the force is being shaped to deliver. But really it can be understood somewhat differently with the shaping of a kill web enabled crisis management force that can scale up through the full spectrum of conflict:

What skill sets are crucial to deliver the desired combat or crisis management effect with the distributed integrated force? How do we measure or assess our ability to deliver the full spectrum of options for the Combatant Commander? How do we conduct training against the backdrop of a capable adversary and their changing behaviors in a crisis up to and including during the high-end fight? How do we execute effective decision-making at the proper point of combat effect?

These are all considerations of what needs to be an effective and adaptive training regime for today's combat force. To understand the nature of those skill sets or proficiencies, I talked recently with Paul Averna from Cubic Mission and Performance Solutions. Averna is an experienced naval aviator who has worked on training systems for many years, and he supports the U.S. Navy and industry's strategic development and transition of the next generation Synthetic Inject To Live Live Virtual Construction (LVC) capabilities for the DoD Air Combat Maneuvering Instrumentation (ACMI) systems, an upgrade for U.S. and Coalition partners to train for the high-end fight.

Averna highlighted some key features of the skill sets required for training in the new strategic environment. The first is the team nature of delivering the desired combat effect. According to Averna:

> "Force capability is taking the key elements of the force and blending them together to deliver the desired effect at the right time and the right level. And to be able to anticipate reactions from the red side, and to evaluate how the red side has been impacted by the combat effect delivered."

The challenge is to not only work proficiently with one's platform but to be able to work in an integrated, coherent, mutually supportive manner in delivering the desired combat effect while staying inside the reactive enemy's ability to respond. The peer fight revolves around the competition to disrupt each side's ability to aggregate, integrate, and deliver effects enabled by secure C^2 and ISR networks.

The use of joint and coalition exercises as a training venue is a key part as well. The goal of exercises expressed in training is to demonstrate to adversaries the blue side's capabilities to operate effectively in the high-end fight. As Averna put it:

> "Training is a lever for the combatant commander because he is able selectively to demonstrate that he can deliver effects when and where he wants with a team which is both U.S. and coalition in character.

"Understanding how rapidly to integrate and deliver multi-domain effects, particularly when those capabilities are distributed is a critical feature of the needed skill set. For the last 20+ years we have had the luxury of conducting operations at will from a persistent sanctuary. This battlespace sanctuary afforded us the time and space to observe, target, mass effects, and assess results in a manner with little concern for the threat's ability to disrupt, degrade, or otherwise hold us at risk.

"When facing a peer threat, we will have to consider how to create sanctuaries dynamically in both space and time as a precursor to or in conjunction with our aforementioned operations. That adversary will work to constrict or pressure the blue side "sanctuary" understood as a maneuver force."

How to aggregate effective force within dynamic sanctuaries? Operating within sanctuaries to be able to generate force to get a desired combat or crisis management effect requires integration of non-kinetic and kinetic capabilities and an ability to operate with resilient and effective C^2 and ISR connectivity. A significant part of the fight as the blue side sanctuaries operate as a maneuver force is keeping combat integrity and disrupting the peer competitor's ability to fight while maintaining signature control and superior understanding of the environment.

Another core skill set is to be able to deliver effective dynamic targeting.[32]

As Averna put it:

"A key challenge for operations in the sanctuary context is to be able to develop effective targeting. The goal here may not be to destroy kinetically, but to disrupt, and disaggregate the adversary's ability to fight. It is not just a classic kill chain; it is dynamic targeting within a kill web."

---

32 Robbin Laird, "The Strategic Shift and Dynamic Targeting: Meeting the Challenge," *Second Line of Defense* (May 28, 2020) https://sldinfo.com/2020/05/the-strategic-shift-and-dynamic-targeting-meeting-the-challenge/.

As Averna highlighted, "I may not want to destroy; I may want to just disrupt and degrade him long enough for the crisis management situation to deescalate. This is a huge problem for lots of the people I've talked to who are still thinking the goal of the kill chain is a kinetic kill. And in an all-out war, I get that. But if what we're really talking about is crisis management and controlling the escalation, we need to train for cross-domain effects appropriate to control the crisis."

An additional set of required skills is learning how to operate your platform within the context of flexible and agile modular task forces. Rather than working a set piece task force, the platform operator needs to become accustomed to working in almost lego block-like task forces, which may well contain ground, air, space, cyber, and maritime elements to deliver the desired combat or crisis management effect.

As Averna noted:

> "We are now able to aggregate information from a variety of air, sea, land, and space platforms to give us a better picture of what's going on in the environment and effectively to shape the grand scheme of maneuver and leverage capabilities such as the electronic order of battle that will determine the limits of my operational sanctuary? How quickly can I aggregate capabilities and deliver the desired effect, and then measure whether or not I was successful in delivering that effect?"

Another key skill set is to operate in a C^2 environment, where both the decision at the edge and at the strategic level operate in a very fluid and dynamic way. On the one hand, tactical decision making at the edge is being empowered by new capabilities such as F-35 wolfpacks. On the other hand, C^2 at a more strategic level is crucial to shape the deployment (long lead-time) tasks and evaluate overall combat effects.

How do we train to ensure effective decision making at the edge and a strategic level as well? The C^2 and ISR revolution we are now facing is reversing the logic of platforms to infrastructure; it is now about how flexible C^2 and available ISR systems can inform the force elements to shape interactive combat operations on the fly. That is, the new capabilities are enabling tactical decision making at the edge and posing real challenges to traditional understandings of how information enables decision making.

It is about learning how to fight effectively at the speed of the network to achieve combat dominance. This obviously requires rethinking considerably the nature of decision making and the viability of the classic notion of the Observe, Orient, Decide and Act (OODA) loop. If the machines are fusing data or doing the OO function, then the DA part of the equation becomes transformed, notably if done in terms of decision making at the tactical edge. The decisions at the edge will drive a reshaping of the information about the battlespace because actors at the tactical edge are recreating the information environment itself. In effect, chaos theory becomes a key element of understanding what C^2 at the tactical edge means in terms of the nature of the fleeting information in a distributed combat space itself.

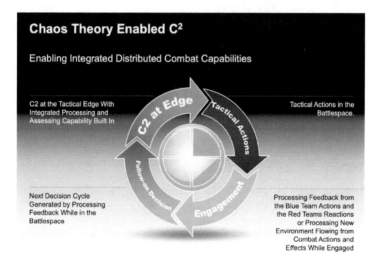

This graphic is credited to *Second Line of Defense*.

The new C^2 and ISR infrastructure enables new warfighting approaches, which need to be shaped, exercised, and executed, and in turn affect how the forces train for the high-end fight. How indeed do you train these skill sets?

By focusing on the sanctuary concept, Averna explained that C^2 operating within a sanctuary or managing several operational sanctuaries is a core capability which needs to be built, trained to, and evolved as well. According to Averna:

> "Who's going to be the battle commander and be able to have the confidence that they have the full picture of information. In some cases, the F-35 may have better situational awareness than say on the E-2 or the Wedgetail. Who's going to make that call?"

In short, the challenge of preparing and engaging in full spectrum crisis management requires new skill sets and capabilities. The training challenge is to shape such skill sets and capabilities.

The Shift in Training

August 17, 2021

Training still proceeds from the core importance of learning to operate your aircraft and to master the core skills required to operate your platform in demanding combat situations.

What is being added is that as the multi-mission capabilities of aircraft expand into multi-domain warfare, the aperture of training needs to expand. And that aperture is wider than what a single or even cross-linked physical training ranges can provide.

Additionally, with the adversary's capabilities to engage the blue side air combat force significantly beyond visual range, accurately replicating those threats is becoming increasingly difficult on training ranges as well. As the blue side works its own capabilities to fight via kill webs, a wide range of the capabilities being shaped, trained, and forged need to be done so in ways that the red side will not get significant information and knowledge about how the blue side wishes to evolve its cross-domain warfighting capabilities.

As a weapons school instructor during his time flying the F-14 in the Navy at NAS Fallon, and later at MCAS Yuma as a MAWTS-1 instructor, Averna noted that Top Gun was set up initially to close a performance gap uncovered in the Vietnam War.

> "When we got to the Vietnam War, we saw a very uneven level of competency from one squadron to another, and we saw some

individual aircrew that were extremely successful at the complex environment the Vietnam air battle presented, including the introduction of technology like radar-guided missiles and integrated Surface to Air Missile systems.

"With the reliance on Beyond Visual Range (BVR) weapons and tactics, highly perishable Basic Fighter Maneuvering (BFM) skills atrophied, and aircrew were making too many mistakes in maneuvering against more nimble opponents. And as a result, the kill ratio went down dramatically. This led to the formation of Top Gun, to deal with the challenge of the inconsistent proficiency in the fleet aircrews.

"The focus was upon training the trainer. Select individuals who are very competent in their aircraft, but also can teach, to help their fellow squadron mates learn how to perform in a building block manner to the point where they can go out and be an effective instrument of national policy when it came to the counter air fight.

"And to complement the new focused Air-to-Air training curriculum, new tools were fielded like the Cubic Air Combat Maneuver Instrumentation system, or ACMI system. And why was that important? You needed to understand where everybody was in time and space to be able to reconstruct what happened. We each have a different mental image of what we did in a particular environment because we're looking through the heads-up display through the canopy bow out over the nose of the airplane.

"And to the extent that I can turn my head around that perception is good probably up to about 10 miles with a limited number of participants. But if I have to keep track of multiple players that are well beyond visual range doing interesting things that I can't directly see, I have a much more difficult time reconstructing what happened. And it's all about that—the accuracy of what happened that helps us develop the correct learning points out of that flying event.

"And that's the way we have trained pilots predominantly from the 70s into the 80s and into the 90s, and it is based on understanding the building blocks that it takes to be able to deliver the right effect for particular missions. For example, in an air-to-air syllabus, one would start out with basic fighter maneuvering, learning how to maneuver and max perform one's airplane.

"Then one would look at how to max perform one's airplane versus an opponent's airplane. Then one would start working in sections and learning how to employ as a section, and then as a division against a limited number and then a larger number to an unknown number of potential adversaries. We were focusing on the skill sets to work the mission against a relatively unsophisticated threat or a near peer threat, but certainly not one that was capable of meeting us in terms of quality and density of a fight."

What Averna described as the training focus was occurring on a physical range, with adversary aircraft or aggressors flying physically against the blue side. With the impact of both what the blue and red side can operate now, physical ranges are a necessary but not sufficient capability, and the red side is not well represented by flying aircraft like F-5s.

Averna put his assessment this way:

"We face a physical range constraint problem, but there's also the challenge of using weapons that we want to use. We don't really want people to know what we're doing with our weapons nor seeing what our tactics are so that we maintain an element of surprise if we need to operate in combat.

"And we have another limitation to our ability today to train well. Even if I was able to find a current contemporary threat system that I might face in a peer fight, I'm not finding it at the local hardware store or the local department store. I'm going to have to acquire it through some means, I might have to decompose it and make sure that I understand all the operating modes on it so that I can present its effects correctly to the aircrew or the team. And that we are interacting the right way in order to defeat it. We don't have that luxury of acquiring those things, they're extremely expensive; it is very rare when we do get our hands on something like that. So, very few people are actually able to work with it."

Expand beyond visual physical ranges are difficult and expensive. Managing training space, ensuring the right kind of training, and getting adequate training time poses the question of resource allocation. How do the DoD and its coalition partners drive down cost and expand capabilities to train effectively?

One way to do so is with the arrival of synthetic training systems, which can target training time to the skill set levels of individual pilots. The arrival of adaptive training systems allows for calibration of the training time needed for individual pilots. Averna explained this capability as follows:

"Let's say that Pilot A is extremely good at low-level flying, and he doesn't need to spend all that much time in doing a lot to train for this skill. Pilot B, on the other hand, has problems with speed rush baseline and needs more time for the low altitude training environment.

"Yet the way that we designed the syllabus is that both get the same amount of flying before they get the proficiency check. Where we are going is a recognition that people learn at different rates and people retain skills at different rates. By moving to an adaptive training environment, we can target the skill sets which those two different pilots have and can tailor training times to generate the required proficiencies."

In other words, it is about making training more targeted and more effective.

We then discussed the multi-mission challenge for training. Earlier, aircraft were more narrowly focused on mission sets than the new aircraft. Those legacy aircraft would be used for single or a smaller set of missions than later aircraft, which are multi-mission focused. The Super Hornet entered the force as a multi-mission aircraft, but the challenge has been to train pilots to be able to switch missions using legacy capabilities.

The F-35's new sensor packages, data fusion, and 360-degree situational awareness expand the pilot's capability to operate in a multi-domain environment. But how to adjust training to be able to maximize this skill set?

The inside of the cockpit of an F-35 Joint Strike Fighter Full Mission Simulator accurately replicates all sensors and weapons to provide a realistic mission rehearsal and training environment for pilots. Photo by Lance Cpl. Gavin Umboh, 2nd Marine Aircraft Wing, February 8, 2016.

These new capabilities impact many facets of the mission, from the way forces mission plan, brief, execute, and debrief. Just take a moment to consider a concept such as mutual support between a flight lead and their wingman. This is how Averna highlighted this change:

> "We've actually started to think differently about concepts like mutual support. If you ask somebody in the early 1990s what's the definition of mutual support, they'd probably say something

along the lines of a mile to a mile-and-a-half and 2000 feet of step up or step down. And that was visual mutual support. You're not in the same plane but you're close enough that you could check your lead or your wingman's tail to make sure there was nobody coming up behind them. That was an integral part of your visual scan of the airspace around you.

"Now with F-35 or F-22, mutual support is several miles plus, and the pilots will not see each other's planes visually. If we can appropriately identify the objects and the space in front of us, and we have the ROE to engage, we're going to take those shots well beyond visual range. And that's where the main training problem exists. We don't expect to ever get into the kind of dogfights we saw in Vietnam. It's now much more about targeting, shorting, getting the off-board queuing, processing that and figuring out how to stay low observable, and yet maintain that dynamic sanctuary. It is about training to different mindset and problem set."

Advanced Training as a Weapon System

September 17, 2021

Having just returned from the Pacific, it is clear that U.S. forces are focused on shaping combat capabilities for the high-end fight. And they want to do so in the context of being able to manage crises and to provide for effective ways to deliver escalation management.

But how do you train appropriately to apply those capabilities consistent with the desired end-state? And how do you leverage dynamic training to shape decision makers understanding of how rapidly changing capabilities provide options for full spectrum crisis management?

War games provide a snapshot of assumptions that are made about what the blue and red sides might do; they don't provide effective means to understand how shaping evolving combat capabilities through operations and training can deliver decisive effects not included in the assumptions of war gamers.

As one PACAF officer put it to me during my visit to Hawaii last month:

> "We operate at the speed of staff but need to work much more
> rapidly to the speed of the operations themselves."

And leveraging those operations generate the data which captures what happened in the real-world interaction between red and blue forces and to translate into the synthetic environment to leverage for the kind of combat learning crucial to delivering the desired crisis management or combat effect. Training which leverages operational dynamics is a combat weapon. Getting better at being able to shape dynamic combat learning provides a tactical and strategic advantage.

I continued my discussions with Paul Averna to understand how this process is underway According to Averna:

> "We're leveraging training to be able to develop better, more
> responsive effects that accommodate for the dynamic nature of
> the future fight. And being able to shape exercises and training
> in an area like the Pacific is a lever. Exercises are designed,
> in many respects, to make sure that people can operate their
> systems as they need to when the time comes. That being said,
> obviously, if you don't train with your systems all that much,
> you're not going to be proficient and be able to deliver to the
> capacity that the system could provide and do so in the many
> creative ways one will need to shape an effective combat force."

In my discussions in Honolulu, a key point that was evident was that finding ways for the fleet to operate much more effectively with the Air Force and to leverage the USMC transformation as a linkage force for both is crucial to get more combat capability from the force we have now. To do so means cross-domain operations, which in turn, are enabled by dynamic, cross-domain training.

How to conceptualize what needs to be achieved and how to do so? What one is trying to achieve with the integrated force are the desired crisis management or combat effects and to do so with dynamic evolving sanctuaries. The challenge is to work ways to shape exercise and training environments which enable cross-domain capabilities to deliver the desired combat effects within dynamic sanctuaries. With the operation of several multi-mission platforms, and an ability to reach out to ISR systems like Triton or space-based systems, how does one as a platform operator leverage multi-domain capabilities? How do I train to do so?

This is how Averna put it:

> "What you are trying to achieve is analogous to chess as a construct. You are moving capabilities on the chessboard, to maneuver to position yourself for dominance while thinking several moves ahead as well. If we are working the ability of the Navy and the Air Force to work together, we are working beyond sequential or parallel operations to integrated operations. Traditionally, we are going to operate in lanes and deconflict in time and space so that we can just deliver effects in sequence, or maybe in parallel, but not integrated.
>
> "The Air Force is very heavily focused on fifth gen, even though the preponderance of their CAF aircraft is fourth gen. They view the first night of operations as an all fifth gen environment. The Navy, in the meantime, is exactly opposite. It's predominantly a fourth gen force. You're going to have a very limited number of fifth gen platforms, at least until the mid-30s and maybe beyond. How you integrate those disparate capabilities together is a key training focus. But where do you build that kind of environment? Where can you train to that kind of capability?
>
> "We are largely focused on doing so on exquisite ranges, like those at Nellis, or the Fallon Training Range, or the JPARC range in Alaska, or the Delamere range in Australia once they can secure it. Those are the environments where we traditionally would say, "Okay, we're going to put all that live hardware into the mix here, but we still have that problem that we are emulating the threat and making assumptions about the threat." A lot of the presumptions that we're making may in fact be wrong,

or that we're not gaining the right lessons learned out of those training events."

The Secure Live Virtual Constructive, Advanced Training Environment (SLATE), program in the Air Force Research Laboratory's 711th Human Performance Wing, concluded a 40-month effort with a Phase III capstone demonstration in September 2018 at Nellis Air Force Base, Nevada. Air Force Research Laboratory Photo, October 10, 2018.

The synthetic environment is a key part of folding in what is learned from operations, to shape ways to understand how to become more effective. The challenge is that the synthetic world is not up to the level where we need it to be to deliver the desired outcomes. But it does provide a key pathway to expanding what a platform operator can train to be able to work with capabilities which are not present in a live training environment.

Averna underscored that even though the synthetic training environment is not fully where it can be, it does provide an opportunity for real operators to work through how they would tap into multi-domain capabilities, which can explore real options for enhanced combat capability.

"The benefit of LVC actually is in the fact that you're injecting the actual live capabilities into a common synthetic environment. Your ability to play out how operational outcomes can vary as one works in an integrated manner with specific assets can be tested by real operators."

With regard to training, it is crucial for the operators to understand and know their platforms. The cross-domain integration piece requires experimentation in interacting across the domains to understand where the strengths and weaknesses can be found to deliver the desired combat effect.

He argued that cross-domain learning is not new, but what is new is the level of integrated effects which can be delivered by a truly joint force. He cited his own experiences working at MAWTS-1 where he flew his F-14 and worked with the Marines in training to the six functions of Marine Aviation to include working with the Marine logistical and strike integration approach to achieving those functions.

He argued that such varsity training required "an ability to put all of the pieces together, end to end, where you have a more mature ability to plan effectively, because you understand how all the assets work together, how they don't fit together as much as how they do fit together. We can actually provide that kind of capability through LVC to bring in all of the new capabilities that are out there into a cross-domain environment."

The Three Ts
October 13, 2021

Training is becoming an advanced weapon system. So much so that the classic formulation of Tactics, Techniques and Procedures upon which training has been built is expanding to now be informed by advanced training that reshapes tactics, techniques, and procedures for the future fight. Multi-domain training encompassing the synthetic environment with a full role for the digital warriors is becoming a key requirement in shaping a 21st century high-end fighting force able to operate in rapidly changing combat conditions.

In my recent visits to forces stationed in the East Coast of the United States and in the Pacific, finding ways to understand the evolving capabilities of the adversary and weaving those into blue side multi-domain warfighting techniques and approaches has been increasingly challenging but also indispensable. Whether a Marine is operating from an expeditionary base employing advanced sensors and needing to understand how the adversary operates and thinks, or pilots are operating against highly integrated multi-domain systems, the challenge is the same: how to spoof, how to deflect, and how to defeat an evolving adversarial force fielded by a peer competitor?

To understand how to shape such a way ahead, I continued my discussions with Paul Averna of Cubic Corporation on the evolution of advanced training. According to Averna, we need to start with the ability to present a realistic threat environment to our blue team. To do so requires a significant shift from how we have done training in the past two decades.

Averna said:

> "Previously, we've been able to approximate red capabilities with fairly inexpensive or lower cost solutions. In other words, we haven't had to fly our current blue aircraft against one another to get quality training. We could get by using earlier generation platforms because what we were focused on was training fundamentals of blocking and tackling in the air problem, or the air to surface problem on the physical ranges with the infrastructure that we've had. After executing a rollback phase, we were able to operate from a relatively static sanctuary to deliver effects in the battle space. We're facing a paradigm shift. We have peer competitors that make it very difficult to establish a secure combat sanctuary and to hold that sanctuary for an uncontested period of time to dominate the battlespace.

> "When you overlay the geographic challenges in the Pacific, it becomes a much more challenging problem. We can solve some of that by prepositioning. And we're talking about the doctrinal concepts that the Marine Corps is espousing to get forward and to be able to deliver ISR and kinetic effects from a dynamic sanctuary. That's the direction that we're going. How do you bring a relevant threat emulation to the training environment so that we can be confident that the tactics, techniques, and procedures we are training to can deliver the right solution in a timely manner?"

I pointed out that with the kinds of mission data we are collecting with systems like the F-35, it is important to be able to translate that information into training usable simulated capabilities as well. Averna underscored how important such an effort is to shape a more effective force.

> "We're collecting some interesting information. But how does that translate into the emulation of the dynamic threat environment that we are facing?"

There is also the question of the evolution of software within both the blue and red systems and the challenge of then translating those changes into a simulated training environment as well.

Averna added:

> "The systems that we're able to put into place have traditionally been singular emulators of a specific system without the ability to rapidly update those system's capabilities. When software changes are made to the threat system, we don't have that corresponding ability to rapidly update and emulate the new techniques which can leverage those software changes."

The question of evolving technologies is one part of the equation. But the other is understanding how various peer adversaries use their equipment or how their TTPs are evolving as well. Averna underscored how significant this challenge was and how the training environment needs to change to deal with this challenge.

> "The way that we have built our emulation of the peer threat to date is not something that translates forward because of the rapid nature of the red side's ability to change their capabilities combined with the quantities of specific advanced systems that can be fielded.

> "For example, if you have a software defined radio, I can operate a wide variety of waveforms within particular brands, and they will look different. Does our system recognize that it's a different waveform? Those are the kinds of things that we are going to

decide. That's new. That requires a different response. We must have a faster way of doing this for both the blue and red sides.

"Part of the benefit of an effects-based LVC training environment is that you can actually update the models that are used to emulate the threat very quickly. You don't have to have that particular update feature tied to the longer development cycle of an OEM operational flight program that has traditionally had an embedded training capability built into it, which is tied to a longer OFP build cycle. We need to look at how we can update the red side threat presentation better, faster, cheaper than we have traditionally done."

In my view, this is why there is a strategic shift in training required to shape dynamic advanced warfighting. The third T needs to lead the traditional TTPs or perhaps it is AT or Advanced Training driven by integration of the simulated with the live environment with an expanded role for digital warriors within the training enterprise.

Averna said:

"I just want to revisit that last point that you're making before we talk about how we do the emulation of the red threat. And that is, in the TTP definition, the classic acronym is tactics, techniques, and procedures. But to your point, there should be a training front end highlighted because this actually changes the way that we fight."

We then discussed how LVC can provide new ways to get to the AT-led dynamic to shape a way ahead for warfighting. According to Averna:

"When you have an LVC training capability where Live, Virtual, and Constructive entities interact in a common synthetic environment, you can exercise capabilities, not constrained by the physical ranges, to open the aperture, and have actual operators evaluating or assessing the impacts of what they're doing in real time, and then debrief what they have learned.

"I can get fidelity on my systems for the beyond visual range fight in an LVC environment. I can have virtual or other live players who are guising as the red threat show up on my systems as they would in combat. And that's the real point where we need to operate. We need to provide realism with regard to the red side threat to the operators so that they can actually assess in real time how well they're executing their game plan.

"We will build game plans based on our best knowledge of the threat and our best knowledge of how to employ our systems. But being able to train to that game plan and understand when the game plan is working poorly or proceeding as we intended, that's the essence of high-quality training.

"In terms of training, we need to be able to recognize multi-domain impacts. I don't typically control multi-domain effects on a single 4th Gen tactical platform, although I might be able to, dependent on the classification and capability of a bespoke system. The fifth-gen systems are much more in that multi-domain capability space. But traditionally, in fourth gen you are typically delivering in a singular lane of effect.

"How you recognize those other participants that are delivering multi-domain effects in concert with what you're trying to do traditionally, has been about timing coordination/synchronization. At this point in time, this thing should be turned off, whether kinetically or non-kinetically. And therefore, I will have sanctuary to go in and do what I want to do.

"After a certain period, if I can expect them to bring that system back up, and then I'm back into a less than optimum sanctuary consideration, and I have to maneuver or do something different. Those are the type of events where we've driven predominantly onto a time-hack model. But when we talk about a dynamic sanctuary, it's about maintaining operational advantage across a window of time. And being able to then assess and apply different techniques to achieve or sustain the desired effect. That's what we want to be able train to."

Another key aspect which LVC brings to advanced training is the ability to use guising as part of working the red side. As Averna explained it:

"In the virtual world, there are different protocols of how we exchange data about the participants. We call them entities. An entity can be a platform. It can be a weapon. It can be a sensor. It can be an effect. And each entity has a whole slew of characteristics or attributes, such as electromagnetic properties.

"And that drives the interaction between someone in a man in a loop simulator, and constructive participant. And we already do this in that we can generate a constructive participant to look like anything we need them to look like. And because of the way that they are built, they will appear across our systems in the virtual world as an intended threat.

"Let's say hypothetically I am an F-15E aircrew in a Tactical Operational Flight Trainer (TOFT) working in a Beyond Visual Range (BVR) training event against a constructive F-16. As I am flying around in the virtual world, I see an F-16 out at range on my systems. Well, that F-16 doesn't exist. It's an entity. And that entity has a whole slew of attributes. And then correspondingly, on my systems, I'm going to detect him at a certain range, and I'm going to be able to see him with a variety of sensors at a given range, target aspect, whether he's in full afterburner, or at idle, whether his radar is emitting, etc.

"In my virtual representation of my actual platform, models of sensors, effects, and weapons approximate the real-world capabilities of my aircraft. What I really want the blue side operator to see an adversarial F-16 operating like an SU-27. The radar cross section of a SU-27 is different from an F-16. And as a result, I would see him at a different range than I would the actual threat that I'm targeting. Why is that important? From a timeline perspective, the distance and the closing rate matters because it gives me a range of options that I have when I'm going to shoot and how many I'm going to shoot at him at that given range.

"If I can show on my live blue platform's systems an SU-27 coming at me, a couple of things happen. First, I'm getting the realistic engagement, ranges, and profile with him. And that drives how I am going to be able to do tactics well. I have real-world physics being applied on me and my platform that impact my physiological and cognitive performance. There's also that psychological element to it, which is I'm going up against a real bad guy as opposed to somebody that I see as a friendly F-16. That is a very important element of realism. In essence, we now have the ability to overcome the physical limitations of our current training ranges and deliver the threat environment our operators need for realistic training."

In short, TTPs need to become TTTPs to get to where we need to go regarding advanced warfighting. In that shift, the training piece expands the role of the digital space and the role of digital warriors in evolving the warfighting capabilities of a multi-domain blue force facing an evolving red multi-domain force, changing both in terms of technology and in terms of concepts of operations.

Training for the Interoperable and Integratable Force

November 29, 2021

To get the kind of combat effect which U.S. forces seek, integratability of key elements of the force is crucial. It is not the old concept of network-centric warfare being pursued, but rather integration of modular capability-based task forces to deliver the desired combat effect in the distributed battlespace through kill webs.

But how do you resolve the integration challenge? And how do you measure the capabilities of the adversary to counter our intentions with their own integrated capabilities and to what extent can they be effective?

Put in other terms, mixing and matching capabilities and training to blend them together into an integrated force package and understanding various potential combat effects from different force packages is a key way for the U.S. and its allies to fight and win against peer competitors.

But as Averna noted, it is not simply acquiring a system or capability and then training to operate that system or deliver that capability, it is about training to generate various integrated combat effects.

Recently, the U.S. Navy successfully completed a training effort which provides a solid foundation for reshaping training in a way that will achieve more effective paths to force integratability. As Carrie Munn and Erin Mangum of PMA-265 put it:

"The F/A-18 and EA-18G Program Office (PMA-265) completed a successful technology demonstration for the Secure Live Virtual Constructive Advanced Training Environment (SLATE) at Naval Air Station Patuxent River, Maryland, last month. The event included four flight tests, supported by Air Test and Evaluation Squadron (VX) 23 and industry partners, The Boeing Company, and Cubic Corporation.

"The demonstration showcased the Synthetic Inject to Live (SITL)—Live Virtual Constructive (LVC) system's maturity and performance in supporting training against near-peer threats, while validating its technology readiness level with the F/A-18E/F Super Hornet and EA-18G Growler. The resulting SLATE SITL capabilities, technical specifications and lessons learned are currently in work for transition into the Navy's Training Program of Record, the Tactical Combat Training System (TCTS) Increment II. Merging the two technologies presents the quickest way to get the best capabilities into the hands of the fleet as quickly as possible.

"The SLATE system connects Live (manned aircraft) with Virtual (manned simulators) and Constructive entities (computer-generated forces) in a robust training environment that replicates the threat density and capability required to prepare military forces for the high-end fight. These LVC capabilities fully link "Live" aircraft with the common synthetic environment used across U.S. Navy and U.S. Air Force training enterprises, providing efficiencies for both Services.

"The SITL LVC capabilities demonstrated by SLATE are essential to providing our warfighters with a complex and realistic training environment that promotes combat readiness," said Megan Sullivan, PMA-265 SLATE Integrated Product Team lead. "The event's completion informs planning and enables more rapid fielding to the fleet."[33]

Mike Wallace, Boeing test pilot with Air Test and Evaluation Squadron (VX) 23, utilizes the Manned Flight Simulator at Naval Air Station Patuxent River, Maryland, during the Secure Live Virtual Constructive Advanced Training Environment (SLATE) demonstration. Naval Air Systems Command, Patuxent River, Md., October 6, 2021

This is a good description of the training effort, but what it does not do is highlight that this really is about training as a weapon system-enabling modular task force integration. That perspective was very clear from talking with Paul Averna of Cubic Corporation who was a key participant in the training effort at Pax River.

---

33 "PMA-265 Conducts Successful SLAT Demo, *NAVAIR News* (October 5, 2021), https://www.navair.navy.mil/news/PMA-265-conducts-successful-SLATE-demo/Tue-10052021-1730.

What the exercise allowed was for the blue side to bring a number of disparate assets into an air-surface offensive and defensive force which confronted a red force operating at much greater range than the live exercise area provided. And the blue force was able to integrate assets against a red force operating a force package designed to attack an air-maritime force operating off of the waters of the Pax River range.

The live range was off of Pax River and the live aircraft—Super Hornets—had SLATE pods attached to them which allowed them to operate with the ground-based testing teams operating both red and blue assets. The SLATE pods allowed for the simulated capabilities to integrate into the live aircraft's combat systems and be part of the integrated air and combat picture available to the pilots of the live aircraft.

There were four live events during the month of September 2021 during which various parts of the technical data package that the technologies and training architecture embodied were tested. The technical data package is owned by the government which allows it to work with industry to deliver capabilities rapidly to the fleet.

The training exercise was the first time that live Super Hornets operated together with virtual F-35s and worked their integration in terms of when they would interact and what they would expect while interacting during a mission working together. They connected with MH-60 Romeo ASW helicopters operating from the simulators at NAS JAX along with surface fleet assets working from an Aegis combat simulator as well. This was the first time that the Navy had fielded their simulated training system in a pod onboard a live aircraft, so testing involved working through the integration between ground test systems and the live flight aircraft.

With regard to the red side, they used guising technologies to turn live training aircraft into simulated advanced red side aircraft with the flight profile and various capabilities of those aircraft. Other peer capabilities were included as well into the red side package.

Averna put it this way with regard to the effort behind this September event:

> "For interoperability and integration to be realized, it is nec-
> essary to determine the aggregate effect of different capabili-
> ties working together. Rather than just acquiring a variety of
> systems and training to get good at using those different sys-
> tems, we need to integrate key force elements and to determine
> aggregate effect for the different ways we might choose to meet
> Commander' Intent. And regarding peers, we know that they
> are fielding capable or potentially capable systems but how good
> are they at force integration?"

The exercise highlighted why DoD needs to pivot to SITL-LVC enabled training. It is crucial to provide realistic threat emulations, to allow red and blue assets to operate beyond the physical ranges themselves, and to provide for the level of security to conduct operational proficiency training for force integration. The September flight events used currently available capabilities developed through the Secure Live Virtual Constructive Advanced Training Environment technology led by NAVAIR's PMA-265 Advanced LVC team.

To put it another way, one of the key aspects of the exercise was that realistic employment ranges were not confined to the Pax River live training airspace. The red force operated well outside of the physical range to operate against the air-maritime force operating within the physical training range. The training environment allowed for multiple skills to be tested concurrently in the simulated combat situation. Live platforms worked with constructive weapons and trained in an integrated manner with the blue force to shape a dynamic sanctuary from which to prevail against the red force.

And with the training technology, they were able to exercise fighter integration TTPs which encompassed both kinetic and non-kinetic effects. With third party targeting capabilities as a key part of the evolving kill web approach, working who the sensor is and who is the shooter is a key part of combat integration needed in a peer fight. The September exercise demonstrated that the training technology clearly can facilitate such combat learning.

The ability of each platform community to figure out how to plug into this training environment is facilitated by the common standards and protocols provided by the training system. This is true for both the air and surface communities in the Navy, with the potential to bring additional Fleet assets into the common training environment through integration of the Minotaur fusion system into the advanced training system already shaped and exercised in September 2021 at Pax River.

This is not a nice to have capability, but a necessary one if winning is the goal of combat. Understanding integrated combat effects generated by diverse force packages is a key way ahead for the kill web force; but training to do so is a work in progress.

Shaping a Way Ahead for Advanced Training

February 7, 2022

The challenge of crafting advanced training solutions is driven by several key dynamics. The first is the nature of the peer adversary. These adversaries are pursuing limited war on an ongoing basis to expand their influence and power in the global competition with the liberal democracies. Limited war is about learning escalation control and management and how to use both military and diplomatic tools in such an effort.

As Paul Bracken, the noted strategist has underscored: "Russia and China' are trying to come in with a level of intensity in escalation which is low enough so that it doesn't trigger a big Pearl Harbor response. And that could go on for a long time and is a very interesting future to explore." How to use U.S. and allied military capabilities to have the right kind of crisis management and combat effects?

In my latest interview with Paul Averna from Cubic Mission and Performance Solutions in December 2021, highlighted the importance of training to work with allies to deliver the right kind of crisis management and combat effects.

"For effective training, we need to discover how to work our various platform capabilities to decisive effects. And it's not just the high-end kinetic end game of a conventional fight between us and a peer competitor. It is down at the lower rungs of conflict to manage escalation points. We need to be able to use asymmetric advantages to shape escalation options, and we need to train to do so

The second is the nature of the new military platforms such as the F-35. These platforms are part of a broader kill web and as such the challenge is to understand not simply their capabilities in a stove-piped functionality but in terms of how they work to deliver integrated capabilities for a modular task force.

Averna put it this way:

"The capabilities of the platforms themselves are now dramatically different from what they have been in the past and in non-traditional ways. For example, with regard to fighter generations of aircraft, they were measured in the performance of the aircraft platform, such as speed, turn rates and types of weapons they could carry. With the fifth generation, the question of the platform and its performance became quite different as the data fusion capability and the ability to work integrated with other fifth generation aircraft in a low observable environment, meant that those aircraft now worked very differently.

"But how to train to understand and leverage those capabilities for the low observable and wider combat force?"

The F-35 training piece is strategic in character because of the emergence of a F-35 global fleet. For example, with the Finns selecting the F-35 and with the Danes, Norwegians, the Dutch, the Belgians, the Brits, the Poles and the Americans all operating in the arc from the High North to Poland, how to train to get the best combat and crisis management effect from the data sharing across the F-35 force and leverageable for the joint and coalition force?

And Averna highlighted another training aspect which the reliance on a high-end system like the F-35 introduced as well.

"We always have had classified capabilities that we don't discuss in public. But the impact of how we utilize those systems, the tactics, techniques, and procedures, typically are held at a secret level. We are moving now into a SAP kind of training world. Such training at a higher level of classification, introduces its own challenges and limits both for the joint and coalition force."

He underscored the importance of "being able to exchange information appropriately across our platforms, whether it's operationally or in training. And we are having to work through the policies with regard to how we share information and what's shareable and at what level of classification."

The third is to train for operating in dynamic sanctuaries as peer adversaries contest the operating areas of U.S. and allied forces. This entails clearly understanding what our low observable platforms can provide as well as how to leverage those capabilities for the joint force operating in the contested battlespace. The problem highlighted above whereby how to integrate U.S. and allied F-35s entails the challenge as well of leveraging that integration then for the joint and coalition force, which need to operate in dynamic sanctuaries against dynamic peer competitors.

Averna noted that "we are struggling right now in the 5th Gen community really to understand how those capabilities can be utilized, i.e., to be distilled into specific tactics, techniques, and procedures. And of course, they are operating in concert with multi-domain assets as well. We are really at the beginning of understanding how to work better together and to determine how best to work together to deliver a real synergistic effect."

The fourth is to craft ways to train against the reactive enemy who is using their evolving technologies to contest the operation of our forces and to work to deliver a decisive crisis management effect with the goal of creating escalation dominance.

The fifth is how to fold in the dynamics of new capabilities and technologies on both the blue and red sides and to train to use those capabilities to gain the desired crisis management and combat effects. This can only be done by creating a simulated environment folded into live training as well.

The live training piece is crucial. Averna underscored that simulation is clearly not enough for realistic training required for full spectrum warfare.

> "Simulators don't account for the real-world physics well. They don't account for the fog of war; they don't count for the physiological and psychological stressors that are going on with actual operators. The pitch of my voice is different when I'm under stress. I may not talk cleanly, clearly, coherently, when I've got a pucker factor going on because I'm being targeted by something I've never seen before, and I feel like it's a lethal threat to me. That is going to come across to the rest of my community or colleagues or participants in an LVC environment, and that will make it more authentic for them as well."

The simulation part folded into the live training environment is key as well given the nature of the dynamic adversaries we are dealing with. The training ranges are too limited to encompass the kinds of new technologies and the combat situations to be anticipated in a dynamic strategic and combat environment.

Put in other words, advanced training encompasses effects-based training but in the context of preparing and engaging in limited war with blue forces operating in dynamic sanctuaries and delivering decisive effect to gain escalation control.

Averna argued:

> "The simulation of the threat provides an ability to deliver the effects as we would see on in night one in our cockpits, so that we can conduct realistic training. Regardless of what the effect we need to achieve, we're trying to understand what is happening around us. With regard to effects-based training, we need to get to a more realistic red side environment and to do better than what we currently have in our physical ranges with our current prop of adversary platforms that we use in training."

In short, training now is not just about mastering your platform, it is learning to adapt in a rapidly evolving combat environment that is inextricably intertwined with the escalation challenges of ongoing limited war with peer competitors

CHAPTER SIX:

THE BLITZKRIEG AFGHAN WITHDRAWAL AND ITS IMPACT

"The Graveyard of Empires"

By Kenneth Maxwell
August 24, 2021

The British House of Lords is an odd anachronism. It has been partly but imperfectly reformed. There are now "life peers". Yet the House of Lords has almost as many members as the central committee of the Chinese Communist Party. It has in effect become a comfortable rest home for former but now redundant political place holders, retired military chiefs, bishops of the Church of England, as well as the few hereditary peers of the realm who remain.

But on occasion it can provide a forum for searing criticism of those who hold real power. And it did so last week when a special session of Parliament was recalled on Wednesday 18th of August to deal with U.S. President Joe Biden's self-created crisis in Kabul.

Lord Hammond, called Joe Biden's decision: "a catastrophic failure of western policy, and more particularly, U.S. policy…" Baroness Manningham-Buller, as the deputy head of MI5 had flown to Washington DC with the head of MI6, and the head of GCHQ, in the immediate aftermath of the attacks of the World Trade Center and the Pentagon on 9/11. It was an occasion she told their lordships when "the world wanted to support America." As the 20th anniversary of 9/11 approaches, the opposite is the case.

Baroness Manningham-Buller headed MI5 between 2002 and 2007 and was an intelligence officer for 33 years. She specialized in counterterrorism. She had been the liaison in Washington with the American intelligence community at the time of the first Gulf War. She warned that Biden's abandonment of Afghanistan would have two consequences: "First there is inspiration. This Taliban victory and its rout of Western forces, as it appears, will inspire, and embolden those who wish to promote jihad against the West. Secondly, the border with Pakistan is porous, and its government is supportive of the Taliban. There is plenty of room to recruit, plot, and grow a new generation of terrorists."

She was not alone. Lord West, that is Baron West of Spithead, former admiral Alan West, former First Sea Lord, who had seen service in the Falklands and Iraq, was more specific. He warned that "in recent months it has become clear that a large number of Islamic fighters of various persuasions, including al-Qaeda, Daesh, and the Chechens, had joined the Taliban."

In the House of Commons, with the chamber full for the first time since the beginning of the pandemic, Boris Johnson, just back in Downing Street from holiday at his family compound in West Somerset, and Foreign Secretary, Dominic Raab, very well-tanned just back from his extended beach holiday at an exclusive luxury boutique hotel on the Greek Island of Crete, cut very lonely figures, attacked most insistently by conservatives from their own back benches. The former prime minister, Theresa May, asked Boris Johnson: "Was our intelligence so poor…did we just believe we had to follow the United States…" Tom Tugendhat, the conservative chair of the House of Commons foreign affairs committee, and an Afghan war veteran, in a very powerful speech, called it "Britain's biggest foreign policy disaster since Suez". He concluded: "This doesn't need to be defeat, but right now it damn well feels like it is."

And it was not just in Britain. Armin Latchet, Angela Merkel's choice to succeed her as next German chancellor, called Biden's decision the "the biggest debacle NATO has suffered since its founding."

And that is precisely the point. The invasion and occupation and war in Afghanistan was a NATO operation, involving over the past 20 years since the terrorist attacks on the United States on 9/11, the deployment of the troops from over 50 NATO members and associated nations. It was the "endless deployment of U.S. forces in overseas conflicts" which Joe Biden claimed was the justification for his unilateral action in pulling the US out of Afghanistan without any consultation with his allies. The war was, he said, "not in the national interest." This was not true. The Afghan invasion was a collective engagement in support of the United States. And in the end Biden forgot this.

And the consequences of his forgetting will be with us all for years to come. Biden has, in fact, returned America to its pre-WW2 isolationist roots. It seemed an easy option for an old Senate hand, used to deal making in the backrooms of the Congress. And it was a politically driven decision with an eye on domestic politics. The overall concept of ending America's "endless wars" is not unpopular in the United States. Biden was right about this.

But its implementation of his decision has been utterly disastrous. Above all, it has undermined the role America had played over the last nine decades of American hegemony and the achievements of the Second World War and America's post war engagement in the reconstruction of war-ravaged Europe and Asia, and Washington's key leadership role in the construction of the network of post-war international organizations.

But isolationism and nativism and nationalistic paranoia had never gone. The "paranoid" style has a deep history in U.S. popular culture as the American Columbia University, historian Richard Hofstadter, explained long ago. And the enemies are already identified. Hofstadter observed that: "It is ironic that the United States should have been founded by intellectuals, for throughout most of our political history the intellectual has been for the most part either an outsider, a servant or a scapegoat."

And he added:

> "There has always been in our national experience a type of mind which elevates hatred into a kind of creed; for this mind group hatreds take a place in politics similar to class struggle in some other modern societies."

Regrettably, this is what we have seen over the last years in America.

President Joe Biden had now put more nails into the coffin of American international engagement and has set the world on a very dangerous new course at a time of increasing international instability and the challenges of powerful authoritarian and aggressive adversaries who will relish Biden's calamitous unilateral decision and are sure to take advantage of the opportunities it offers them.

Not in Afghanistan in all probability if the new authoritarians have any sense. But on the broader international scene where the tectonic plates are already shifting. It has become a platitude that Afghanistan is the "graveyard of empires." President Biden has now entered into the role which Afghanistan has played in world history.

Checking Out of Hotel Afghanistan

By Ambassador (ret) Jon D. Glassman
August 23, 2021

Thirty-two years ago, January 30, 1989, ten American diplomats and U.S. Marine Security Guards, including I, the U.S. Charge d'Affaires, departed Kabul as 120 thousand Soviet troops evacuated the country across its northern border. We were ordered out by the incoming Bush administration for fear that we would be massacred in error by mujahidin rebels expected to storm the Afghan capital after Soviet departure.

Sharing the belief that the fall of the Soviet-backed Afghan regime of Najibullah was imminent, I told the New Delhi press that the Afghan quasi-Communists would collapse in six months. This, however, did not occur for three years until mujahidin forces took the capital in 1992, decisively empowered by the collapse of the Soviet Union, its military and food supply chain, and its financial support of the client regime.

Najibullah, a brutal former Secret Police director, fled to the UN compound from whence he was extracted and hung in 1996 by Taliban forces mobilized by Pakistan to end the chaos of mujahidin coalition rule.

The expected and genuine outcome of the Soviet evacuation is relevant now as we cope with the debacle of U.S. evacuation and withdrawal. The

Soviets and their Afghan partners took extreme measures in the last days of large-scale Russian presence to buttress their respective post-withdrawal positions vis-à-vis the mujahidin resistance, neighboring Pakistan, and, most importantly, each other.

Abandoned Soviet tanks rust away in the field next to Combat Outpost Red Hill, Oct. 12, 2011. Parwan Province, Afghanistan, photo by Spc. Ken Scar, 7th Mobile Public Affairs Detachment.

Measures that the Soviets and their clients undertook will not, and cannot, be repeated now, nor could any post-withdrawal arrangement that might eventually ensue be undone by the collapse of the United States, as occurred with the Soviet Union.

Yet, it is worthwhile to recapitulate the extraordinary effort the Russians and their Kabul allies put into guaranteeing their post-withdrawal equities. As we contemplate new and more modest U.S. involvement in Afghanistan in the future, we might want to consider whether we will achieve better results than the aggressive Soviets, notwithstanding the greater resilience of our polity.

On August 17, 1988, a C130 aircraft carrying Pakistani President Zia ul Haq, Pakistan JCS Chairman General Akhtar Abdur Rehman, my good friend U.S. Ambassador Arnie Raphel, and U.S, Defense Attaché BG Herbert Wassom crashed in Bahjawalpur, Pakistan. Immediately, speculation arose that the Soviets had assassinated President Zia, the linchpin of Afghan mujahidin resistance.

Indeed, Soviet Ambassador in Kabul Nikolay Yegorychev, former First Secretary of the Moscow Communist Party, told me a few weeks earlier that some "Pakistani patriot" would likely shoot down a U.S. resupply flight into the neighboring country unless the U.S. stopped its provision of Stinger anti-aircraft missiles to the mujahideen.

But only hours after the crash, Ambassador Yegorychev called on me—in his one and only visit to the U.S. Embassy —to claim that the Soviet Union had nothing to do with the Zia crash. When reminded about his Stinger statement and questioned about Afghan regime involvement, Yegorychev said he could say nothing about the Afghans, implying by failure to deny that the Najibullah government may have been responsible.

Even if this were the case, the embedded Soviet presence in the Afghan intelligence apparat made Russian complicity at some level an inescapable assumption. Whoever had the lead, red and green tracer fire raced across the sky that night as interested parties in Kabul celebrated the demise of their arch-enemy Zia ul Haq.

On November 2, 1988, returning from a diplomatic lunch to the U.S. Embassy, I encountered a large trailer truck carrying what appeared to be a ballistic missile. Judging from its dimensions, it was clear that this was something much bigger than a FROG tactical missile.

Shortly, thereafter, overhead imagery confirmed that the Soviets had deployed SCUD medium-range missiles to Kabul and began firing them with immense roars against putative mujahidin concentrations in the direction of Pakistan. This was clearly a warning to Pakistan to stand back as the Russians departed.

During these months, there were also reports that the Soviets were upgrading their bombing volume at selected points in Afghanistan, using for the first-time Tu22 Blinder/Backfire medium bombers.

On one occasion, a member of our Afghan national Embassy staff went to the approaches of the Salang Tunnel, a chokepoint on the resupply road from the Soviet Union and found widespread areas containing many dead civilians–suggesting that these bombers may have been delivering wide-area, fuel air explosives to maximize indiscriminate kill.

Again, the message was: do not obstruct the regime lifeline or there will be hell to pay. While these military measures were being applied, a new Soviet Ambassador, Yuliy Vorontsov, formerly deputy to Ambassador Anatoliy Dobrynin in Washington, was dispatched to Kabul. Vorontsov proclaimed to the press that Soviet troop withdrawal was not a certainty and was dependent on the creation of political conditions that would guarantee stability according to the Soviet vision.

It was surely hoped that the U.S. and Pakistanis would deliver a political arrangement that would favor Moscow's post-withdrawal permanent influence. What confounded the Soviet plan was that the U.S. Embassy, through the development of widespread contact and other efforts, knew with certainty that Soviet withdrawal preparations were proceeding, notwithstanding Vorontsov's posturing. Additionally, the Ambassadors of the Soviet Warsaw Pact allies, all nominally Communists but admiring American ideals, briefed me in detail on Soviet plans as soon as they were told by the Russians–often before they reported to their own capitals.

Later, when Yuliy Vorontsov returned to Washington as Russian Federation Ambassador, he told me that the Soviets had also tried to reach a political deal with elements of the mujahidin to guarantee Russian interests. Vorontsov said he had arranged a meeting with Afghan Tajik resistance leader Ahmed Shah Massoud (assassinated by an al Qaeda suicide bomber in 2001) but the meeting did not take place because its site was bombed by Najibullah's Afghan Air Force, fearing a Russian sellout. The Soviets tried but could not achieve a favorable political accommodation.

This meander through the history of the Russian withdrawal leads to the conclusion that, notwithstanding willingness to undertake extreme military and political moves, the Afghan problem evaded facile solutions by the Soviets and Najibullah regime.

When I lived in Kabul, I walked through the city for hours unguarded and alone every weekend without weapons, body armor or rescue capability—no protection needed. My street conversations in Dari and Russian were tolerated by the Soviets and their clients. But there was an additional element.

During these walks, I sometimes heard praise for President Reagan even from Afghan Communist soldiers. This impunity for U.S. personnel and latent support, even among our enemies, was possible because the U.S. was perceived as aligned with Afghan national values. The Soviets were the hated outside infidels that America was helping to expel. Regrettably, we assumed the Soviets' mantle with our focus on train and equip and counterinsurgency over the last twenty years.

Historical Images and Memories

August 31, 2021

The Biden administration's decision to withdraw from Afghanistan and removing the U.S. military and support for the Afghan Air Force has been followed by a rapid takeover of Afghanistan by the Taliban.

Such an historic event generates images for the living and for future generations. The most viewed image in the United States is the parallel to the escape from Saigon. The pairing of images of the escape from Saigon and from Kabul does obscure a significant difference in how this happened. With regard to the Saigon events, it was generated by the Democratic Congress pulling the money from the executive branch which was working with the South Vietnamese forces. This time the Democratic executive branch made unilateral decisions about withdrawing and acted on their plans. It was an executive branch "planned" withdrawal.

But for European allies, the images are different historically. For the French, the historic images are also built on their post-war military engage- ments, ranging from Indochina to North Africa. I discussed this with French native and co-founder of *Second Line of Defense*, Murielle Delaporte. Delaporte is the editor of *Opérationnels SLDS*, a Paris-based defense quarterly she founded in 2009.

Question: What images come to the various generations in France with regard to the entrapment of civilians, and the contested withdrawal from Afghanistan by the Americans?

Murielle Delaporte: For my parents' generation, the images of Dien Bien Phu (1954) are vivid. Here the French government negotiated with the enemy while the French Army was fighting for its life. The French military had asked for help from the United States but were left in large part abandoned to their own fate.

The parallel with Kabul's fall today is striking in the sense that it highlights the gap—or even antinomy—between the political logic of negotiating and the military logic of fighting. Announcing in advance that you are leaving on a very specific day is already giving ammunition to the enemy. It drives a significant sense of betrayal, and resentment from the veterans has to be felt under such circumstances.

The second image which is shared by my parents' generation and the first segment of the post-war generation is the Suez Crisis (1956). Here the British and the French worked with the Israelis against the Egyptian takeover of the Suez Canal.

Again, the United States not only did not come to the aid of the two allies but took the side of the Egyptians and the Soviet Union and enhanced a sense of U.S unilateral decision making — as well as great power order feared during the Cold War—with little consideration for allies.

The nuclear program already underway in France was indeed accelerated in response to this event.

These historical events reinforced the French Gaullist instincts to promote independence from the Americans, which can be seen today in the Macron government. The current Biden administration approach certainly will reinforce these historical images and experiences.

Question: Will this reinforce the need for the British and the French to have an independent nuclear deterrent?

Murielle Delaporte: It is already the case, but it might deepen the commitments. The current French government is deeply committed to this capability, but it might help in keeping public commitment to protect French independence. I would add that the Vietnamese experience involved a significant problem of trying to protect those Vietnamese who worked with us as well.

And the Algerian War which followed, and the civil war had a key impact on French identity as well. With the conflict in Algeria, the challenge of saving those who worked with us against the Algerian nationalist forces was a significant one.

For the military, the Indo-Chinese experience, and the sense of helplessness to prevent the abandonment of those who fought along the side of the French military have been a determinant factor and a painful memory. Indeed, to this day, the question of the Algerian engagement remains deeply seared in French historical memory and is part of the ongoing very sensitive debate about Islam, immigration, and France.

The Americans from this point of view were more able to bring about some form of collective healing over Vietnam, in particular through movies trying to explain what the war was all about (*Platoon, The Deer Hunter, Apocalypse Now…*).

In France, except for Pierre Schoenderffer, there were no cinematographic productions (or debate for that matter) allowing to turn the page early on and in an appeased manner on traumatic military engagements, like Indochina and Algeria.

The Americans have faced with both Iraq and Afghanistan a significant challenge of coming to terms with their historical responsibility of the fate of those who worked with them against their opponents in both Iraq and Afghanistan. And this follows a decades-long war against "global terrorism," which is entering a new phase.

Question: The French clearly fought in Afghanistan and have led the fight in Africa against Islamic terrorists. Images from Mali must come to mind for the current French generation as well. How do you see that?

Murielle Delaporte: They might, but it could play both ways: the spillover effects from the impacts throughout the region of the return of the Taliban will probably feed the arguments of those pressuring for a withdrawal of the

French forces from the G5 Sahel countries (Mali, Chad, Niger, Burkina Faso and Mauritania), where the Barkhane Operation is already being redefined.

On the other hand, the renewed fear of international terrorism fed from the old Afghan safe haven could have the opposite influence supporting the counter-argument about the need to keep the battle against terror in the front lines,

The Impact of the Afghan Blitzkrieg Withdrawal Strategy
September 5, 2021

There is little question that there is a significant impact of the Afghan Blitzkrieg Withdrawal Strategy on the U.S. military as it engages in a strategic shift from the land wars to a focus on great power competition.

The first key impact starts with the question of the legacy of the land wars. Nearly a million Americans served in Afghanistan along with thousands of allied soldiers and officers. Because this was a lengthy engagement, characterized as stability operations and nation building, those soldiers and officers trained and worked with Afghans closely to shape a way ahead, because that is the very heart of managed transition. Then suddenly those relationships are cut by the U.S. leadership leaving those soldiers and officers in the position of having to confront the loss, death, torture, or relocation of those very persons with whom they worked for a "new" Afghanistan.

A key element of military service is honor. This disruption and the way it is done is not in the best traditions of military honor for sure. And a generation of officers and soldiers cannot be thrown into a political memory hole and simply asked to march forward.

The Western militaries are voluntary forces. Citizens need to want to serve and doing so with honor to the values of their countries. It is difficult to see how the nature of the withdrawal does not create a major set of problems for the military going forward.

The second major impact is with regard to shaping a military strategy going forward. The Obama Administration promised a Pacific pivot, which largely did not happen because of the demands from CENTCOM and the Middle East, including the rise of ISIS and the Syrian civil war. In fact, it might be remembered that President Biden was Vice President Biden during the period of fighting the "good war" in Afghanistan.

The military focus was on counterinsurgency, nation building and that most ambiguous of terms, stability operations. Shifting from this skill set to preparing for full spectrum crisis management and the high-end fight is significant. How will this happen? Will the U.S. shape a new counterterrorism strategy in the Middle East which significantly reduces demand on U.S. forces? If not, then frankly, the demand side is beyond what the U.S. military can provide for a strategic shift.

A third major impact flows from the second. CENTCOM's credibility is seriously in doubt given its performance over many years in the outcome—a failed Afghan military capability. And with that comes the question of why the U.S. Army is in any leadership role for preparing for full spectrum crisis management and the high-end fight? The strategic shift prioritizes air and naval forces, and those land forces which can support crisis management which is largely about the USMC and its transition to the high-end fight.

Closing up shop. U.S Air Force personnel assigned to the 317th Airlift Squadron, 315th Airlift Wing, Joint Base Charleston, South Carolina, support the Afghanistan withdrawal airlift on August 17, 2021. Photo by Master Sgt. Donald Allen, U.S. Central Command Public Affairs.

A fourth major impact is precisely the question of crisis management. In addressing the strategic shift, my colleague Dr. Paul Bracken has focused on the central role of escalation management, inclusive of the nuclear weapons elements. I have focused on full spectrum crisis management and have underscored the importance of reshaping civilian capabilities to be able to use an agile military force able to respond to and provide for escalation control

The play out of the Afghan withdrawal was hardly a textbook case in how to do escalation control or crisis management. As Dr. Bracken has put it: "If our actions in Afghanistan are indicative of U.S. competence in future crises, the world is in serious trouble."

A fifth major impact is in working with allies. For the U.S. military either in the Pacific or in Europe, that working closely with allies is the foundation for a credible crisis management or deterrence strategy. And working with allies means changing how the United States military integrates with allies and partners to shape a distributed force.

Or to put it more bluntly, the United States is not able to compete with multiple authoritarian powers and to prevail without changing how the U.S. military works with allies. This is being done on the military level, but the experience of the "runs of August" is not a reinforcing experience.

If one would take just one case: In June 2021, President Biden launches a new Atlantic Charter. In July 2021, Sec Def Austin signs a new carrier agreement with the UK. And in August?

In short, the U.S. military faces several challenges flowing from the Blitzkrieg withdrawal strategy. How will these challenges be addressed and met?

Its Impact on Crisis Management and Allies

August 22, 2021

Recently, I talked with Dr. Paul Bracken, the noted strategist and nuclear weapons expert, regarding how he saw the near to mid-term consequences of the Biden Afghan withdrawal and the swift seizure of Afghanistan by the Taliban. For Bracken, one key takeaway is that this would accelerate further global polycentrism and reduce the ability of the United States to lead global coalitions. Given that the major threat is the global conflict between authoritarian and liberal democratic powers, the role of the United States is not only reduced but the threats to the liberal democracies are enhanced as well. According to Bracken:

> "What we are seeing is an acceleration of polycentric nationalism. Everybody's relating to everybody else, nervously of trying to keep the balance, and very reluctant to join rigid blocks a la the Cold War because they want to preserve their independence.

> "This situation leads to significant distrust of alliances and enhances the desire to want to have something they can fall back on in the very worst case, which would be nuclear weapons. If we take the case of a low hanging fruit with regard to nuclear weapons proliferation, namely Iran, we shall see renewed emphasis to become a nuclear power. They didn't need a nuclear weapon when Obama came into office. They could calculate that the U.S. together with Israel was not going to hit them. Israel was not going to hit them because it doesn't have the wherewithal to do it. And the U.S. was not on board.

> "My view has been that they wanted to negotiate the money that we owe them more than get a bomb. I think that can be reevaluated now, that the neighborhood has in some sense gotten more dangerous. But in addition, the number of nuclear weapons Pakistan is getting each year is getting quite high, like in the hundreds. So the region is getting more dangerous. Merely to hold your own against Pakistan, India, Russia, Israel, and the United States, Iran will increasingly need the bomb. I bet if I ran a war game with people from DoD and CIA playing Iran, they would opt to go nuclear, i.e., to acquire nuclear missiles than can at least cover Israel and Europe."

With accelerated polycentrism, we see both a reduced U.S. role in shaping global coalitions, and a growth in how the key liberal democratic nations approach managing their security and defense relationships with each other.

Of course, the United States remains an important nation, but we're not a superpower. We're not the global guarantor of the West. We're in a period of time where authoritarian leaders will interpret what we're doing and the allies are doing, or partners are doing, and could frequently be wrong. Our allies will be making calculations about what we'll do, and they could be frequently wrong. And we will be making calculations about adversaries and allies alike which could be significantly wrong. And the intelligence performance in Afghanistan is certainly not a reassuring corrective to meeting this challenge.

Bracken underscored that such developments makes shaping an appropriate and effective military force for the United States and its allies increasingly challenging. As Bracken put it:

"The authoritarians, Russia and China, could make a move. They could do that and make a big mistake. The potential for convoluted, complex scenarios that take you close to war goes up quite a bit.

Tomasz Siemoniak, Poland's Minister of National Defense walks the troop line during a ceremony on the Polish helipad on FOB Ghazni. The minister visited on the 69th anniversary of the Warsaw Uprising to congratulate Task Force White Eagle on a job well done and to receive brief backs on current operations. Photo by U.S. Army Staff Sgt. Bryan Spreitzer, August 1, 2013.

"Why? Not only because of the evolution of technologies, but because there are just so many decision-making centers. To manage the way ahead, will require a generation of military thinkers, which the Afghan experience certainly has demonstrated are in short supply."

He then discussed a very specific aspect of the military competition which gets harder with the widening of conflict points and of the evolution of technology.

"I've been really worried about this whole ISR buildup in the following way. It can tell you if the Chinese are moving missiles around and the Russians are too. But it's like looking through the problem through a straw, as the intel people say.

"It's highly dependent on Signals Intelligence (SIGINT) which the decision maker is only getting the signals that the algorithms sort through and present to him. And it's really short-term. It gives little or no insight about where the country's sentiments, the leadership of the country's sentiments are going."

The Afghan situation and the way it was done have reduced the credibility of U.S. decision making in the eyes of allies and adversaries. It's not an event in and of itself. It's within an acceleration of global disaggregation and re-aggregation. And it doesn't make the U.S. a non-player. We're still an important player. But now we have to see some skill sets we haven't seen for a while in how to actually use what power assets we've got.

CHAPTER SEVEN:

THE AUSTRALIAN
SUBMARINE DECISION

September 19, 2021

The recent announcement of the decision by the Australian government to cancel their diesel submarine contract and to acquire nuclear attack submarines is significant. There is much already written about the announcement and its consequences, but what can get lost in the noise is really the key point: this decision launches the next phase of Australian strategic development, but down a path which has been evolving for some time.

At the heart of the reason the Aussies have done so is clearly the Chinese behavior and virtual war with Australia. Australia as a continent is a key challenge for Chinese ambitions in the region. They are a continent which can stage long-range forces against Chinese military operations. The Chinese Communist leaders have done what they should not have: Awakening the quiet power in the Pacific to shaping a longer-range defense force, closely allied with the major competitors of China.

Only Australia really counts in terms of deterring China in a fundamental geographical way: they are a firmly liberal democratic country, and they reject Chinese Communism. And as such, the Chinese economic and political engagements in Australia, coupled with the political and cyber warfare that the Chinese have engaged in with the clear desire to destabilize Australia have been met with firm resolve. And the Chinese have responded by escalation up to and including direct military threats against Australia.

This is the driver of the decision. Period. It is not about not loving the French, and an inability to work with France or ignoring their contractual obligations under the contracts signed earlier. When Australia made the decision to go with the French Naval Group and build a long ranger diesel submarine, the strategic context was very different than it is today.

When the premise of your decision changes, it is important to recognize that and to recalibrate, reload and rethink what you are doing and why. For the Australian government, the expensive effort to build a new class of diesel submarines was a key part of dealing with the regional dynamics changing in their region. But in only five years, the Xi government has pursued a course of action which is changing the direction of Pacific defense by the liberal democracies and their allies.

I am writing this article while in my digs in Paris, France. But I have spent the last few days talking with a number of my Australian and French colleagues. This is a strategic event—to quote one of my Australian colleagues:

"This is the most significant defense acquisition in my lifetime
by the Australian government."

But it also is a launch point for the next phase of Australian strategic development, which is itself part of a trajectory launched earlier. During my visits to Australia since 2014, I had a chance to work with the Williams Foundation and then became a Fellow with the Foundation. I have published a book which lays out what I learned during my visits in terms of shaping a narrative built around the seminars held twice a year by the Foundation. Those seminars and my book on Australian defence strategy provide a very clear record of how the ADF has rethought its place in the world and how to operate more effectively.

The F-35 acquisition decision at the beginning of my visits was more than a platform choice; it was the next step in RAAF modernization but one which reached out to the joint force and has driven the ADF voyage on building a fifth-generation force. Now the nuclear submarine decision is the keystone to the next phase of this journey, one which is about extending the reach of the ADF throughout the entire Indo-Pacific region.

The precursor for this decision lies not in submarines but a growing concern with the need for the ADF to have longer-range strike capability. In 2018, one of our seminars dealt directly with the long-range strike requirement. In terms of reference for the seminar held on August 22, 2018, this key point was made:

> "The ability to strike at range brings a new dimension into any unfolding strategic scenario which, in itself, may often deter escalation into armed conflict. While in the event of escalation occurring, the absence of a long-range strike capability both limits Australia's options for strategic maneuver and concedes to an adversary the ability to dictate the terms of engagement.
>
> "An independent strike capability expands the range of options to achieve Australia's strategic ends; signals a serious intent and commitment about Australia's national security; and has the capacity to influence strategic outcomes short of resorting to armed conflict."

The Morrison government announced its defense strategy in July 2020 and that announcement is where I started my book and then looked backwards. I labeled that strategy as a strategic reset. And that reset began with weapons, not platforms. On March 31, 2021, the Prime Minister announced a new effort in the weapons area.

> "The Morrison Government will accelerate the creation of a $1 billion Sovereign Guided Weapons Enterprise, boosting skilled jobs and helping secure Australia's sovereign defense capabilities. The Department of Defence will now select a strategic industry partner to operate a sovereign guided weapons manufacturing capability on behalf of the Government as a key part of the new Enterprise. The new Enterprise will support missile and guided weapons manufacturing for use across the Australian Defence Force."

In doing so, the Australian government opened up discussions with the Trump Administration with regard to acquiring not only weapons but an ability to produce those weapons on Australian soil. A key element of this discussion revolved around naval weapons, which also highlights a key aspect of how the ADF has worked with the United States military over the past few years. The ADF has a close working relationship with the U.S. Navy and the USMC. In fact, the RAAF has bought and operated a number of naval air platforms over the years in addition to the close working relationship with the U.S. Navy in operations and training. And it is currently operating a number of key systems, which will interact nicely with the new submarine, notably Triton and the P-8.

In the course of these discussions, the aperture opened on the possibility of the acquisition of a platform which could carry some of these weapons deep into the Pacific, namely the nuclear submarine. Because the nuclear navy is in many ways the crown jewel of the U.S. military, the ADF leadership has full confidence in them as partners. For the U.S. Navy, having worked for a long period with the British Navy, and in the case of the Astute class having engaged through its contractors in direct support for the UK at home in building the new nuclear attack submarine, a template was available which could be applied to the Australian case.

The reset of Australian defence is wide-ranging and includes reworking Australia defense ecosystems for greater resilience, logistical depth, and shifts in geographical focus, namely towards Western Australia and the Northern territories. Having visited Western Australia in 2020 just prior to the pandemic shut down of Australia, it is clear that a buildup of infrastructure in this area up to and including the Northern Territories is a core aspect of any strategic reset.

And the logical next step for the RAAF to join in this journey would be to acquire a long-range bomber. But the journey begins with the new submarine.

Shaping a Way Ahead for the ADF

September 24, 2021

The decision to build a fleet of nuclear attack submarines is clearly not a simple platform decision. And its impact is not limited to the Royal Australian

Navy or to the allies who are part of the agreement to shape such a force. The ADF has been on a journey for joint force development for some time. Notably, the acquisition of the F-35 clearly drove consideration for how to shape a fifth-generation force. Now it is about a long-range fifth generation force.

It must be remembered that when the diesel submarine decision was taken, the Japanese were the presumptive favorites. At least until the decision was announced. There was much disappointment and concern in Tokyo about the shift to buying a French to be designed submarine. Yet today, the Japanese-Australian relationship is stronger than ever in the defense domain. In part, it is so because of the same factor that reshaped Australian thinking about the submarine, namely Chinese Communist behavior and military developments.

It also needs to be remembered that the Australians were NOT buying an off the shelf French submarine. On one hand, they were drawing upon the Virginia-class combat system and had contracted Lockheed Martin as the prime contractor for the new build diesel submarine, while on the other hand, the new build submarine was never the "deal of the century" as proclaimed by the French government. It was a series of contracts which could eventually lead to the build of a new design submarine. In effect, the program was shaped to work design, and then make the build decision. In effect, Naval Group had been hired as a design consultant with the expected decision to build that submarine in Australia as Naval Group and the Commonwealth resolved the manufacturing build challenges.

It also needs to be remembered how the Royal Australian Navy and the Commonwealth had shaped their new shipbuilding program. It was about taking a two-pronged approach. First, there is a focus on the combat systems and integratability across the fleet. Second, there is a focus on the platform build itself. With the decision to move to a nuclear submarine, the combat system trajectory already in place for the new build diesel submarine can clearly be leveraged going forward.

When I was last in Australia, in March 2020 before the pandemic impact, I worked on a report on the first new build Australian ship, namely, the

Offshore Patrol Vessel. After my discussions with the Capability Acquisition and Sustainment Group or CASG in Canberra, this is what I concluded about the new approach:

"Clearly the Department is focusing on a new approach in launching this ship, but a new approach which is seen to provide a template for the way ahead. It is not about simply having a one-off platform innovation process; it is about launching a new way of building this ship and in so doing setting in motion new ways to manage the initial build and the ongoing modernization process.

"It is not about having a bespoke platform; it is about shaping an approach that allows leveraging the systems onboard the new platform across the entire fleet and Australian Defence Force modernization process.

"In part, it is selecting a platform which physically can allow for the upgrade process envisaged with the new emphasis on a fleet mission systems management model. The Royal Australian Navy has clearly gone through a process of choosing a ship that has a lot of space, a lot of margins, the ability to adapt to missions by its space on deck, and under the deck for a modular or containerized solutions, extra power to operate for what comes in the future, and the ability to adapt the platform through further evolution of the design to take on different missions into the future. The platform is important; but the focus is not on what the systems specific to the ship allow it to operate organically as an end in of itself but as part of wider operational integratable force."[34]

What this means in blunt terms is that the platform has changed but the focus on an integratable combat system has not. The first was the focus with Naval Group; the second was always the focus with the Lockheed Martin team and will almost certainly continue.

---

34   Robbin Laird, *Joint by Design: The Evolution of Australian Defence Strategy* (2021), Chapter Eight.

The nuclear attack submarine choice is obviously a significant step in shaping new capabilities for the ADF and for the Commonwealth. But before discussing this aspect, we again need to focus on the continuity aspect. That revolves around theater anti-submarine or underwater warfare. The RAAF is adding significant capability to work the Royal Australian Navy in this domain, most notably in terms of the P-8 and Triton capabilities. The Australians do not have a separate Naval Air Force as does the United State, so RAAF and Royal Australian Navy (RAN) integration is crucial to shaping a joint force moving ahead. What the new nuclear submarine will add is reach, range, speed, and enhanced survivability, which enhances ADF capabilities overall. The context has not changed, but the capability to be operate more effectively in that context will.

There are significant eco-system impacts of the nuclear submarine decision. Australia will build its basing structure to accommodate this class of ships, which means that they can host from time to time its allies who have such submarines, whether French, British or American. It also means a challenge for crewing as the Collins class to the Virginia class is nearly three times increase in crew size.

It is about coming to terms with Western Australia and the need to build up infrastructure literally to support basing and to do so on the Eastern side of Australia as well. This will take time, money and a long-term commitment.

The impacts of this decision reach beyond the Air Force and Navy. The impact on the Australian Army is significant. The turn towards a need for Northern Territory and Western Australian defense clearly is ramped up. The need to operate effectively from the West of Australia out to the First Island Chain becomes even more significant, and the Australian Army role is clear in this regard: a more USMC-like force is required.

In short, acquiring a nuclear attack submarine is the next step in the evolution of the ADF. And it is one about extended the reach of the ADF in the Indo-Pacific and reinforces the strategic shift under way for Australia's role in the region.

The Ripple Effects

September 26, 2021

The Morrison Administration made a strategic decision to change course with regard to their procurement of new attack submarines. That decision was in line with ADF thinking with regard to the need for the force to have longer range strike capability to deal with the changing threats in the Indo-Pacific region. This decision has sent ripple effects into the Australian alliance structure, ripple effects which need to be worked through in the coming months.

The first ripple effect is with regard to President XI and his administration. Is he really the leader for life? His performance over the past three years leaves much to be desired from a Chinese national interest point of view, as well as the Chinese Communist point of view and the two are clearly not the same.

What he has done has significantly worsened the Chinese situation. By unleashing the global pandemic, inadvertently or not, and doing whatever the opposite of full transparency is, he has highlighted that his regime is one of information war, not responsible global engagement.

The impacts of his regime's behavior towards the liberal democratic states over the past few years has been to work to undermine those states and their values. It has been about conducting political warfare against them. This coupled with the decisive effect which the pandemic has unleashed has significantly disrupted the kind of globalization which has benefited the growth of Chinese economic power and political influence.

In part to cover their failures, the Chinese regime engages in a very active policy of information warfare to drive wedges where possible within and among the liberal democratic states And is statesmanship is not generated in the next few months by the leaders of these liberal democracies, then the Chinese will clearly have enhanced possibilities for success in this part of their global policy.

In Australia, the recognition of political warfare against Australia has become firmly grasped. This plus the pandemic has led to a significant focus on how to build reliable and secure supply chains for the island continent.

The second ripple effect is with regard to the United Kingdom and its evolving role with Australia and the "five eyes" countries. Global Britain is a reach at best. The role of the Royal Navy is significant but generated in large part due to its relationship to the U.S. Navy. And the newest British nuclear attack submarine has been built with very significant U.S. manufacturing assistance as well.

As a RAND report published in 2011 highlighted:

> "In 2003, the MOD solicited the help of General Dynamics Electric Boat through a foreign military sales agreement with the United States. Approximately 100 experienced Electric Boat designers and managers—about a dozen of them on-site at the Barrow shipyard and the rest back in the United States—began to interact with BAE Systems and help with the design effort.

> "The Electric Boat designers helped set up the design tool and processes at the prime contractor and started to develop the detailed drawings necessary for construction through a secure data link between Barrow and Groton.

> "Electric Boat also began to transfer production knowledge to the shipyard. It passed along modular construction techniques that it had developed for the Ohio and Virginia classes, including the advanced outfitting of the submarine rings using a vertical method rather than the traditional horizontal process.

> "It helped develop an integrated master plan through a separate contract with the MOD's integrated project team, which further developed the earned value management system being used to track program progress. Eventually, an Electric Boat employee was assigned as the Astute Project Director with BAE Systems at the Barrow shipyard responsible for all aspects of delivery.

> "Through the interactions with Electric Boat, the growing exper-tise of the prime contractor, and the increased involvement

of MOD, the design portion of the Astute program started to make progress."[35]

The template shaped for Astute between the UK and the U.S. Navy is clearly a solid starting point for any Australian-build process going forward. Perhaps without it, no deal would have been reached.

The third ripple effect is with regard to the evolving ADF working relationship with the United States military as well as with other core allies in the region. In effect, the U.S. Navy, Japan and Australia are working through new ways to deliver ASW or USW capabilities. This means that Japan along with Australia are key players in how the U.S. Navy reworks with its allies an Indo-Pacific approach to ASW or USW in an advanced kill web or team sport approach.

The final ripple effect which I will discuss is with regard to Europe and its place in the world, and evolving perceptions within Europe with regard to strategic reality. To some extent, the reactions among some European commentators remind me of my time in Europe in the 1980s during the Euro-Missile crisis. The Soviet Union was deploying new intermediate range nuclear missiles clearly designed against theater targets, which enhanced their capability to decouple Western Europe from the United States. The Reagan Administration generated a two-track approach—of negotiation to get rid of those missiles while deploying new missiles in Europe targeting Soviet military targets.

During the 1980s, European critics considered this an unwarranted nuclear escalation by the United States. Authoritarian powers are very good at ratcheting up threats and then characterizing any response of the liberal democracies to those threats as "escalation".

And the Communist leadership of China has certainly done this with regard to the Australian decision, despite the fact that a nuclear attack submarine force is really a defensive move, clearly protecting Australia from the buildup of Chinese military power and after the Chinese directly threatened Australia with long-range strikes.

---

35 John F. Schank, et.al., *Learning from Experience, Volume III: Lessons from the U.K.s Astute Program* (Rand: 2011), p. 44.

That is not surprising, but the logic is clear: if you respond to our intimidation, you are escalating the crisis. The problem is that a number of European commentators have echoed this sentiment, calling this a new cold war in the Indo-Pacific region, far from them, and criticizing the Australians for making such a move.

And at the same time, recent public opinion polling in Europe clearly indicates that for most Europeans, the conflict between China and Australia or between China and the United States is not really about them. As Eszter Zalan wrote in the *EUobserver*:

> "Most Europeans think that there is a new Cold War unfolding between the U.S. and its rivals, Russia and China—but do not think their own country is involved, a new polling-backed report by the European Council on Foreign Relations (ECFR) has found. The report, published on September 22, 2021, and based on polling 12 EU countries, also shows that Europeans consider EU institutions to be more likely than their own governments to be in a Cold War with China and Russia alongside Washington.

> "The report warns that it could also be explained with a growing gulf between European public opinion and the US, as well as between national approaches and the more hawkish position of the EU's political leadership in Brussels. If this new polling has captured a lasting trend, it reveals that European public is not ready to see the growing tensions with China and Russia as a new Cold war," Ivan Krastev, co-author of the report, and chair of the Centre for Liberal Strategies said. So far, it is only European institutions rather than European publics that are ready to see the world of tomorrow as a growing system of competition between democracy and authoritarianism," he added."[36]

In short, the Australian strategic decision on attack submarines is an inflection point at which global dynamics might move in very different directions.

---

36   Eszter Zalan, "Europeans Think Cold War is Here: But Not for Them," *EUobserver* (September 22, 2021), https://euobserver.com/world/152987?utm_source=euobs&utm_medium=email.

It does not cause global change, but it clearly is an accelerator to change in terms of the competition between the liberal democracies and the 21st century authoritarian states.

But these events added to other recent events should put to rest the persistent forecasters of 2030 and the appropriate force structure for 2030 or 2040 in the defense of the interests of the liberal democracies. In 2019, how many people projected a global pandemic and its crushing impact on globalization? In 2021, how many anticipated the Biden administration Blitzkrieg withdrawal "strategy" and its unfolding impact on allies and adversaries alike, not the least of which its impact on the United States and its military? In July 2021, how many were forecasting an Australian nuclear attack submarine decision in September of this year?

All of this should lead to modesty with regard to our confidence in accurately projecting the future of conflict in the region or of the optimal force design to deliver the desired crisis management and combat effects.

The Perspective of VADM (Retired) Tim Barrett
October 19, 2021

The Morrison Administration's decision to pursue a nuclear attack submarine highlighted an 18-month period with Vice Admiral Jonathan Mead in charge on the Australian side of negotiating within the new nuclear submarine alliance to deliver Australian solutions. I interviewed Mead when he was head of Navy Capability in 2016.[37] He then went on to be Commander Australian Fleet and then Chief of Joint Capabilities and Command of Joint Capabilities Group. He has a strong ASW background as well as working closely with the other member of the Quad, namely India. He is now the Chief of the Nuclear-Powered Submarine Task Force.

There is much to be determined with regard to how Australia will proceed but given the dynamic changes in the strategic environment and the working relationships with allies in the region, there are a much wider

---

37   Robbin Laird, "Rear Admiral Jonathan Mead Focuses on the Way Ahead for the Royal Australian Navy," *Second Line of Defense* (August 30, 2016), https://sldinfo.com/2016/08/rear-admiral-jonathan-mead-focuses-on-the-way-ahead-for-the-royal-australian-navy/.

array of options than with the short-fin Barracuda program. With the United States clearly seeking to expand its operating areas in the Pacific, and with Australia building capabilities to operate its own nuclear submarines, it would be no surprise if nuclear submarines began operating within the Australian first island chain. It would be no surprise if there might be mixed manning solutions onboard U.S. or UK nuclear submarines in anticipation of the future Australian submarine. It would be no surprise if Australia sought alternatives to full build of nuclear submarines on Australian soil and find something more akin to F-35 solution sets.

To be clear, this is a work in progress but one that will not be a replay of how the Australians addressed the replacement of the Collins class with a full build Australian vessel on Australian soil. The pressures to defend Australia, and to engage the Japanese and Americans in a more effective undersea warfare set of capabilities is a pressing not long-range challenge.

I had a chance to discuss these issues on October 14, 2021, in a phone interview with Vice-Admiral (Retired) Tim Barrett, with whom I have had the opportunity to discuss maritime issues since 2015. As the exact nature of what will happen in the program is a work in progress and not really open to public disclosure until that 18-month period is completed, we focused on the context and how one might assess that context.

Vice-Admiral (Retired) Barrett made three key points. First, the nuclear submarine effort was a strategic one, which was about Australian defense and not primarily focused on a priority on ship building on Australian soil. It is crucial to understand that this is about adding core defense capabilities earlier rather than later and would almost certainly encompass interaction between shaping the eco system for the operation of Australian nuclear submarines and the presence of allied nuclear submarines working with the Australian eco system.

The second key point was that the priority needed to be focused on adding nuclear submarine capability to the evolving USW or ASW capability which Australia was already building out. The Australian government recently decided to add another squadron of Romeo helicopters to the fleet and has procured P-8s and Tritons as part of an expanded ASW or USW warfighting capability. The submarine is not a silver bullet for ASW, or USW mission sets but part of the evolution of the kill web approach to ASW and USW missions going forward.

The submarine decision is part of a broader set of decisions with regard to how the ADF should respond to the challenges in the Indo-Pacific. This was a deliberate and considered position from the Navy's perspective, but the political and geopolitical circumstances have changed. "This is not the first time that Australia has sought or considered the acquisition of a nuclear submarine." The decision is based on the need to provide more capability to the coalition to conduct USW or ASW in the region. In that way, it is analogous to the Growler decision taken a few years ago.[38]

The third key point was that flexibility and innovations will be part of working out a way ahead and he noted that Mead had worked with him previously. For example, when Barrett was Commander of the Australian Fleet, then Commodore Mead was instrumental in working an innovative plan to manage a temporary capability deficiency for fleet fuel tanking. To shore up a gap, the RAN 'leased' a Spanish Navy oiler for 8 months, and the RAN crews trained on the ship and operated the ship in support of the Australian Fleet. Eventually, the RAN acquired two new Spanish oilers, but the kind of innovation demonstrated in this example, will almost certainly be part of the way ahead in meeting the challenges of accelerating the operational acquisition of nuclear submarine capacity in support of Australian defense.

According to Vice Admiral (Retired) Barrett: "The strategic environment has changed. We need to reconsider the balance between sovereign capability for a thirty-year build and the need for creation of capability in the near term. The earlier 30-year period build approach should not be the dominant approach; the capability and its presence to shape deterrent capabilities is crucial and work out over time how the build side of this effort is clarified and put in place. The program needs to be driven by the need for creative capability options first."

---

38 Robbin Laird, "Group Captain Braz and the Coming of the Growler to the Australian Defence Force," *Second Line of Defense* (April 14, 2017), https://sldinfo.com/2017/04/group-captain-braz-and-the-coming-of-the-growler-to-the-australian-defence-force/.

CHAPTER EIGHT:

SECURITY DYNAMICS AND DEFENSE

Shaping Resilience

October 18, 2021

Recently, I had a chance to discuss with Air Vice-Marshal (Retired) John Blackburn the work he been engaged in since I was last in Australia in March 2020. The team has recently released a final report on the challenges facing Australia to become a more resilient society as well as their report on challenges facing Australia in the energy sector as well to build out resilient capabilities.

Prior to the pandemic, Blackburn was pursuing several issues affecting resilience, initially from a largely defense point of view, but then broadened his lens to a wider set of issues. Now with the nearly two-year pandemic impact, the issue is clearly not a niche issue.

Question: Your work on resilience preceded the pandemic, but obviously has now been informed as well by the impact of the pandemic on supply chains, medical manufacturing and fuel and energy issues as well. How would you describe your journey?

Blackburn: "In 2019, I was asked to present at the Australian Navy Institute in 2019 on maritime trade and the risks to that trade. I had previously worked on resilience issues in the energy, economy, and environment arenas. However, in preparing for the Navy Institute seminar I came to realise that we were in a similar situation with respect to maritime trade, i.e., little resilience to deal with potential trade interruptions.

"When we looked at the total system, the lack of resilience was clearly obvious. When Second Line of Defense brought attention to the work of Rosemary Gibson on the dependence of the West on the supply of medicine by China, we started to focus on a medicine supply chains in Australia as well."

Question: To be clear: prior to the pandemic you were focusing on the resilience issue. The impact of the pandemic highlighted the strategic significance of the issue. But there seems to be a desire to get "back to normal" without realizing that the pre-pandemic world is not coming back, notably regarding how globalization with China at the epicenter was playing out prior to 2020. How do you see this shift?

Blackburn: "Politicians try to boost the voter's confidence in a crisis "Hey, we'll get back to normal soon." Unfortunately, that pre COVID "normal" is gone. That was business as was. We're not going back there. You can't. We've really got to say, "We're uncertain of where we're headed, but we know it's not where we were before," and here's an opportunity. Do a reset, taking account of our resilience issues and vulnerabilities. We have to design the future that we're heading towards very rapidly, because we can't just go back."

Question: But certainly, in the United States, the capacity to grasp reality through the vortex of current political rhetoric and debate is probably at an all-time low. How do we get back on track?

Blackburn: "You are right… I think the United Kingdom, at present, is probably one of the best examples of what you are pointing out. Because of the concerns that were raised about Brexit and where they have ending up, they seem to be in a state of denial and distraction. In Australia, it is an unusual situation because we essentially drew up the drawbridge and said, "Well, fine. We're just going to isolate ourselves," and then we pumped up debt at an incredible rate.

"But why did we do that? Because we didn't have the hospital capacities, the medicine supply capabilities, the production capabilities to deal with vast spread COVID-19. We had no choice, but to draw up the drawbridge and isolate ourselves. But we're still not facing the reality because, faced with the risk of voter's losing hope, the politicians are still not facing the full reality of the situation we are in and are not preparing adequately for the risks we are likely to face in the next few years. Specifically, COVID variants and supply chain failures.

"There's a lot of positive spin about … "The end of the pandemic is coming up shortly. We'll all be back to normal. Things will be great." So, we're not able to have a very honest, apolitical conversation, which is the first point that we highlighted in our national resilience project. If you can't have an honest conversation about where we are, what the assumptions are, what the risks are without blaming somebody else for being in that situation that we're in together, then there's no way you can work out where we need to go in terms of a more resilient and secure society."

Question: Australia has been engaged in serious conflict with the epicenter for generating the pandemic, namely China. There has clearly been enhanced realization that China is not Australia's friend in terms of the survival of a liberal democratic society. How do you see the Chinese threat feeding into a resilience perspective within Australia itself?

Blackburn: "It clearly does but we have a compounding challenge to face, namely, the short-term perspective of politics here, driven by the three-year election cycle. The Chinese Government has implemented trade sanctions against us as they attempt to bully us into being subservient. That will not happen. However, the Chinese actions have been anticipated but we have lacked a long-term strategy to address this threat and so we are constrained to just reacting and pleading for help from the USA.

"We don't have a coherent view of where we need to be in 10, 15, or 20 years. It's all about the next election. It is very hard to develop a resiliency strategy and a strategy for dealing with China if your political focus is short term."

Question: How might we get to a place whereby we can take a long-term view?

Blackburn: "As we conclude in our report, we don't prepare for crises. That's just not in our culture. We react. Unfortunately, a lot of our reactions, particularly at the political level, are too little too late and too shortsighted. We get caught in this reaction loop and you don't get people with the brain space to step outside of that process.

"The military concept of preparedness doesn't really exist in civil society in Australia. In our resilience project, we highlighted that we could learn from the military. In my work on Plan Jericho, there were two things we focused on. First, was the need for vastly improved, shared situation awareness, and second, the ability to operate as an integrated team, because Plan Jericho wasn't really about air force—it was about how do we trigger a joint force.

"So, what we did in the project was to take those two themes and add preparedness and mobilization. In the project report we suggest that there are three characteristics or attributes critical for a society to be resilient. One is shared awareness, by having an honest conversation about what the issues are, as well as the threats, the assumptions, and problems. The second characteristic is the need to work as a team. In our country, particularly with our federation structure, that has been a bit of a challenge. Thirdly, if you've got the first two, is the ability to prepare for a range of risks/scenarios.

"In the military, we trained, simulated, and exercised; it's not that you assume you're going to exactly see what you have trained for but rather that you are building the skill sets and experience to be able to deal with a wide range of crises.

"For each of the nine areas we looked at in the project, the same challenges or blockages came up. We have individuals with incredibly deep expertise, but we don't have shared knowledge in the society because it's blocked either for political reasons, by bureaucracy or by IP issues in industry."

Blackburn then described an example of a strategic opportunity for Australia, given its robust ability to generate electric power from solar sources, or if the country faces reality, nuclear power. "If we're going to be able to have control over our transport, our logistics, our basic systems that support our way of life, then we're going to have to get off imported fuels as fast as we can, in terms of transport and logistics. Everything from trucks to vehicles, to trains, to ships, needs to be changed so that we can have control over the energy necessary to run the logistics of our society. We need to electrify our transport and logistics systems as much as possible.

"From a wider perspective, electric cars are more about our security as a nation than just about emissions; BEVs, Hydrogen Fuel Cell vehicles, and renewable ammonia powered ships can result in a significant reduction of our imported fuel dependency. We can have control over these parts of our national systems by having control over the energy used to power them. But the current electricity grid system in this country is very fragile. We're going to need to grow it to two to three times its current size as we transform our energy systems through electrification.

"Most everything is connected. What I find is that the domain experts largely stay in their lane way. There are not enough whole of systems experts in this country. The result is that we don't get that broader shared awareness we need to think strategically."

The New Warfare
August 1, 2020

The strategic shift from the Middle East wars to the question of 21st century global conflict among the core global powers is occurring in the context of a thirty-year process of globalization. This means that the classic understanding of national or allied defense industrial bases has been turned on its head as global sourcing has created a very new situation in which the challenge is to actually know what the critical processes and capabilities are to have under national control in times of conflict or crises where global supply chains are disrupted or shut down.

What does it mean to have a nation and its military or security forces sustained through a period of crisis? And this question is not an idle one for since the People's Republic of China (PRC) has joined the World Trade Organization (WTO), it has pursued a deliberate policy of leveraging globalization to position itself for strategic dominance.

This has not happened simply by the Chinese pursuing what one might call a distorted (for a Western point of view) or a directed globalization strategy. They have been added by the enthusiastic support of Western politicians, industrialists and publics who have seen lower costs at home and profits abroad as the mark of economic development. As Western business schools churned out a generation of theorists who focused on lean supply chains and on core value of a firm, which meant getting rid of organic supply capabilities within a firm, Chinese Inc. was only too willing to define itself as the supplier of choice for the West.

The only small problem is that the PRC is not following Western rules of law and the PRC leaders have a global strategy, which relies on distorted globalization to gain strategic advantage. As Ross Babbage, the noted Australian strategist, underscored in his recently published report on political warfare:

> "China's very large economy and the authority of the Party within it gives Beijing extensive scope to persuade, bribe, and coerce national and regional governments to accept large infrastructure developments and other Chinese involvements within their societies. China Inc. can afford to purchase key foreign enterprises, offer funding for uneconomic infrastructure projects, and heavily subsidize the entry of Chinese corporations into strategically important markets, even within strong Western societies. This provides Beijing with strategic positioning options that Moscow cannot afford and is not well-structured to undertake."[39]

In their ground-breaking book, *China Rx: Exposing the Risks of America's Dependence on China for Medicine*, Rosemary Gibson and Janardan Prasad Singh provide significant insights into how distorted globalization has put the United States and the Western world into a situation of dependency which clearly provides tools for the Chinese leadership in a future crisis.

They described the strategic shift from pharmaceutical leadership to dependence on Chinese production as follows:

> "In the 1990s, the United States, Europe, and Japan manufactured 90 percent of the global supply of the key ingredients for the world's medicines and vitamins.

---

39   Ross Babbage, *Winning Without Fighting* (CSBA, 2019), p. 44.

"Now, China is the largest global supplier. American dependence on China for the active ingredients in many medicines is so significant that a headline in a 2012 pharmaceutical industry newsletter, FiercePharma, blared, "Dangers Aside, Drugmakers Can't Live without Chinese Active Ingredients."[40]

This shift provides the grounds for concern either through disruption of the supply chain by design or not on the Chinese part.

"The centralization of the global supply for essential ingredients for drugs in China makes it vulnerable to interruption, whether by mistake or design.

"If disruptions occur for an essential ingredient made in China, the United States will wait in line along with Europe, India, and other countries to obtain it. If a global public health crisis occurs,

"China will likely keep its domestically produced medicines at home and stockpile them to secure access for its citizens before seeing to the needs of other nations."[41]

You don't have to be a genius to then focus on what this means not only for civil society but the military as well. While there has been much focus on the potential threat of bioterrorism, there has been virtually no focus on the U.S. and the West putting into the hands of the Chinese, the means to cripple Western militaries in terms of medical supplies.

Their book provides significant detail on how this situation has happened as well as paths to recovery. The path to recovery requires focusing on the restoration of the supply base within the United States and the West to ensure that key elements of both the manufacturing and stockpiling chain are resident within the liberal democracies, and not dependent on the goodwill of a country which has clearly signaled its intentions with regard to how it is using distorted globalization to its strategic advantage.

---

40   Rosemary Gibson and Janardan Prasad Singh, *China Rx: Exposing the Risks of America's Dependence on China for Medicine* (Prometheus, Kindle Edition), p. 33.

41   Gibson and Singh, *China Rx: Exposing the Risks of America's Dependence*, p. 33.

Robert D. Atkinson, president of the Information Technology and Innovation Foundation, said during testimony at the U.S.-China Economic and Security Review Commission, "It's become clear that the path we thought China was going on to become more market-oriented, more rule of law, more respectful of intellectual property — that path hasn't emerged. You could argue there's significant backsliding. Not enough people understand. The old strategy was about gaining commodity production, largely in manufacturing, largely through low cost, largely through inducing U.S. firms and others to go there. That was very successful…

> "The new strategy is to go after our core competencies and technology. That's a very different strategy. We could have a trade balance with China tomorrow, and it wouldn't address that problem, which is going after the kinds of advanced industries in which the United States is still competitive in. That's the new war."[42]

Information War

October 2021

The coming of the Wuhan virus marked a significant global disruption and has created an historical fault line between a before and after global development event. This means that post-pandemic, what will be the "new normal." Hidden in plain view is a key aspect of the "new normal" between the global authoritarian states (China and Russia) and the liberal democratic states, namely, information war for global dominance.

It is hidden in plain view in part due to the fact that the Russian leadership has made it very clear that this is what they are all about in global engagement. The Russians have released an updated National Security strategy on July 2, 2021. One bit of irony here is that July 2 is the actual date the American declaration of independence was signed, but this document spells out the priority on Russian recovery.

What is asserted is the priority for Russian values against Western values. And in this defense of Russian values, information war is highlighted

---

42   Gibson and Singh, *China Rx: Exposing the Risks of America's Dependence*, p. 211.

as a key reality facing the Russian federation as the West is characterized as using the various modern means of information, such as the internet, to seek to disrupt the Russian value system and way of life. This means that the Russians feel free to do the same, and to use information warfare to do the same. Indeed, the document does not use the word cyber warfare whatsoever. It focuses on political warfare and information security.

And in the Russian military mind, information war is an ongoing element of the global competition which allows them to get inside the adversary's decision-making cycle, and inside the debates and conflicts within Western societies and in their alliances, and to do so in ways that weaken the West and lead to disintegration of Western values.

It is not just about intrusion for classic military effect; it is about a much wider agenda of undercutting Western values, protecting the "Russian way of life," and preparing the way for the Russians to use various lethal means to achieve its objectives short of widespread direct armed conflict.

Recently, I had a chance to meet with and discuss with Jean Louis Gergorin in Paris how the Russians and its authoritarian partners are shaping their way ahead in the information domain. Gergorin is the co-author of well-regarded assessment on cyber conflict which labels cyber war as the "permanent war."

Gergorin started by underscoring that for the authoritarians, information war is a key tool for preparing the battlefield. It is a way to win without fighting with traditional military means. It is a tool that allows them to operate inside the Western societies and to play off of the conflict and disaggregation within and among Western states.

He highlighted the UK Parliamentary report which underscored how the Russians played into the Brexit debate providing an enhanced push for a leave vote. He noted how the Russians are playing out the Gerasimov doctrine whereby Russia works intensive information and political operations to shape the environment for Russian success rather than having to use classic conventional military means to ensure strategic success.

The so-called Gerasimov doctrine, which is named for General Valery Gerasimov, Russia's Chief of the General Staff calls for developing a "new-generation warfare" concept. This concept or approach is an amalgamation of kinetic and non-kinetic means across various domains to gain dominance in a conflict. Gerasimov published what has become a famous article in 2013 where he argued that the rules of war had changed, in which non-kinetic means of achieving political and strategic goals can be more effective than kinetic ones in achieving dominance in a conflict.

The use of cyber tools has been evident in both their takeover of Crimea and the pressure on the Baltic states. In each instance, the Russians have used cyberspace as part of the political warfare phase preparing the ground for enhancing pressure on the Ukraine in the one case, and on Estonia on the other.

The updated military strategy further expands on the importance of such an approach and Gergorin highlighted how the Russians are doing so. They are hosting several cyber-criminal organizations on their own soil. Putin is following the Queen Elizabeth I model of using privateers to fight the enemy indirectly. In addition, the Russians have stepped up their game of placing digital Trojan horses directly into Western infrastructure systems.

The Russians are perfecting their capabilities and using cyber intrusions as messaging tools as well. He cited the example of attacking the Czech Republic after a decision was announced to symbolic denigrate the Russian role in liberating Prague from the Nazis, by launching a series of cyber-attacks against Czech Republic institutions.

He argued that the Russians have focused on use of ransomware to both send messages and to be able to place trojan horses into infrastructure systems to provide for crisis management tools in future crises.

The Chinese have also been heavily engaged in such activities, as well as North Korea. In the North Korean case, a key motivation has been to obtain currency to get around Western sanctions.

The interplay between domestic divisions in the West and the evolving warfare approach of the authoritarian states can be seen in the importance of re-tweeing. Divisions in the West tend to spawn extremist groups on various sides of the political spectrum. Through social media, messages are generated which then can be identified by the authoritarians and retweeted by AI systems for much wider diffusion.

He argued that we need to recognize that information war is a permanent feature of the "new normal" and needs to be treated as such. Part of the response needs to be to curb the Western obsession with digitalizing everything. Secretary Wynne has suggested that there is an opportunity to return to analog systems in many cases within infrastructure systems, a view which makes sense to Gergorin.[43]

A key challenge facing the West is that we tend to separate cyber from information warfare. We have cyber commands which focus on the cyber interpretation of digital warfare and have specialized commands like SOCOM which deal with information warfare. But for the Russians, both are managed by the same command. This creates a fundamental challenge on our side of seeing cyber defense as technical problem.

He argued that a dual approach was necessary going forward dealing with the authoritarians and their political warfare and information warrior capabilities. On the one hand, retaliation in kind was required and to have the tools and policy framework for doing so. On the other hand, it is necessary to have a dialogue with them about this area of warfare. President Macron has done so, with mixed success, but cyber intrusions needed to be discussed and managed as part of a broader Western deterrent strategy. As he put it:

> "You fight and talk at the same time." It is necessary to have both a retaliation capability and not hesitate to retaliate but at same time to craft a negotiation strategy with the authoritarians at the same time."

---

43 Michael W. Wynne, "Shaping a New Approach to Cyber Defense: Time for Analog," *Second Line of Defense* (November 27, 2016), https://sldinfo.com/2016/11/shaping-a-new-approach-to-cyber-defense-time-for-analog/.

CHAPTER NINE:

THE LEAD INTO THE UKRAINE CRISIS 2022

Looking Back and Looking Forward: The Case of Ukraine

January 29, 2022

My first visit to Ukraine was shortly after it became an independent state with the collapse of the Soviet Union. The team I was working with visited Belarus, Ukraine, and Russia, with a focus on securing the nuclear weapons which the Soviet Union had controlled but abandoned inside what was now Ukrainian territory.

This was the wild west period in post-Soviet history, when in Kiev or Minsk or Moscow, the collapse of the Soviet Union left behind a society in shreds, struggling for identity.

Much of the next thirty years would see these states re-focusing on their way ahead as societies and coming to terms with the Soviet past. A major part of the Ukrainian challenge comes from the existence of divisions within Ukrainian society about how to look at their Russian neighbor compared to their European neighbors.

The focus of the United States in the early 1990s was to ensure that the former Soviet Union's nuclear weapons came under control. The agreements reached, which saw nuclear material removed from both Ukraine and Kazakhstan, may have secured the world from a "loose nuke" concern, but in retrospect dramatically strengthened Russia's nuclear position. Although there were no explicit security agreements to defend Ukrainian territory in case of Russian aggression, certainly giving up nuclear weapons put Ukraine in a dependent position. And from my discussions with Ukrainians, there seemed to be an assumption that becoming a non-nuclear power — the country signed the nuclear Non-Proliferation Treaty in 1994 — meant the West had some sort of responsibility to work with them on their defense.

Since then, NATO and the European Union have expanded, but without both Ukraine and Belarus, the two key former Soviet republics viewed by Russian leaders to be part of the own security areas. The two have instead served as buffer states between a resurgent Russia and the new European order built since 1991. I did a study for Net Assessment in the early 1990s which focused on how challenging and dangerous this buffer zone could be to any future European order, and now here we are playing out the challenge of Ukrainian sovereignty versus the Russian view of buffer states that are part of their zone of security and influence.

During my Euro-missile work in Europe in the 1980s, a contemporary observer in terms of watching these events was Vladimir Putin. Operating in East Germany, he saw the significant struggle for European opinion, and the response of the United States and NATO to Russian military developments. He saw the divisions; he saw the conflict; and how saw how different the perspectives were among the European members of NATO.

Putin sees the fissures and dynamics of change in Europe and in NATO and has developed information war and hybrid war means to enhance his ability to shape an agenda to his liking. Putin has made it clear that the collapse of the Soviet Union in his view was a major disaster for Russia and has worked throughout his presidencies to restore a credible role for Russia in the world. At the heart of that approach is expanding the Russian influence and its defense perimeter.

But now he faces a very different challenge than did the Soviet leaders. Now he faces several European states who are keenly aware of the Russian threat. The Nordics have closely cooperated; Poland, the Baltic States and Romania, states with very clear proximate interest, have all focused on expanding their defense capabilities since the Crimean seizure in 2014.

What this means is that Europeans most significantly affected by any takeover of Ukraine by Russia are prepared to respond forcefully in ways that make sense to them; Washington, in my view, is clearly challenged if it wishes to direct a whole-of-western response and shape a way ahead as the crisis is worked and resolved.

This change is really a dramatic one, and my extensive travels in Northern Europe and recent travels to Poland certainly highlight the scope and nature of the changes within the alliance since 2014. Now, key European states are often leading the deterrent effort for NATO rather than waiting for guidance from Washington.

Putin is also playing off of the U.S. relationships – economic, political and security – with Ukraine. There have been ongoing suggestions of corruption in those relationships, and whatever the truth of these charges, the Russians and Ukrainians certainly know what is either true or can be plausibly argued to be true. But simply put: in any analysis of the current U.S. position towards Ukraine and its security, it is crucial to unpack what has gone before to determine the credibility of any U.S. response.

With regard to Putin's objectives, one can go back to look at his disputes with George W. Bush during the period of the Orange Revolution in Ukraine, to see clearly what he wants. He wants Ukraine to be like Belarus: a state dominated by leaders willing to be the loyal allies of Russia and to be part of the permanent war with the West, which was described in the July 2, 2021, Russian military doctrine statement.

While Bush simply brushed off Putin's objections, Putin never felt persuaded to act differently; instead, he took it as a sign to wait for an appropriate time to achieve the objective of protecting the Russian security zone – Belarus and Ukraine – and rolling back Western influence. That Putin would eventually act on those desires should never have been in doubt.

As Murielle Delaporte and I put it in our book on European defense:

> "The Orange Revolution in Ukraine (2004-2005) and the prospects for Ukraine to become a member of the EU and perhaps even NATO was a flash point for Putin where the new narrative

of the Russian nation was to be joined by the action of seizing the Crimea and 'returning' it to Russia, or in this case, the new Russian republic. Put in another way, the narrative about Russia and its legitimate rights to shape its own ethnic destiny and its role as a Euro-Asian power was backed by actions. And the seizure of Crimea was very popular in Russia, to say the least. The Putin narrative underscores that revolution and state collapse is inherently bad, and the linking of the protection of Russians 'abroad' with the role of the manifest destiny of the Russian state is a core ideological challenge to modern Europe."

And the current Ukrainian crisis can be seen in a wider context of European developments as well. The Russian threat to Ukrainian sovereignty is simply not about Ukraine. It is about the stability of the current European order.

The region cutting through the European continent from the Black Sea north has been an unsettled part of the post-Soviet European order. To simply take this year, the Black Sea crisis of this summer where we saw significant information war, and the "migrant" crisis generated by the Russians through Belarus against the Poles, the Balts, and the European order more generally are all part of the wider challenges which Russia is generating against the post-Soviet European order.

How Europeans and the United States shape their engagement with the Russians going forward will shape the next phase of the European order. This is not simply a Ukrainian crisis; it is much broader than that.

This is not a static thing but a moving process, whereby Brexit and the Turkish de facto exit from NATO have been key parts of reshaping the European order and the Russian pressure on their former territories is now playing a forcing function to determine who is serious about maintaining the current European order and who is not. German actions in this crisis will be critical in determining how the states who are seriously concerned about the Russian challenge and threat proceed.

After the Afghan Blitzkrieg withdrawal strategy of President Biden, how the United States shapes its response, and whether that in any coherent way represents a way ahead for the European states most affected by the Ukrainian invasion threat will be determined by actions not simply zoom meetings.

It is also the case that Russia's challenge to the European order is part of the wider challenge of 21st century authoritarian powers to the global order as shaped by the United States, the European Union, and the democratic powers in Asia. Whatever transpires in the Ukrainian crisis is not limited to Europe.

In short, we have entered a new historical epoch which will be shaped by the concrete actions of key states and what the results of such actions will be both in fact and perceived reality.

History is on the move once again, and with it the shaping of new global anarchy or order.

Putin's Perspective on Ukraine

By Paul Dibb
February 13, 2022

Why has Russia's President Vladimir Putin become so aggressive in his attitude to the US, NATO and Ukraine? In my analysis, I begin by examining the disintegration of the former Soviet Union and how it is still seen in the Kremlin as a great humiliation. Then I turn to the enlargement of NATO, and how Putin claims to see Ukraine and Russia as 'one people' and why he is risking war. I conclude by sketching out how Putin sees opportunities in a friendship with China that 'has no limits' and in which China opposes 'further enlargement of NATO' and supports Russia's proposals to create long-term, legally binding security guarantees in Europe.

I need to stress at the outset that by trying to understand Moscow's hostile stance and the way it is currently threatening to use military force against Ukraine, I do not endorse Moscow's belligerent attitude or the dictatorial role that Putin is playing in what is now a potentially very dangerous situation for peace in Europe and, indeed, globally.

If we are to attempt to understand why Russia is behaving in this potentially very dangerous manner, we need to begin by recalling what happened to the Soviet superpower as it collapsed in 1991 and how that calamity continues to affect current strategic thinking in Moscow.

Putin recalls the Soviet collapse as a time when gross injustice was done to the Russian people: 'It was only when Crimea ended up as part of a different country that Russia realised that it had not been simply robbed but plundered.' The UK ambassador to Moscow from 1988 to 1992, Rodric Braithwaite, observes that the disintegration of the USSR at the end of 1991 was a moment of triumph for the West, but for the Russians it brought national humiliation, domestic chaos, great poverty, and even famine.

Former CIA director and U.S. defence secretary Robert Gates recently stated that almost everything Putin does at home and abroad these days is rooted in the collapse of the Soviet Union in 1991, which for him marked the collapse of the four-century-old Russian Empire and Russia's position as a great power. Gates remarks that Putin's current actions 'however deplorable, are understandable'. Since becoming president in 1999, Putin has been focused on returning Russia to its historical role as a major power and its historical policy of creating a buffer of subservient states on its periphery—the so-called near abroad.

Readers who wish to consult the definitive account of the USSR's collapse are strongly advised to read the just published authoritative book called *Collapse: The Fall of the Soviet Union* by Vladislav Zubok, a professor of international history at the London School of Economics. Braithwaite describes it as a deeply informed account of how the Soviet Union fell apart and how we have once again come to the brink of a major armed stand-off between Russia and the West.

Zubok concludes that the speed and ease with which the Soviet central structures collapsed baffled even the most experienced Western observers. He believes Mikhail Gorbachev's leadership, character and beliefs constituted a major factor in the Soviet Union's self-destruction. His fumbling policies of reform generated total chaos that legitimised runaway separatism in the Baltics and, ultimately, in the core Slavic territories of Russia, Ukraine and Belarus.

In the summer of 1991, the expectation of a new Marshall Plan among the Soviet elites became almost universal. But many in Washington wanted to break up the Soviet Union for security reasons. Treasury secretary Nicholas Brady advised President George H.W. Bush that America's strategic priority was to see the Soviets become 'a third-rate power, which is what we want'. During the 1990s, Zubok claims that 70–80% of Russians lived in poverty with the old Soviet social safety net gone and with rampant crime and mafia-like rule in most towns and regions.

Regarding the prospect of the incorporation of a democratising Russia into a larger Europe and NATO, the view was that the post-Soviet geopolitical space was too huge and unpredictable for integration within the Western orbit. The enlargement of NATO took place quickly, because the newly independent Baltic countries and Poland wanted to be free of the Russian military menace. Boris Yeltsin wanted Russia to join NATO, but the new U.S. administration under Bill Clinton chose to offer Russia only 'a partnership' with the alliance because the general view in Washington was that Russia was simply too big to fully belong to NATO.

Yeltsin warned that NATO's enlargement could lead to a new division in Europe. The U.S. Secretary of State, James Baker, reassured Gorbachev that NATO would 'not shift one inch eastward from its present position' once it had safely taken in a reunited Germany. Those words were never recorded in any mutually agreed formula.

Neither was the issue of Crimea raised when the leaders of what became the new countries called the Russian Federation, Ukraine and Belarus, met in secret in the Viskuli hunting lodge near Minsk on 7 December 1991. It was there that they agreed to the dissolution of the Union of Soviet Socialist Republics.

According to Zubok's book, before Yeltsin's departure from Moscow his adviser, Galina Starovoitova, suggested he offer the Ukrainian leadership an option of negotiated changes to the borders of Ukraine after a moratorium of three to five years. She was concerned about Crimea.

This option would have helped to placate Russian public opinion and leave open the possibility of settling the territorial issue according to international law. Yeltsin, however, didn't raise this issue in the Viskuli nego-tiations. The subsequent attitude of his state secretary, Gennady Burbulis, was that all this could be resolved by skilful diplomacy. And the rest, as they say, is history.

Turning now to the NATO issue, Braithwaite's view is that, under relentless U.S. pressure, NATO's borders have advanced until they are 'within spitting distance of Russia and Ukraine'. That is how it's seen in Moscow, but it is ridiculous in my opinion to suggest that current NATO members Estonia, Latvia, Lithuania and Poland present any realistic military threat to such a powerful country as today's Russia.

Putin, of course, takes an entirely different point of view. He believes that the Americans conspired to break up his country and encourage the creation of a separate country called Ukraine.

We are now in a situation where the animosity between Moscow and Washington over NATO's future and the existence of an independent Ukraine has become central to the future of peace in Europe. As Gates observes, Putin's embrace of the strategy of securing Russia's near abroad is seen in his actions in Belarus, Moldova, Transnistria, Georgia, the 2020 Armenia–Azerbaijan conflict, Kazakhstan and now—most dramatically—Ukraine.

Putin regards Ukraine as a critical security risk for Moscow—a dagger pointed at the Slavic heart of Russia. Gates believes that Putin has overplayed his hand on Ukraine because he finds himself in a situation where Russian success is defined as either a change of government in Kyiv—with the suc-cessor regime bending the knee to Moscow—or Russian conquest of the country. Resolving this serious threat peacefully is going to be an immense challenge to the resolve and unity of the Western alliance. Already, Germany is looking like a key weak link because of its dependence on Russia for half of its natural gas supplies.

Putin is proclaiming that Ukraine's membership of NATO is a 'redline' issue for Moscow and that he wants written guarantees from the U.S. that Ukraine NATO membership will never be allowed.

In July 2021, he allegedly wrote a 7,000-word article titled 'On the historical unity of Russians and Ukrainians'. In it, he asserts that Russians and Ukrainians are one people—'a single whole'. He argues that 'modern Ukraine is entirely the product of the Soviet era. We know and remember well that it was shaped—for a significant part—on the lands of historical Russia.' He goes on to claim that the U..S and EU countries systematically pushed Ukraine into 'a dangerous geopolitical game aimed at turning Ukraine into a barrier between Europe and Russia, a springboard against Russia'.

Putin asserts that what he terms 'the formation of an ethnically pure Ukrainian state, aggressive towards Russia' is 'comparable in its consequence to the use of weapons of mass destruction against us'. He ominously concludes: 'And we will never allow our historical territories and people close to us living there to be used against Russia. And to those who will undertake such an attempt, I would like to say this way they will destroy their own country.'

So, in effect, there is Putin's declaration of war if the U.S. and NATO do not for ever ban Ukraine from NATO membership. But there is a further potentially dangerous international complication.

Russia and China are increasingly looking like a de facto alliance. Last week, Putin visited China and met with President Xi Jinping. In a joint statement, the two leaders agreed that friendship between their countries 'has no limits; there are no 'forbidden' areas of cooperation. The two sides specifically agreed to 'oppose further enlargement of NATO', and the Chinese side proclaimed that it 'supports the proposals put forward by the Russian Federation to create long-term legally binding security guarantees in Europe'.

This is China's most explicit support to date of Moscow's confrontation with the West over NATO membership. The joint statement of this meeting between the leaders of the world's two major authoritarian powers includes 'serious concern' about AUKUS and 'strongly condemns' the 'decision to initiate cooperation in the field of nuclear-powered submarines'. The statement marks an increasingly serious joint confrontation with the West. What we are witnessing now is Beijing's encouragement of Moscow's hostility against the U.S. over NATO membership.

Xi will now be closely scrutinising how Washington reacts to Moscow's military threats against Ukraine and the implications for Beijing's military intimidation of Taiwan.

This article was published by ASPI on February 10, 2022 and is republished with the permission of the author.

A Nordic Perspective on the 2022 Ukraine Crisis
February 13, 2022

I have had the opportunity over the years to visit what I refer to as the defense arc from the UK through the Nordics to the Balts to Poland. The CEO of Risk Intelligence, Hans Tino Hansen, has been a key guide for me to thinking through the process of change in defense and security affecting Northern Europe over the past decade and a half.

On February 8, 2022, I had a chance to discuss with him what he sees as the view from the Nordic side of the current Ukraine crisis and its implications.

Question: How does the current Ukraine crisis fit into the evolving history of European direct defense?

Hans Tino Hansen: "With the preoccupation with the Iraq and Afghanistan wars, the West has in a certain sense had its head in the sand and developed a geopolitical blindness with regard to European geopolitics. Putin has not. And he has been working his approach to determine who in the West is willing to do what in meeting his ongoing demands.

"He proposed several demands which he knew – as a self-fulfilling prophecy – the West could not accept. But what he is observing is that the European states along with the United States and Canada are laying out their real red lines. The Western written response to his demands stated very clearly in paragraph 12 of the reply that NATO would act to defend any NATO member.

"This means from Putin's perspective, that NATO states would not directly defend Ukraine."

Question: Let me pick up on your point about geopolitics. I think it is safe to say that for many in the United States policy community, with globalization and a focus on climate change, geopolitics seems to have been lost in the shuffle. Both President XI and Putin are refocusing attention, but we seem to have very different perspectives coming from modern Europe and the Biden Administration about what this crisis is about compared to what Putin thinks it is about.

What is your take on the apparent disconnect?

Hans Tino Hansen: "It is if the two sides are playing the well-known strategic game, Risk. But the two sides are using different playbooks.

"For Putin, a key objective is to reinforce his position that the West is the aggressor and will not meet his "legitimate" demands about creating a buffer zone between the West and Russia."

Question: Indeed, in both the Russian military doctrine statement issued in July of 2021 or Putin's presentation last fall to the Valdai Discussion Club Meeting 2021, it is clear that his position is that Russia is in a state of permanent war with the West, and to use Putin's words, the inferiority of the West is proven by the simple fact that there is a debate in the West about who is man and who is woman. We are talking about big cultural gaps, and those gaps are also replicated within divisions in the West as well. Is this not just the next phase in Putin's approach to determine who his friends and committed enemies in the West really are?

Hans Tino Hansen: "For Putin, this is a fight about long-term survival of the current Kremlin leadership, which makes it all the more dangerous. To him, it is legitimate to use virtually all means to achieve his objectives. For Western publics and leaders, this appears so old fashioned and antiquated, but not to a number of former Warsaw Pact states who see the Russian threat as very real indeed.

"I think for states who take the defense threat seriously, and certainly Nordic states increasingly do so, there is a recognition that some of the lessons learned in the Cold War need to be applied again but in the new context. It is not so much history repeating itself but the need to remember and relearn what is relevant from that history and applying to a new technological and cultural context. But it most certainly is about geopolitical conflict.

"We have cleaned the chalk board of the realities we faced militarily in the Cold War. There was nothing left of the knowledge and experience from the Cold War, and nothing left about geopolitical analysis and understanding of geopolitical threat. After the 30 years of the collapse of the Soviet Union and the military being sent to distant realms.

"The direct defense of Europe in a modern geopolitical context has simply disappeared as a core subject of analysis and focus of attention for the general public and its politicians."

Question: What will now be the response within Europe going forward?

Hans Tino Hansen: "The closer you are geographically to Russia the more focused you are on a direct threat, so for Finland, Poland, Estonia, Latvia and Lithuania or for Norway, the Russian challenge is not ever far from sight. For a state like Germany, energy, inflation or climate change is more pressing than a Russian take-over of Belarus for example.

"For us it cannot be.

"The Russian de facto swallowing of Belarus connected to their ramped-up presence in Kaliningrad poses a direct threat to the Nordics, the Balts and the Poles. Kaliningrad, while on one side a military stronghold, it also puts Russia into a more vulnerable position than many realized, and one response to this crisis could well be significantly enhanced cooperation among those states who take the threat seriously.

"But with regard to Germany, with what I call the "Schröder-Merkel trap" their leaders have tied Germany tightly into the Russian spider's web and significantly reduced their freedom of maneuver in political, energy and military terms."

"And looking forward, there will be greater cooperation in our region on defense matters. And we have some significant equipment in common which will allow us to do that, notably the F-35 will be flown by Poland and Finland, along with Denmark on the way and Norway is already doing so.

This will not be limited to F-35 for new submarines and surface ships will come online in common as well over the next decade.

"Putin has done more to ramp up the common defense in Northern Europe and between the Nordic countries and the Poles and Balts than any NATO meeting could have."

A Polish Perspective on the Ukraine Crisis 2022

By Robert Czulda
February 14, 2022

In a geostrategic dimension, Moscow's goal is to ultimately destroy international rules, which were created after the Cold War. After the aggression on Ukraine in 2014 Russian commentator Fyodor Lukyanov, Editor-in-Chief of Russia in Global Affairs magazine and Chairman of the Presidium of the Council for Foreign and Defense Policy, explained a Russian approach: "after the end of the Cold War, we got tangled up in some misunderstandings. Supposedly everyone knew who won, what is the new world order, but no one defined it formally. New rules were not written in any international documents, acts or agreements. Now Russia tried to set new rules, because those that have been in force until now have not been beneficial to Russia".

Robert Czulda moderating a panel on air power modernization at the Defence 24
Conference on September 27, 2021. Image Credit: J.Sabak

Now many experts and some officials – French President Emmanuel Macros has been among them for the last couple of years – claim that Russia must be included in a new European security system.

However, it is impossible to reach a solid agreement with Putin's Russia without significant concessions. Moscow's demands are as long as absurd - the Kremlin expects the West to fully abandon Ukraine (all foreign advisors and arms delivered to Kiev are to be withdrawn, NATO has to stop any military exercises with Ukraine, which would be forced to become a neutral country).

Moreover, Russia expects NATO to halt its enlargement. In return, Russia offers nothing. Moscow has been playing on dividing the West and weakening Central and Eastern Europe, which it still considered by the Kremlin as a Russian sphere of influence. Russia does not want to conquer this part of Europe militarily, but is ready to use non-military yet still hostile instruments to achieve subordination, which would be ultimately recognized by the West.

An open war or even a limited armed conflict would be a massive disaster, but that does not mean that we should yield to the thug. If the West – both NATO and the United States - want to preserve its position – it must draw a red line. Of course, Ukraine is not in NATO, and it will not be defended by NATO troops, but the Ukrainians know that. Lithuania, Latvia and Estonia - the most vulnerable NATO member states - are a different story. Their security is also a security of the whole transatlantic security system. The failure of their defense would mean the end of NATO as a security provider and the United States as a superpower and protector.

Russia has already achieved an important goal.

What many Western analysts fail to notice is the fact that during the current crisis, Russia has completely absorbed Belarus, which no longer exists as a separate state. Security apparatus and armed forces have been closely integrated and Belarus has lost its defense and political independence. Polish security expert Andrzej Wilk put it bluntly: "Belarusian military and its defense industry are parts of Russian system."

Now, the whole was accomplished – Russia deployed its troops in Belarus, which will remain there after the current crisis is over. Moreover, Russia moved a potential frontline with NATO several hundred kilometers to the West. A length of NATO's border with the Russian Federation was expanded too.

France and the 2022 Ukraine Crisis

By Pierre Tran
February 15, 2022

President Emmanuel Macron's Feb. 7, 2022, flight to Moscow could be seen as the doves' diplomatic attempt to defuse the crisis over Ukraine, a counterbalance to the hawks dispatching troops and weapons to warn off Russian forces massed on the border with its neighbor.

Macron spent five hours in talks behind Kremlin closed doors with Russian president Vladimir Putin, with the French head of state flying the next day to Kyiv to meet Ukrainian president Volodymyr Zelenskiy, and then on to Berlin to see German chancellor Olaf Schulz.

The French aim was to "de-escalate" the crisis rising from Russia gathering some 130,000 troops and armor on the border with Ukraine, previously part of the former Soviet Union.

Moscow may have denied any plan to invade Ukraine, but there is deep concern Moscow will order a military move, such as seen in 2014 by seizing the Crimean Peninsula and Donbas region, eastern Ukraine.

Macron had assumed the role of peace broker, carrying the badge of French political leader, as he may hold the six-month rotating presidency of the council of the European Union, but he knew he had no mandate to speak for the 27-strong EU. And France may be a NATO member, but Paris also had no remit to speak for the transatlantic alliance.

Macron had actively taken up the role of the nation's top diplomat, spending precious political time in search of a peaceful solution to a perceived Russian threat on an East European nation. France is due to go to the polls in April, and Macron has yet to declare candidacy in the election for the five-year tenancy of the Elysée president's office.

That diplomatic whirlwind may well have been a French drive, but it may also be seen as part of Macron's wider mission of boosting the role of Europe in world politics, his pursuit of the concept of European strategic autonomy, including a military capability, separate from NATO and Washington.

Among the points Macron and Putin agreed at the Moscow summit was resumption of talks over the territorial dispute in Donbas under the 2015 Minsk agreement. Officials from France, Germany, Ukraine, and Russia met Feb. 10, but the four members of the Normandy format came away with little to show for resolving the low-level conflict in the region.

Macron also discussed a new security order for Europe at the Moscow summit, as Russia has demanded a roll back of the NATO membership and missiles deployed around Russia. France has urged grave caution but has not advised French nationals to leave Ukraine, pointing up a distinct approach from at least 30 other nations, which afternoon daily Le Monde reported Feb. 14 have told nationals to leave the country.

Paris insists on an independent verification of threat, a cornerstone of its pursuit of strategic autonomy. France has its own intelligence gathering means on land, sea, air and in space, and will have access to intelligence gathered and shared by NATO partners. That independent approach could be seen in the decision by the then President Jacques Chirac to stay out of the U.S.-led 2003 invasion of Iraq, a decision which bruised relations between Paris and Washington for years.

After the Moscow meeting, the Russian spokesman disputed media reports that Putin had assured Macron that there would be no further military moves around Ukraine.

Russian intelligence agencies reportedly have a common practice of recording events, perhaps prompting the question whether there is a recording of that high-level exchange of views, perhaps resolving who said what and when.

NATO Reinforces its Eastern Members

The UK defense minister sparked controversy after the *Sunday Times* reported Feb. 13 that Ben Wallace said there was a "whiff of Munich in the air." British authorities sought to play down that remark, which implied Russia might play the role of Adolph Hitler, the BBC reported the following day.

NATO was undergoing brain death, Macron told *The Economist* in 2019. But the crisis seems to have sparked something of a cerebral recovery, with NATO members rallying around to show support for Ukraine, which seeks to join the military alliance.

A first batch of U.S. airborne troops landed Feb.4 in Germany, part of a 2,000-strong deployment to Poland and Romania, with 1,000 soldiers moving from Germany to Romania.

The UK was sending 350 Royal Marines to Poland, adding to the 100 army engineers already there, helping to strengthen the border with Belarus. Germany was sending 350 more soldiers to Lithuania, reinforcing the some 600 German troops already there and accounting for around half the battle group.

Russia has drawn a red line against NATO ever accepting Ukraine as a member, and it remains to be seen whether the alliance will accept Kyiv's application, which would pledge collective defense in the event of an attack. Russia has demanded a NATO retreat from its borders, with weapons and troops pulled out of former Soviet bloc states which joined the Atlantic alliance after 1997. Moscow has also called for the NATO withdrawal of intermediate-range missiles from Europe, and recognition and autonomy of the Donbas region.

Russia has issued Russian passports to Ukrainians in the region, underlining its territorial claim.

U.S. president Joe Biden has clearly said there would not be armed conflict with Russia, which would spell another world war. The Western partners, including the European Union, have pledged to take severe economic sanctions if there were a Russian invasion.

Europe vs Putin

After the Kyiv meeting, Macron flew to Berlin, allowing a late working dinner with Scholz and the Polish president, Andrzej Duda, bringing together the three leaders of the Weimar Triangle, the cooperative group of France, Germany, and Poland. "Our common goal is to avoid a war in Europe," Scholz said.

Scholz was just back from meeting Biden in Washington for talks. Before Macron flew to Moscow, he twice called Biden, and called Duda, UK prime minister Boris Johnson, Putin, Scholz, NATO secretary general Jens Stoltenberg, and Zelenskiy, clearing the ground for the meeting with Putin, *The Economist* said on social media.

That was a departure from Macron's previous meetings with Putin, notably in 2019 at the Brégançon medieval fort, the French official holiday retreat on a Mediterranean island, and in 2017 at the Versailles palace, west of the capital. The Elysée reportedly did not brief Western allies before those meetings.

Putin appears to have changed.

"These more than five hours of talks make us realise how different the Putin of today was to the Putin of three years ago," said a French source briefed on the Moscow talks, Reuters reported. The Russian leader spent most of the time "rewriting history from 1997 on."

Putin told the BBC that he had been forced to moonlight as a taxi driver in the 1990s as he earned so little after the collapse of the USSR. "Sometimes I had to earn extra money," Putin said. "I mean, earn extra money by car, as a private driver. It's unpleasant to talk about to be honest, but unfortunately that was the case." Putin's remarks were in the BBC documentary film, *Russia, Latest History*, which aired Dec. 12, 2021.

Putin worked for the KGB intelligence service and resigned after the 1991 coup against President Mikhail Gorbachev, which led to the collapse of the Soviet Union. Putin went on to work with Anatoly Sobchak, mayor of St Petersburg.

Putin reportedly used the familiar French "tu" rather than the more formal "vous" form of address when he saw Macron at the meeting. Macron had declined to agree to give a Russian request for a DNA sample for a Covid test, which meant the meeting was held at a long table, sparking many visual jokes on social media.

A View from Latvia

The Latvian deputy prime minister and defense minister, Artis Pabriks, told Feb. 7 the German Marshall Fund of the United States, that while the U.S. informed Latvia and the other Baltic states on U.S. negotiations and plans with Moscow, it was not clear the Latvian government had been informed of Macron's "talking points" before he flew to Moscow. Macron made a call Feb. 5 to Latvian prime minister Krisjanis Karins, before the meeting with Putin, the list from *The Economist* on social media shows.

Are those who are negotiating with Putin "representing the West or are they mediators between the West and Moscow?" Pabriks said, adding that Russia's demands extended beyond Ukraine, and Moscow was seeking expansion against the West, Europe, the US and Canada.

Pabriks evoked the then UK prime minister Neville Chamberlain and the 1938 Munich agreement - and referred to the film *Munich: The Edge of War* which recently started showing on Netflix. Macron should have flown to Kyiv first and discussed the "concessions" before going to Moscow, Pabriks said.

Franco-Russian ties

France has strong links with Russia. That can be seen in the then leader of the Free French forces, Gen. Charles de Gaulle, sending French pilots to fly alongside the Russians on the Eastern Front in the Second World War.

Those French air force pilots formed a squadron, dubbed Normandie-Niemen, flew Yakovlev Yak 1 fighter planes 1943-45, and supported Russian troops in the battle of Kursk. Moscow awarded the French squadron the distinction of Hero of the Soviet Union.

The present Normandie-Niemen squadron flies Rafale fighter jets from Mont-de-Marsan air base, southwest France.

In 2011, the then president, Nicolas Sarkozy, backed a controversial sale worth €1.2 billion ($1.4 billion) of two Mistral class helicopter carriers to the Russian navy, with options for two more. The Baltic nations, the U.S., Ukraine, and other central European allies criticized that deal, which stood to boost Russian force projection.

Sarkozy's successor, François Hollande, cancelled the Mistral carrier deal in 2015 and repaid Russia €948 million, comprising €893 million for building the two warships and €55 million for adapting Russian equipment for fitting on the vessels. The French authorities declined to pay the French shipbuilder, Naval Group, an estimated €200 million payment for building the two warships, Vladivostok and Sevastopol, which were later sold to Egypt.

CONCLUSION:

GRAY ZONES OR LIMITED WAR?

Western analysts have coined phrases like hybrid war and gray zones as a way to describe peer conflict below the level of general armed conflict. But such language creates a cottage industry of think tank analysts, rather than accurately portraying the international security environment.

Peer conflict notably between the liberal democracies and the 21st century authoritarian powers is conflict over global dominance and management. It is not about managing the global commons; it is about whose rules dominate and apply. Rather than being hybrid or gray, these conflicts, like most grand strategy since Napoleon, are much more about "non war" than they are about war. They shape the rules of the game to give one side usable advantage. They exploit the risk of moving to a higher intensity of confrontation.

Russia is doing this right now in Ukraine. China, likewise, is doing it in the South China Sea and in the Sea of Japan. It's critical to understand this point, and terms like gray zone operations and hybrid war don't capture the challenge of escalation control.

There are two games being played. One game is over the immediate contentions of the major powers. Ukraine and Taiwan must be protected from attack. But the second game is just as important, it asks what limits should be crossed to manipulate the risk of going to a higher intensity of competition?

In the Cold War these limits defined the "system dynamics" of the competition. Shaping them was important, because they were the foundation for winning a war that might erupt, or toward stabilizing a competition in a way that gave advantage to one side or the other. Seen this way Korea, Vietnam, Berlin, etc. were about winning those local wars. But they were more importantly about shaping the global competition between the United States and the Soviet Union.

Quite elaborate rules were worked out for this. It took substantial time during the evolution of the Cold War (to make sure that it was indeed was a cold war from a global conflagration point of view) for this learning curve to develop. Limited wars, like Korea, produced know how about escalation control and dominance.

The problem today is that we are only at the earliest parts of this learning curve for our age. We're in a long-term competition with authoritarian powers, but it's like it was 1949 in terms of our know how for managing this rivalry to our advantage. The problem isn't simply to defend Ukraine and Taiwan; it's to do it in such a way that doesn't lead to crazy escalations or that doesn't scare the daylights at of our allies. Taiwan and Ukraine are not sideshows to global conflict; they are the early test cases of competition in a second nuclear age.

Recently, I discussed the question of how best to describe the terminology to describe peer conflict with my colleague Dr. Paul Bracken the author of *The Second Nuclear Age*. According to Bracken, it is preferable to use the term "limited war" to describe the nature of conflict between the authoritarian powers and the liberal democracies.

> "A term was invented in the Cold War which is also quite useful to analyze the contemporary situation, namely, limited war. This term referred to conflict at lower levels and sub-crisis maneuvering. And that is what is going or today in cyber and outer space, to use two examples. But it also applied to higher levels of conflict like limited nuclear war. The notion of limited war focuses escalation as a strategy. What is the difference between limited and controlled war?

> "That's a really important question with enormous implications for command and control. Today, for example, limits are determined in a decision-making process whereby the Pentagon goes

to the White House and says we'd like to do this operation. The White says yes or no.

"Left out of this is any discussion of building a command-and-control system for controlled war. This means keeping war controlled even if things go wrong — as they always do. Without an emphasis on controlled war, and not just limited war, I would estimate that the United States will be highly risk averse, that is, the fear of an escalation spiral will drive the United States toward inaction.

"Look at the Ukraine. The first U.S. reaction to the Russian buildup was to immediately take military options off the table. The White House refocused its strategy on financial sanctions instead. It looked as if the United States was desperately searching for ways not to use force. Soft power, gray zone operations, the weaponization of finance — these are clearly important, and I think we should use them.

"But they look like a frantic attempt to any use of force, like British foreign policy in the 1930s.

"Our language shapes our strategy. An image of war that blows up, that's unlimited, or that you've declined to fight because of your fear that it would become so is where we are. In academic studies and think tanks the focus is overwhelmingly on "1914" spirals, accidental war, entanglement, and inadvertent escalation.

"If it's going to be controlled or limited, how are you defining that it is limited? Is it limited by geography? Is it limited by the intensity of operations? Is it limited by the additional political issues that you will bring into the dispute?

"These are never specified in discussions that I see of hybrid or gray zone warfare. To use a very sensitive example. In a Taiwan scenario, will the United States Navy and Air Force be allowed to strike targets in China? I see a real danger that this isn't being thought through. If we think it through only in a crisis, we're likely to find a lot of surprises in how the White House and Joint Chiefs of Staff see things differently.

These expressions – hybrid war and gray zone conflict – are treated as if they self-evident in term of their meaning. Yet they are part of a larger chain of activities and events.

We use the term peer competitor but that is a bit confusing as well as these authoritarian regimes do not have the same ethical constraints or objectives as do liberal democratic regimes. This core cultural, political, and ideological conflict who might well escalate a conflict beyond the terms of what we might wish actually to fight.

And that really is the point – escalate and the liberal democracies withdraw and redefine to their disadvantage what the authoritarian powers wish to do. Bracken noted:

"That's a good distinction too, because it brings in the fact that for 20 years, we've been fighting an enemy in the Middle East who really can't strike back at the United States or Europe other than with low-level terrorist actions. That will not be the case with Russia, China, and others.

"The challenge is to define limited war, and I would add, controlled war. Is it geographic or Is it the intensity of the operations? How big of a war is it before people start unlocking the nuclear weapons? Every war game I've played has seen China declare that its "no first use" policy is terminated. The China player does this to deter the United States from making precision strikes and cyber-attacks on China. This seriously needs consideration before we get into a real crisis.

"Russia and China' are trying to come in with a level of intensity in escalation which is low enough so that it doesn't trigger a big Pearl Harbor response. And that could go on for a long time and is a very interesting future to explore."

Limited war requires learning about escalation control i.e., about controlled war, which when one uses that term, rather than hybrid war or gray zone conflict, connects limited war to the wider set of questions relating political objectives of the authoritarian powers.

Bracken concluded:

> "I believe using those terms adds to the intellectual chaos in Washington. It prevents us from having a clear policy discussion of what the alternatives for escalation control and management are in any particular crisis. This is a lot more dangerous than mishandling the Afghan exit, or the COVID pandemic."

CONTRIBUTORS

Robert Czulda

Robert Czulda is an Assistant Professor at the University of Lodz, Poland. He is a former Visiting Professor at the Center for International and Security Studies at Maryland (CISSM) under a Fulbright Senior Award.

Dr. Czulda is an Alum of the Young Leaders Dialogue of the U.S. Department of State (2010– 2011), and has lectured at universities in Iran, Brazil, Indonesia, Ireland, Lithuania, Turkey, and Slovakia, as well as the National Cheng-chi University in Taipei.

He is a freelance defense journalist as well and has published widely on Polish defense and related issues. Dr. Czulda's area of expertise is international security and defense.

Paul Dibb

Paul Dibb is emeritus professor of strategic studies at the Australian National University. He was a deputy secretary of the Department of Defence, director of the Defence Intelligence Organisation and head of the National Assessments Staff. He is the author of *The Soviet Union: The Incomplete Superpower*, first published in 1986.

James Durso

James Durso is a regular commentator on foreign policy and national security matters. Mr. Durso served in the U.S. Navy for 20 years and has worked in Kuwait, Saudi Arabia, and Iraq.

John Glassman

Dr. Jon Glassman is a consultant on defense and strategic matters residing in Washington, DC.

A career diplomat, Dr. Glassman worked at American Embassies in Madrid, Moscow, Havana, Mexico City, Kabul, and Asuncion (Paraguay). He was Charge d'Affaires (Chief of Mission) in Afghanistan during the final two years of the Russian presence.

George Galdorisi

George Galdorisi is a career naval aviator whose thirty years of active-duty service included four command tours and five years as a carrier strike group chief of staff. George is the Director of Strategic Assessments and Technical Futures at the Navy's Command and Control Center of Excellence in San Diego, California.

Kenneth Maxwell

Dr. Kenneth Maxwell was the Founding Director of the Brazil Studies Program at Harvard University's David Rockefeller Center for Latin American Studies (DRCLAS) (2006-2008) and a Visiting Professor in Harvard's Department of History (2004-2008).

Ed Timperlake

The Honorable Edward Timperlake is the former Director Technology Assessment, International Technology Security, Office of the Secretary of Defense, and served on the Board of The Vietnam Children's Fund, a pro-bono project that has built 48 elementary schools in Vietnam.

Previous positions he has held include serving on the Professional Staff, House Committee on Rules focusing on illegal foreign campaign donations to the American political process. As an Assistant Secretary, Department of Veterans Affairs, he was a member of The White House Desert Shield/ Desert Storm Communications Task Force. He created the "TASCFORM" analytical methodology for measuring the modernization rate of military aircraft worldwide for both the Director Net Assessment and Central Intelligence Agency and was Principal Director Mobilization Planning and Requirements/OSD in President Reagan's first term.

Pierre Tran

Pierre Tran is a Paris-based journalist who focuses on French defense policies and was a Reuters correspondent for many years and is a regular contributor to *Second Line of Defense* and *Defense.info*.

ABOUT THE EDITOR

Dr. Robbin F. Laird

A long-time analyst of global defense issues, he has worked in the U.S. government and several think tanks, including the Center for Naval Analysis and the Institute for Defense Analysis. He is a Columbia University alumnus, where he taught and worked for several years at the Research Institute of International Change, a think tank founded by Dr. Brzezinski.

He is a frequent op-ed contributor to the defense press, and he has written several books on international security issues. Dr. Laird has taught at Columbia University, Queens College, Princeton University, and Johns Hopkins University. He has received various academic research grants from various foundations, including the Fritz Thyssen Foundation, the United States Institute for Peace, etc.

He is the editor of two websites, *Second Line of Defense* and *Defense. info*. He is a member of the Board of Contributors of Breaking Defense and publishes there on a regular basis. He is a regular contributor to the Canadian defense magazine *FrontLine Defence* as well.

He is a frequent visitor to Australia where he is a Research Fellow with The Williams Foundation in supporting their seminars on the transformation of the Australian Defence Force (ADF). Recently, he has become a Research Fellow with The Institute for Integrated Economic Research-Australia. The Institute is focused on a number of key macro social/defense issues which revolve around establishing trusted supply chains and resiliency in dealing with the challenges posed by the 21st century authoritarian powers.

He is also based in Paris, France, and he regularly travels throughout Europe and conducts interviews and talks with leading policymakers in the region.

SECOND LINE OF DEFENSE
STRATEGIC BOOK SERIES

The Return of Direct Defense in Europe (2020)

The Return of Direct Defense in Europe: Meeting the 21st Century Authoritarian Challenge focuses on how the liberal democracies are addressing the challenges of the 21st century authoritarian powers, in terms of their evolving approaches and capabilities to deal with their direct defense in Europe.

As General (Rtd.) Jean-Paul Paloméros, former NATO Commander and head of the Allied Transformation Command put it with regard to the book: "One of the many great values of *The Return of Direct Defense in Europe* is that (it directly addresses the need) to meet the challenge of XXIst century authoritarian powers. Because the great risks that lie in front of our democracies deserve to be named: national selfishness, divergence of strategic and economic interests, trampling on fundamental and commonly agreed values."

As Professor Kenneth Maxwell underscored: "This is a fascinating and very timely account of the major shifts and challenges which have transformed post–Cold War Europe and outlines in troubling detail the formidable challenges which lie ahead in the post-COVID-19 pandemic world. It is essential reading for all those who forget that history must inform the present."

Joint by Design:
The Evolution of Australian Defense Strategy (2021)

In the midst of the COVID-19 crisis, the prime minister of Australia, Scott Morrison, launched a new defense and security strategy for Australia. This strategy reset puts Australia on the path of enhanced defense capabilities. The change represents a serious shift in its policies towards China, and in reworking alliance relationships going forward.

As one reviewer commented: "It is obvious that Laird is not a simple military and security analyst. By reading his book, it turns out that thanks to his editorial work, he is also an experienced narrator with the necessary skillset to tell a complex story in an exciting way. Therefore, overall, it is important to note that *Joint by Design: The Evolution of the Australian Defence Strategy* is not just an academic book that develops the context and the making of the new defence and security strategy of Australia, but because of the wealth of reports about seminars and quotes from key actors, it is also a very credible source for historians. This is particularly valuable when its main topic is one into which it is very rare to gain such deep and detailed insight."

Training for the High-end Fight:
The Strategic Shift of the 2020s (2021)

"Training for the High-end Fight" highlights the essential strategic shift for the U.S. and allied militaries from land wars in the Middle East to the return of great power competition. The primary challenge of this strategic shift will be the need to operate a full spectrum crisis management force. That means training a force capable of delivering the desired combat and crisis management effect in dealing with 21st century authoritarian powers. The book looks at how the U.S. forces are reshaping training to compete effectively with peer competitors.

As Air Marshal (Retired) Geoff Brown commented: "Robbin Laird uses his significant research over the last seven years and his unprecedented access to USN, USAF and USMC senior warfighters to detail the major shift in thinking that is underway as the U.S. works through the training requirements of Allied Air Power when all the domains are contested by a capable adversary."

2020: A Pivotal Year? Navigating Strategic Change at a Time of COVID-19 Disruption (2021)

This book addresses the impacts of the COVID-19 disruption on global politics and provides assessments of the ripple effects felt throughout Europe and Asia. The book focuses on the significant changes we see in building out post-pandemic societies and how the conflict between 21st century authoritarian states with the liberal democracies is reshaped. Authors based in Europe, the United States, and Australia have all contributed to this timely and unique assessment. It is the precursor to the current book and the two books read together provide readers with a overview of defense and security issues during the 2020-2022 period.

As one reviewer commented: "The post-COVID-19 world will be different. What will it be like? Laird's *2020: A Pivotal Year?* points out the factors that will shape the post-COVID-19 world – a highly recommended read!"

Preparing for the High-end Fight: The USMC Transformation Path (2022)

This book focuses on the USMC in the strategic shift from the Middle Eastern land wars to the return to great power competition and the high-end fight. The path whereby the Marines have generated their capabilities to engage in full spectrum crisis management began with the introduction of the Osprey in 2007, and then entered a new phase with the introduction of the F-35 and now has entered another phase whereby the Marines are working ways to more effectively distributed the force through enhanced mobile and expeditionary basing.

As George J. Trautman III LtGen, USMC (Ret) Former USMC Deputy Commandant for Aviation underscored in the forward to the book: "Only time will tell how the Marine Corps navigates this treacherous transformation journey, but it's not the equipment that will make the Corps successful on the future battlefield – it's the Marines. Their imaginations, ideas and creativity will lead to innovative employment of the tools they are given. That's true of every piece of equipment in use today and it will remain that way in the future. The USMC Transformation Path: Preparing for the High-End Fight makes a valuable contribution to the professional dialogue that must occur by giving voice to those who are charged with managing the change."

And in the afterword to the book, LtGen Brian Beaudreault, USMC (Ret), and former II MEF Commander noted: "Robbin Laird has masterfully woven the transformation story of the Marine Corps that began well before 2019 with the 2007 fielding of the revolutionary, long-range, assault-support, tiltrotor MV-22 Osprey, followed by the fielding of the Fifth Generation F-35 stealth jet fighter and the future fielding of the CH-53K heavy lift helicopter.

"Robbin has exhaustively interviewed current high-level commanders and consequential leaders across the Navy and Marine Corps enterprise and has pieced together a fantastic body of work that guides the reader towards a comprehensive understanding of the current challenges as well as the opportunities to be exploited by U.S., allied, and coalition forces within the Indo-Pacific and European theaters.

"Robbin has crafted fresh ideas and makes solid recommendations throughout this work that can help the Commandant and Chief of Naval Operations reduce near and mid-term risk while enhancing the sensing, striking and sustainment power of naval expeditionary forces through more innovative employment of existing capabilities."

Forthcoming Titles (2022 and 2023)

A Maritime Kill Web Force in the Making: Deterrence and Warfighting in the 21st Century

The book focuses on that new context and how the U.S. Navy and USMC are reshaping their capabilities to operate as an integrated distributed force functioning through interactive kill webs to deliver the kind of crisis escalation dominance which the United States needs in confronting the 21st century authoritarian powers.

We are focused on the fighting forces and their innovation. It is about the combat effect to be delivered in the mid-term which is at the heart of our book. We argue that the template being created for a maritime distributed force—or what we prefer to call an integrated distributed force, for which we include relevant joint and allied capabilities—is laying down the foundation for the way ahead. Such a template will be able to incorporate new technologies such as new weapons, and autonomous systems within an agile fleet that will be then able to make decisions at the tactical edge within the context of broader mission command C^2.

French Defense Policy Under President Macron (2023)

Emmanuel Macron became President of France on May 14, 2017. He is the youngest President of France in the Fifth Republic and the youngest head of state in France since Napoleon. The legislative elections which followed his election were dominated by the party which he established to support his reform agenda and policies.

During the Macron Presidency, there has been a clear focus on maintaining a balanced force structure, in the face of economic growth challenges and reform efforts. The nuclear force remains a key part of the French policy, but increasingly France is working with the United States, NATO, and its European allies on ways to better integrate French forces into a broader defense set of capabilities. This reader provides a detailed look at the evolution of defense capabilities and policies under President Macron.